PRINTING HISTORY

THE CALGARY HERALD EDITION

First Printing .... November, 1961
Second Printing .... December, 1961
Third Printing .... February, 1962
Fourth Printing .... June, 1962

CANNIFF EDITION

First Printing .... November, 1967

$2.50

ACKNOWLEDGEMENTS

We are grateful to The Calgary Herald for permission to publish this new edition of the original Alex Munro Gardening Book. To Mr. Gerald Brawn of The Calgary Herald (who helped prepare the original manuscript), we acknowledge our appreciation for his advice in the preparation of this new edition.

We extend our thanks to Mr. Tom Beck and Mr. Art Brown of Calgary for the use of their color photographs that illustrate this book.

—The Publishers

ALEX MUNRO'S
GARDENING
BOOK

By ALEX MUNRO, FRHS

Printed and Published by

CANNIFF PRINTING
(1964) LTD.
1510 - 6 Street S.W.
Calgary, Alberta, Canada

PRINTED IN CANADA

ALEX MUNRO, FRHS

Before his death in 1966, Alex Munro was "Mr. Gardener" to countless Calgarians.

He was born in Evanton, Ross-shire, a small village in northern Scotland, on May 13, 1895, started gardening when he was a schoolboy, and at 17 became an apprentice gardener on a Scottish estate near his home. He gardened on various Scottish estates until 1920, with the exception of wartime service with the Seaforth Highlanders during the First World War.

In 1920 he came to Alberta, and in 1923 first joined the City of Calgary's Parks Department. He was appointed superintendent of city parks in 1949 and retired in 1960.

In 1939 he was appointed a Fellow of the Royal Horticultural Society. He designed the beautiful Burns Rock Gardens on 10th St. N.W., and also helped a former city parks superintendent, W. R. Reader, lay out the Reader Rock Gardens.

He was president of the Calgary Horticultural Society in 1949 and served as official horticulturist of that society and of the Calgary Garden Club. He wrote a weekly gardening column for The Calgary Herald, and was in great demand as a judge of flower shows and was unofficial adviser to thousands of gardeners who wrote or asked him for help.

FOREWORD

Alex Munro's Gardening Book was originally published by The Calgary Herald in 1961. It rapidly gained recognition as a "best seller", with sales totalling over 17,000 copies.

Although five years have elapsed since the last edition was sold out, inquiries for the book have never ceased. For it was this same demand that brought about the publication of the original edition. From the time Mr. Munro began writing his weekly gardening column for The Calgary Herald in 1955, there was a steady stream of inquiries as to whether his columns could be published in book form. If ever a book was created in response to popular demand this was it.

The text for this new edition is the same as the original one, with the addition of an index and some color illustrations.

Gardening in Alberta requires enthusiasm, skill, and perseverance—for this is a province that has a temperamental climate and capricious seasons. This book will help gardening enthusiasts meet this challenge.

CONTENTS

PERENNIALS

Perennials are like trusted friends whose annual visit one can depend upon.

While annuals are still being nursed in the greenhouses and covered frames, these hardy plants are providing pleasure and color around our homes.

No grounds are complete without the introduction of at least some of these, if not a perennial border.

There are hundreds of hardy perennials which will thrive here, and this is a very extensive subject.

Although this is a very severe climate on perennials, despite it all we can grow some of the finest specimens. Perennials are those plants which have a perpetual rootstock, but whose growth above the ground dies down annually, reviving and making new growth with the return of spring.

The word "perennial" refers to plants that continue more than two years.

Wonderful progress has been made in the development of perennials.

This has not, however, been at the expense of the old-fashioned flowers that our grandmothers grew. On the contrary, no class of plant has received greater attention in recent years, and the improvements of many of the species has been so remarkable that one can scarcely recognize the homely stock from which they sprang.

More and more people are growing these charming perennials and the reason is that, no matter how carefully designed and planted an annual bedding scheme may be, it falls behind in real interest when compared with a well-planted perennial border.

Every week there are new interests added from early spring to late fall. You may find blooms before it is even safe to plant out the annual bedding plants, and long after frost has destroyed the latter we can still enjoy lovely little bouquets of perennials. No other class of plants will give us such good returns for such a small outlay of time and money as perennials. Because of their permanent nature, these plants make an interesting hobby to be pursued throughout the years.

It would be a good idea for you to make a plan of the perennial bed or border first, showing where each variety is to be placed. If a perennial garden is planted intelligently, you will achieve a more pleasing effect.

The taller plants must, of course, be placed at the back of a border, but it is a mistake to carefully arrange the plants from the largest to the smallest. If this is done, the plants will lose their individuality and much of the charm and beauty of the border also.

A good rule is to group the taller plants in threes and the intermediate and dwarf varieties in groups of fives. A few of the taller plants should be brought forward, as this helps to loosen any "banked up" look and also relieve any formal effect.

1

Try to imitate nature as far as possible. One must also take into consideration the season of blooming of the various plants so that all parts of the border will blossom throughout the year.

(A list of perennials, by size, color, and normal blooming time, will be found at the end of this chapter.)

It is suggested that strong colors, such as red and yellow, be planted first, taking care to space them attractively, but at the same time breaking any straight lines that might appear; then the more pastel shades can be placed between these strong colors, to give a very delightful effect.

I have been asked on many occasions if the perfect color scheme has ever been achieved? According to experts, no. Something always seems to go wrong, but nevertheless, some wonderful displays of color have been seen.

The preparation of the soil is very important. In the fall, the ground should be dug deeply, with a liberal quantity of manure added. The soil should be turned over and left as rough as possible so that the snow, frost, sun, and air can act on it.

In the spring the ground should be lightly forked over and then raked. If the first digging has not been done in the fall, do it as early in the spring as possible so that the ground will have time to settle.

Plant the perennials as soon as the frost is out of the ground. Be sure to give them enough room, so that none of the roots will be twisted or crowded, but on the other hand, do not plant them too deep either, or the crowns will be smothered.

Perennials do not require a great deal of care, although if there is a dry spell, a good soaking once or twice a week is better than a sprinkling every day. Stake and tie up your taller flowers early, or they will become straggly and unattractive in appearance.

The chief requirements of the herbaceous (perennial) border are annual dressings, shallow forking up of the surface and regular attention to watering, staking, keeping them weed-free, etc.

In selecting the plants, one that will add a great deal of beauty is the monkshood (botanical name, aconitum). There are three species: Aconitum napellus which is bicolored; napellus, blue; and a creamy white named napellus albus.

The delphinium is familiar to many, but perhaps the new and improved varieties of these stately flowers are not so well known. During the last two decades, quite a few new and strikingly lovely delphiniums have been hybridized, which has resulted in the introduction of many new colors and traits. Before that, they came nearly all in blue.

The variety I recommend is the Pacific Giant, which comes in pink, white, violet, lovely blue and purple shades. The flowerlets of the Pacific Giants are large, measuring 2½ to 3 inches across.

Some good yellow perennials for the back of a border are: golden glow (rudbeckia), mullein (verbascum olympium), and sephalaria alpina. Although the verbascum is only a biennial, it is really worth planting in any border because of its silvery foliage and small hollyhock-like flowers, and what can take the place of the stately hollyhocks which are so effective as a background?

Then again, we have the meadow rue in shades of white, mauve, or yellow. These three colors have beautiful flowers and foliage, and will add certain distinction to a border.

A delicately-toned pink is the perennial mallow, while a good red is the loosestrife, which has deep rose-colored spikes.

There is the gorgeous Oriental poppy which is especially desirable now that there is such a range of color — pure white, pink, salmon, and a vivid deep crimson.

Of the dianthus family, the pinks should find a place in the garden, as they have a delightful fragrance. Peonies are another old-time favorite and in their season, are the glory of the garden. The iris (see the separate chapter on irises) has been greatly improved and is now produced in beautiful shades of red, pink, blue, white and yellow. There may be as many as four blooms on a stalk at one time.

Phlox dominate the garden in their season because of the color masses, great beauty, and also because they blossom when many of the other perennials are past.

The Canterbury bell, though old-fashioned, is still a favorite with many, even though it is a biennial. The speedwells (or veronica) are the most accommodating of plants, growing in any garden soil.

The dahlia, too, has received more attention in the last few years, and it would be difficult to surpass some of the blooms grown in Calgary (See chapter on dahlias).

First let's consider some of the perennials suitable for herbaceous borders here, according to heights, starting first with the taller ones, then the intermediates and then some of the smaller or dwarf kinds. After that I'll deal in more detail with several of the many beautiful perennials suitable for any kind of garden display, whether in a border or floral bed.

Tall Perennials

One of the most pleasing of the taller perennials is loosestrife (lythrum). This is a hardy plant of vigorous growth reaching a height of almost 4 feet.

It bears reddish-purple or rose-colored flowers, requires lots of water, and may be grown from seed started indoors, or by propagation.

Then there are mulleins (verbascum) which are both biennial and perennial, some having long woolly leaves. They bear tall spikes of flowers, yellow in color, reaching a height of 3 to 4 feet and making a fine show.

Purple cone flowers (echinacea) are another hardy perennial. They have large flowers with cone-like centres, and grow to a height of around 3 feet.

Another hardy perennial is the globe thistle, whose botanical name is echinops. This bears round heads of thistle-like, pale blue flowers, and grows 3 to 4 feet tall.

The willow herb (epilobium) is a hardy plant which grows wild in many parts of the world and in Alberta, and will add much color to any border.

The foliage of the ornamental sea kale (crambe) is as the name suggests most ornamental and also it has large panicles of white flowers. It is hardy and grows from 3 to 6 feet tall.

Pink, crimson and white flowers make the valerian, another hardy perennial, a delight in our gardens. This flower generally grows from 3 to 4 feet.

The sunflower (heliopsis), another of the taller hardy favorites (3 to 4 feet tall), bears orange or yellow blooms.

3

Henry's lily (lilium Henry ii) is a Chinese lily shooting up to 6 feet in height, and bearing 12 to 20 apricot-colored flowers on each stem.

Intermediate Size Perennials

There is a very large group of desirable perennials which grow to a medium height.

Among the most popular are the columbines (or aquilegia). These delicately-tinted flowers are among the most beautiful of all hardy plants. To see them cultivated in the garden you might find it hard to believe that the columbines are really hardy perennials of the Northern Hemisphere. The aquilegia canadensis, which grows wild east of the Rockies, is a yellow color, tinted with red. The hybrids, which I recommend, have large blooms and much longer spurs than the wild species such as the canadensis.

The hybrids such as the Mrs. Scott Elliott strain are among the finest of the columbine family. The colors range through shades of lavender, mauve, purple, white, creamy yellow and red. One of the most vividly colored hybrids is the Crimson Star, which has red petals and a white centre. A few more of the finest hybrids are Longissima, Yellow, Copper Queen and Coerulea Blue. Columbines grow to a height of 30 to 36 inches, and will grow in sun or shade.

Another must for a perennial border is the delicately beautiful gypsophila, the very familiar baby's breath. Most people know how very extensively it is used for dressing up a bouquet. Two kinds of the gypsophila are the double white paniculata flora plena and the pink-colored rosy veil. The pink gypsophila is, I think, unsurpassed for decorative purposes. Both kinds grow best in a hot, sunny location and require a rich, limey soil.

The bellflower (or campanula) is also of a large family. Among the best species are persicifolia or peach leaf, which is either blue or white, and the variety Telham Beauty which has large bells of china blue. These both grow to a height of 30 to 36 inches, and like a sunny spot in the garden.

Next is a biennial, the campanula medium or the Canterbury bell; these are in shades of dark blue, lilac, rose and white. They grow from 24 to 30 inches tall, and also like lots of sun. There are single or double varieties, both of which are lovely.

Tall delphiniums are excellent for the back of the border, but there are intermediate ones in this family, too. The chineuse or Chinese delphinium is dainty and may be obtained in white, gentian blue, Cambridge blue and azure blue. It grows to 36 inches and likes lots of sun, also.

The bleeding heart (dicentra spectabilis) is an old and well-loved plant, requiring a sheltered, sunny spot in which to grow. It is of a graceful habit, having soft, pink heart-shaped flowers.

The gaillardia, or our own brown-eyed susan which grows wild in Alberta, is a worthy introduction to any garden. Two kinds of these which I recommend are the portola hybrids and the monarch strain, which like a sandy or even a gravelly soil, and must be in a sunny location.

The lychnis chalcedonica, known also as Maltese cross, Jerusalem cross, and scarlet lightning, sounds like and is a very exciting flower. It has been cultivated for many years and is a brilliant scarlet in color; however, the stems are very tender and lychnis should be kept staked at all times.

The papaver orientale or the Oriental poppy is, as the name implies, an exotic plant which provides a gay spot of color in your garden, almost resembling a tiny open parasol. Two kinds which I would suggest to you are the Beauty of Livermere, which is blood red with very dark blotches, and Mrs. Perry, which is a lovely salmon rose.

The pyrethrums or painted daisies, sometimes called painted ladies presumably because of their lovely coloring, are a great asset to any border. They belong to the chrysanthemum family, compositae, and are splendid for cut flowers.

Pyrethrums, with their daisy-like blooms, and many attractive colors, do best in well-drained soil.

They should also be planted in sunny positions.

There are many beautiful single and double varieties, including:

Singles — A. M. Kelway (rose), Avalanche (white), and James Kelway (crimson with yellow centre);

Doubles — Aphrodite (white), Lord Rosebery (reddish), Queen Sophia. (pink), and Queen Mary (pink).

The trollius or globe flower is an appealingly beautiful flower. The tallest of the intermediate species is ledebouri, a golden orange color with yellow anthers. This plant requires an acid soil, lots of water and a shady spot in the garden.

Polemonium coeruleum or Jacob's Ladder comes in a white and a blue and has finely-cut foliage and is a good hardy perennial.

Another charming flower is the perennial phlox which is grown in the colors of cherry red, light salmon pink, soft lavender, carmine rose, white, deep purple and bicolors. This lovely flower brightens up a border late in the season when some of the others have faded.

Phlox subulata in shades of rose, lilac, and white, are found among the early flowering plants. They need a hot, sunny place in a rock garden. They are propagated by cuttings from the current year's growth, or from seeds.

Physalis or Chinese lantern may not be so well known as some, although it is a showy and attractive perennial. It has large, bright orange-scarlet, lantern-shaped seed pods when it ripens in the fall. These pods are the main beauty of the plant and may be cut and dried for winter decorations in the home. The only species which does well here is physallis franchettii.

Most of these perennials should be grouped in threes and fours for effective arrangement, and placed about 18 inches to 24 inches apart.

Dwarf Perennials

The smaller and dwarf perennials are needed to fill out the front of perennial borders.

This, of course, has reference to the larger borders where tall, intermediate and dwarf varieties will be used. For those of you who have a narrow border, measuring perhaps 24 to 36 inches wide, the small varieties alone would make an attractive display. The average height of the dwarf varieties which I will name will be approximately 9 to 18 inches high.

One of the earliest of the little beauties is the flower of adonis, also known as pheasant's eye (aestivalis).

There are two kinds of the adonis which I can recommend to you; they are the vernalis and pyrenaica, both being delicate yellow in color with fragile, almost transparent petals and fern-like foliage.

5

They grow about 9 inches high and should be grouped in threes and fives for effectiveness, about 9 inches apart. They are one of the earliest flowers to bloom in the spring and surely that in itself will provide incentive for you to plant the adonis. We have so long to wait for spring flowers that some of the earliest kinds should be chosen.

Next to bloom after the adonis in the spring are the beautiful anemones or wind flowers. Four kinds of these which grow well here are halleri, pulsatilla, ochroleuca, and patens, the latter being our own wild anemone called locally the prairie crocus. They are in shades of creamy white, blue and mauve, and thrive in the sun, growing up to about 12 inches high.

The anthericum liliago, or St. Bernard's lily, has beautiful white bell-shaped flowers and is most fragrant. It grows 15 inches tall and is charming, as are all lilies.

The columbine also comes in the small-growing species. There are several of these which will enhance the front of a border. They are jucunda, alpina, flabellata nana alba, and truncata. All these grow 12 inches to 15 inches high and bloom in several lovely shades.

The jucunda is, I believe, the queen of the columbines — it has large, soft blue petals and white centre. It is a strikingly lovely flower, almost fascinating in its beauty.

The jonsii is a native of the Olympic Mountains, and is the smallest columbine (about 4 inches) known to horticulturists. The foliage is a greyish-green with dark blue flowers and short spurs. It is an extremely dainty plant and, like the jucunda, one of the earliest of its species.

The old-fashioned bachelor's button or corn flower (centaurea) is another attractive addition to any garden. Three kinds of these which thrive here are dealbata, moschata, and montana. They are grown in white, pink and a lovely vivid blue, and will grow in sun or shade.

The spurge (euphorbia) is related to the poinsettia and bears a strong resemblance to its lovely relative excepting the bracts or top leaves are a rich yellow instead of red. It grows about 15 inches high and requires a hot place with dry and light soil. It, too, is one of the early perennials. The best variety of the euphorbia is the Polychroma.

The perennial geranium or crane's bill is a splendid hardy perennial. It is in colors of blue, white, red and purple. Three species of this plant which I can recommend are argenteum, sanguineum, and endress which will reach a height of 9 to 18 inches.

The hemerocallis or the day lily is a lovely flower, which blooms in shades of deep orange to pale yellow. It is called the day lily because of its unique ability to produce a new bloom daily on each of its spikes. It has grass-like foliage and grows well in any good garden soil in sun or shade. The varieties of the day lily to obtain are the Flava, Minoe, and Fulva.

The coral bell (heuchera) is, as the latter name implies, a pretty coral-colored flower. It grows about 15 inches high and is dainty in form. Heuchera Sanguinea and the white variety called Alba are the best.

The iris, sometimes called the poor man's orchid, is a flower which deserves more prominence than is given to it. In recent years, many lovely irises have been developed. The new colors in these are rich beyond description, lovely enough indeed to be called the rich man's orchid. They need a hot, sunny location, and light soil. A little lime added is beneficial to their growth. When you plant irises be sure to keep the rhizomes, which are the fleshy rootstocks, above the ground.

6

The blazing star (liatris) is a native wild flower of our own province which has been cultivated for sale. It is of a very erect habit and is bright rose, red, and purple and grows from 16 to 20 inches high. Three of the best species are Montana, punctata and squarrosa.

The evening primrose (oenothera) is a charming little flower of a bright yellow color and is called the evening primrose because of the opening of blooms in the evening. There are biennials and perennials found in the family of the evening primrose. The perennials species which I recommend include speciosa, glauca and ameona.

One of the most colorful of all perennials is the Japanese peony (paeonia tenuifolium), in lovely shades of dark crimson and pink. These gorgeous early-blooming flowers are a must for a garden. The peony family resent farmyard manure but favor bonemeal cultivated around them (See separate chapter on peonies).

The garden gloxinia, known botanically as the incarvillea delavayi and grandiflora, is a hardy perennial with thick fleshy rootstocks, and is chiefly native of China and Turkestan.

The incarvillea thrives best on a sunny border or rockery in rather light, well-drained loamy soil, enriched with decayed manure.

In this part of the country the crowns must be covered with strawy litter or peat moss as a protection against excessive moisture and thawing out of the soil during the winter. Planting of the incarvillea should be done about the end of April.

Propagation by the division of the clumps or crowns is best done in April so that any roots broken or damaged make new growth quickly.

Seeds of incarvillea are sown in March in shallow boxes filled with a sandy loam and placed in a warm greenhouse, or seeds may be sown in boxes in May and set out in coldframes and covered with sheets of glass (which have paper over the glass) until the seeds germinate.

There are several kinds of incarvillea but the best known is incarvillea delavayi. It has lovely, pinnate leaves 12 inches long, and large trumpet-shaped rose-purple flowers with yellow throats, 8 to 10 blooms in a bunch in early summer.

Incarvillea grandiflora has shorter leaves than incarvillea delavayi and larger rose-crimson flowers with golden throats, 4 or 5 in a bunch and 3 to 4 inches across.

The garden gloxinia is truly a gorgeous plant and catches the eye as soon as you enter the garden.

In addition, the following dwarf perennials also do extremely well in Calgary and may be recommended to gardeners who give them their correct place and proper soil:

The houseleeks (sempervivums, which is the Latin word meaning living forever) are a species of fleshy herbs found widely scattered in the mountainous countries of the old world. They are mostly hardy perennials and stemless, and increased by rosettes which are sent out from the parent plant, thereby suggesting the popular name "hen and chickens." They can also be readily raised from seed. Thirty species of them grow on the Reader Rock Garden.

The houseleeks are cultivated more for foliage plants than for flowers, and are popular for carpet bedding, rock gardens, and for covering dry banks and bare sandy places. They are of the easiest culture and are quickly multiplied by means of the offsets or rosettes.

7

The aubrietia is a perennial and more or less an evergreen trailer. It is excellent for the rock garden and edging. It is propagated by seed, layers, or cutting.

Rock cress (Arabis) is a small perennial or annual herb with white or purple flowers grown mostly for rock work. It is found growing in temperate regions and several species are native to this country.

The cerastium tomentosum, which is Greek for horn, alluding to the shape of the seed pod, is a decumbent perennial. It has weak slender stems, small white leaves, and white flowers. It is commonly called snow-in-the-summer, because of the very white leaves and flowers. It is valuable for rockery work, or for bedding and edging horders. It is extremely dainty in leaf and flower.

The golden tuft (alyssum saxatile), sometimes called cloth of gold, is most appropriately named with its golden yellow, numerous and compact clusters of flowers. It is also valuable for rock work or dry steep banks in that it forms a spreading mat and blooms early in the spring.

The saxifrage, from the Latin rock and to break, possibly refers to the fact that many of the species grow in the clefts of rock. This family is also a large one. At one time the city parks grew 70 kinds here in Calgary.

The saxifrage are herbs, mostly perennial, with perfect small, white, yellow, pink, or purplish flowers. Most of the species in cultivation are grown as rock garden plants.

The gentians are among the most desirable of alpine plants and of blue flowers in general. They are chiefly perennial herbs, rarely annuals or biennials. They thrive well here when planted in partly shaded spots.

THE POPPIES

Now, having described a few of the perennials recommended for the herbaceous borders, according to heights, let's take a look at some other popular perennials suitable for any kind of garden bed in Calgary.

Among the most popular and colorful of our Calgary perennials are the poppies.

Poppies flourish in ordinary soil with most kinds preferring a well-drained garden spot. They must be grown in a sunny location, and are not successful in shady places.

Some poppies, if planted for the herbaceous border, are intermediate in size (including the Oriental) and some are dwarf (including the Iceland and Flanders).

The Iceland poppy, known botanically as papaver nudicaule, is the glory of the cold regions of Canada. It ranges over an immense territory and varies remarkably both in the wild and in the garden.

The colors of the Iceland poppy have been greatly improved over the years. Today, you can have them in shades of pink, rose, yellow, deep yellow, orange, white, whitish pink, and even a pale red, but the flowers never obtain the brilliant scarlet of the Flanders poppy.

Although the Iceland poppy is a perennial, it is short-lived and is commonly treated as an annual. The Iceland poppy is known for the satiny texture and crimpled character of its petals. The flowers are excellent for cutting, especially if the young flowers are selected and cut in the early morning, a principle which applies to many flowers often supposed to be useless for home decoration.

8

The Oriental poppy, papaver orientale, is a long-lived perennial, and although it has the largest flowers of any species in the genus, it has nothing like the fame of the opium poppy.

The alpine poppy is a dainty dwarf species and most suitable for the rock garden. The flowers are small and dainty with fern-like foliage; a charming plant which is to be recommended for a rock garden or in the front of the perennial border.

The best way to raise Oriental poppies is from seed. The poppy does not like to be disturbed and this you would have to do to take root cuttings. Raising Oriental poppies from seed is a simple matter. Seeds develop profusely on established plants. The pods should be gathered before they are open and the seeds saved until spring or, of course, seeds may be purchased at that time.

The seeds should be sown in a box of sifted, sandy soil about the beginning of March. They will be ready to bed out at the beginning of June. The varieties of Oriental poppies which are grown here are Barrs White and Lord Lambourne, scarlet blotched with black spots; and Princess Louise, pink with black blotch.

Poppies vary greatly in size, from the tall Oriental poppy 24 to 36 inches high, to the low-growing alpine poppy 9 inches tall.

The Oriental poppy is a hardy herbaceous perennial with large deeply-cut leaves which bear immense cup-shaped flowers of various brilliant colors in early summer. It is one of the most striking of all the flowering plants which are in full beauty in June and July.

The Oriental poppy has thick, fleshy roots and becomes established rather slowly and flowers little, if at all, until the second year after planting.

It is better to plant all poppies where they are to remain indefinitely, for the plants increase in size annually for many years. It looks best in small groups in the herbaceous border. Poppies should be placed in the middle, or towards the back of the border, as their flowers are rather early to bloom and afterwards the large leaves look rather untidy and some ripen off.

The seeds of all poppies are very small and fine, and the soil in which they are to be planted should be broken down finely with a fork and a rake. Sow the seeds thinly, and cover lightly, for if they are planted too deep they will not germinate.

When the plants are 2 to 3 inches tall, thin to about 12 inches apart. Pick all the seed pods off as soon as the petals drop, unless one desires to save the seed.

There is no way in which the lover of color in flowers may gratify his taste so cheaply and so fully as by growing a good selection of poppies. No other flower will make such a gorgeous show in the border during the months of May, June and July and the first half of August.

It was during the year 1939 or 1940 that W. R. Reader, then Calgary's park superintendent, introduced the meconopsis, bailejii, or meconopsis betonicifolia, the blue poppy, into the Reader Rock Garden.

It is a perennial although it sometimes happens that the plants will rush into flowers the first year before they have developed side growths, with the result that when the single central rosette has flowered, there is nothing in the way of side shoots by which the plants can carry on for the following year.

This is probably caused by poor cultivation. If the plants are raised in good time and kept growing vigorously all the season, they will develop several crowns,

9

the strongest of which will flower the first year, while the others will flower for the second and third seasons.

It is this premature flowering of immature or ill-grown plants that has led some horticulturists to state that this poppy is not a perennial. Well-grown plants of this fine species have lived to flower for four or five successive years.

Meconopsis betonicifolia forms rosettes of large stalked leaves 6 to 9 inches or more in length. In June and July, the plants reach a height of 24 to 36 inches and carry a loose head, large blue poppy-like flowers of satin texture, each 2 to 3 inches across and a handsome corona of golden anther.

The color of the flowers is pale sky blue, and a group of plants well placed with a green background and the advantage of shade is one of the most splendid things that modern gardening has produced.

These plants may be bought so cheaply, and seeds are so reasonable in price and easy to raise, that even the amateur may grow these superb flowers.

LILY-OF-THE-VALLEY

Lily-of-the-valley, known botanically as convallaria majalis, is hardy and easily grown in Alberta in partly shaded places and moderately rich soil, with lots of leaf mould or peat moss. Few cultivated plants give so much satisfaction at so little cost as the lily of the valley. It is one of our earliest flowering spring plants, and may be planted in out-of-the-way places where other plants will not grow.

Lily-of-the-valley can be bought in pink or rose-colored varieties, double kinds of white, and varieties with foliage striped with white. This perennial is much prized for its delicate sweet-scented flowers and is supposed to be the one referred to in the Sermon on the Mount.

When preparing a bed outside in the garden for lily-of-the-valley, it is a good plan to select a partly-shaded spot. Remove all the old soil to a depth of 12 inches. A mixture of two parts fibrous loam, three parts peat moss or leaf soil, and a scattering of bone meal, mixed well together, forms the ideal mixture for the bed.

Planting should be done outdoors about the last two weeks in April provided that the weather is favorable.

The pips or crowns should be planted one inch below the level of the soil, and about 3 inches apart, and kept well watered until they are properly rooted. They love a top dressing of peat moss yearly. Once planted in the proper location and compost, they will thrive and spread rapidly. Care must be taken, however, that they are kept in bounds or they will over-run other plants that are close by.

PERENNIAL PHLOX

Phlox, which is a popular flower with Calgary gardeners, is one of the most important groups of garden plants. Some phlox are hardy, while others are half-hardy. They are invaluable in the herbaceous border, rock gardens, and flower beds. They are extremely dainty and appealing in the many soft, lovely colors in which they are grown.

They are natives chiefly of North America and belong to the Jacob's ladder family, polemoniaceae. The word phlox, meaning flame, alludes to the brilliant coloring of the flowers. The tall herbaceous perennial phlox which provide such an imposing display of blooms in late summer are descended from phlox decussata (paniculata) which is found wild in North America.

The flowers of the modern varieties show a wide range of color varying from white through to blush to rose, crimson and scarlet, and through lavender to purple and bicolors.

Hardy phlox can be regarded as the backbone of summer gardens, producing exquisite large flower heads of rich, satiny masses of color during July and August.

These plants need a deep rich soil and appreciate slight shade. They will thrive in full sunshine providing the soil is deep and remains moist in hot, dry weather, but they are not a success in poor, light soil which dries out in summer.

If the soil in your garden is light, it is wise to plant phlox in a partly shady border, as, for example, one facing west or north. In the average garden which consists of loamy or well-cultivated clayey ground, they may be set in a sunny border. Part shade is, however, an advantage even then, for the plants will last longer in full beauty should hot, dry weather set in. But never plant phlox in deep shade.

Phlox should not be planted too closely. Give them plenty of space for the natural development of the plant, cultivation and good circulation of air.

Never water overhead. Foliage must be dry, particularly before nightfall. The best way is to let the water run slowly out of the hose, placing it on the ground.

Always remove the faded flower heads, for if the seeds are allowed to ripen and fall to the ground they will germinate, grow and smother good varieties.

Phlox provide such a splendid display that it is worth while taking pains with their cultivation. The soil should be dug about 18 inches deep, well-rotted manure being put into it. The best time to plant is in early spring after all danger of frost is past.

Phlox are surface-rooting plants; therefore, they must be kept moist. This may be accomplished by mulching the soil round about them with decayed manure. If you cannot obtain the decayed manure, peat moss or lawn mowings will do, though these do not feed the plants as the manure does.

During hot dry weather, water should be given plentifully to the phlox while they are in full growth. When they are growing freely, it is wise to look them over for the purpose of pulling up all thin, weak shoots, for these will not flower and merely hinder the proper development of the better and stronger shoots.

The pieces that are pulled up will form roots if set in pots of sandy soil, placed in a coldframe, and kept closed for a week or two.

As a rule, phlox need little staking, but it may be necessary to support vigorous plants of the taller varieties by a few stakes encircled by string or raffia. This support should be given if it is required to keep the stems upright.

When the leaves have fallen in autumn, the stems should be cut down to within about 2 or 3 inches of the ground. After the first hard frost has occurred, it is necessary to mulch phlox with leaves, strawy litter or peat moss.

Keep a close watch on the plants during their early growing stages and dust the foliage with fine flower of sulphur. Be sure the upper and undersides of the leaves are thoroughly covered to check mildew and rust. If the foliage turns a light green, and eventually yellow, you can be almost sure that 'the plants have been attacked by the spider mite which can be controlled by spraying with Aramite or Dimite. Directions for the use of these sprays are specifically given on the package.

Dark brown circular spots on the leaves are what is commonly known as rust. The squeeze duster (Roseleaf) can be used for its control. This dust can also be used effectively in eliminating beetles and other leaf-chewing insects.

There are innumerable varieties of the large-flowered herbaceous phlox, and here are some of the attractive ones which can be used in your garden in Calgary:

Salmon Glow, best of all salmons; Starlight, fiery and robust with graceful branching habit; World Peace, a lovely white; Lillian, soft cameo pink; Sir John Falstaff, outstanding variety of rich salmon pink; Etna, salmon scarlet; Europa, white with carmine centre; F. A. Buchner, white; General Van Hentz, reddish salmon; G. A. Strohlein, orange scarlet; Jules Sandeau, rose pink; Le Mahdi, purple; Pharaoh, rose and mauve; Selma, pink; Thor, salmon.

A well-known species is phlox subulata, also called moss pink or trailing phlox. It grows 4 to 6 inches high and is perfect for borders, as edgings for walks and driveways, and especially for rockeries. It is ideal as bank binders to prevent soil wash-out and does well in hot and dry locations, also in part shade. This variety forms a dense carpet-like foliage which remains green all winter.

The low mound-like plants are covered with a profusion of brightly-colored flowers of blue, white, bright pink, dark pink, lilac color, vivid crimson. These dwarf phlox do well here in Alberta provided they are covered over in the fall with a top dressing of peat moss. The peat moss may be removed in the spring about the last two weeks in April.

Next, we have phlox divaricata, known as the wild blue phlox. They bloom in early spring and blend well with the blue-flowered Virginia Cowslip (mertensia). The wild blue phlox produces large fragrant lavender-blue flowers on stems 10 to 12 inches high, and is suitable for borders, rockeries, and naturalizing in large or small areas, especially under large trees, and is also excellent as ground covers.

All phlox should have a covering over them after the ground is frozen to prevent the plants from being heaved out of the ground during the winter.

DIANTHUS (Carnations and Pinks)

The important group of hardy plants known generally as dianthus includes all the pinks and carnations as well as the sweet william, which are all closely related.

In this group are found annuals, biennials and perennials.

Carnations in these parts are thought of by most people as flowers which may be purchased at a florist's shop. It is true that we get a good supply of lovely carnations from out florists, but they can also be grown quite successfully outdoors in Alberta.

The carnation or dianthus carejophilus is a half-hardy herbaceous perennial. Indoors it grows to a height of 24 inches, and outdoors in our climate to a height of about 18 inches.

It is a native of Southern Europe and is occasionally met in the wild state in England, particularly the southern part where it was introduced through cultivation. The carnation is perhaps one the oldest flowers which we cultivate, and has been grown for more than 2,000 years. Originally, it was flesh-colored only, hence the name carnation (from the Latin caro, meaning flesh). Today, they come in many varieties and colors.

Those who plan to raise carnations for outdoor planting should certainly purchase early varieties, such as the hardy Grenadin, the giant Malmaison, and the giant Chabauds. These come in many shades and colors.

Some of the hardy kinds will winter out here if they are well mulched in the fall.

The carnation is rather a heavy feeder, and quantity and quality of blooms depend largely on the nourishment supplied. The necessity for feeding depends upon the richness of the soil, and over-feeding should be avoided because this could prove disastrous.

The dianthus is essentially a European genus, there being but one of the species native on this continent known as dianthus alpinus, found in the high northern regions and also in Europe.

Among the gems of the genus are various pretty little alpine tufted sorts as dianthus neglectus, dianthus glacialis, dianthus delioides, and dianthus alpinus, all of which are dwarf, and of close habit, not exceeding 3 to 6 inches in height, and having lovely, single flowers of the brightest colors. These are suited only for rock gardening.

Dianthus love a light, warm soil, and one that will not become too wet at any time, and especially in the fall when the perennial kinds are grown. They are often killed not so much from the cold as from too much moisture around them.

Chinese pinks, or Indian pinks as they are often called, and which are descended from dianthus chinensis, are showy plants which bear large fringed flowers of various bright colors in the summer. They are used for planting in the summer flower beds. They are treated as biennials and are raised fresh from seeds each year. These plants reach a height of 9 to 12 inches, bloom freely all season long, and come in various shades and colors.

The Japanese pinks, varieties of dianthus heddewiggii, grow 9 to 10 inches tall and bear a profusion of large fringed flowers of varied coloring from July to freeze-up. They are usually treated as half-hardy annuals and raised from seeds sown in a heated greenhouse in February or early March.

All pinks will flourish in various kinds of soils if the following advice is followed. When the soil is light, sandy and poor, spring planting is recommended so that the plants become established before hot, dry weather begins. The advantage of light soil is that the dianthus plants will have free drainage during the fall and winter and begin to grow earlier in spring.

Cultivating the soil once a week in bright, dry weather will help to keep the roots cool and moist. Frequent top dressings of peat moss and lots of sharp fine pea gravel are most suitable for them.

Dianthus should never be planted in a heavy clay soil, but if clay soil is prevalent in your garden it can be made suitable by working in lots of sharp sand and slaked lime.

It is desirable and advisable to keep plants compact. To do this, the old blooms must be removed as soon as possible after flowering; cutting them back immediately above the cuhion foliage that surrounds the stems.

It is important that all dianthus be mulched over with strawy litter after the first hard frost to protect the persistent foliage, that is, the green-crowned leaves that stay above the soil level.

Other types of dianthus grown successfully here in Alberta are allwoodii rock pinks, a race of hardy annuals suitable for the rock garden or flower border. One of the most popular pinks is dianthus casius, commonly known as the

13

cheddar pink because it grows wild on the cliffs of the Cheddar Gorge in England. It is a charming little tufted plant, 6 inches tall, and bears a profusion of rose-colored blooms.

Dianthus arenarius, the sand-loving pink, 6 inches tall with white flowers marked with a carmine ring on the petals, is another good flower.

TROLLIUS

The globe flower, or trollius, is one of the most admired and early flowering perennials which does well in this part of the country, and no garden should be without it.

It is a group of ornamental herbaceous perennial plants belonging to the buttercup family. One type, trollius europaeus, the common globe flower, is a native of Britain. It is a beautiful plant which has been used in the raising of many fine garden hybrids.

All the trollius enjoy rich, loamy soil and ample moisture at the roots. Many of them are superb plants for the flower border as well as for the bog garden, for ponds and poolside planting, and for moist, well-manured and shady places. There are several dwarf kinds suitable for planting in the rock garden.

The globe flower, too, is invaluable as a cut flower, lasting well because of its moisture-loving habits.

Trollius may be increased by division of the roots in spring or fall, or by seeds which should be sown as soon as they ripen in flats of soil, peat moss and sand, well mixed together. These seeds are sown over this compost, covered with the same compost, watered, and placed outside for the winter.

They are usually slow in germinating, the seedlings often taking a year or more to come up, though they are fairly certain germinators in the end.

By sowing the seeds in the fall, and placing them outside during the winter, you advance the germinating period by approximately 12 months.

Trollius europaeus, although a native of Britain, does exceptionally well in our cold climate, and gives us a lovely show of blooms about the end of May and early June. It grows 18 to 24 inches tall, with erect stems carrying large, globe-shaped, yellow flowers with curiously rounded incurved petals which are really sepals. The true petals are small, inconspicuous and concealed within the flower.

Trollius europaeus is well worth a place in the rock garden, and should be planted in the lower parts where it will catch any moisture.

Trollius acaulis is a dwarf plant from the Himalayas, growing to about 6 inches tall with large golden, wide-open flowers like handsome buttercups carried singly on erect stems. It does best in rich loam in the rock garden.

Trollius altaicus, the altaian globe flower, grows 12 to 18 inches tall and has pale yellow sepals arranged like a wide-open buttercup. Trollius laxus grows 18 inches tall and has pale yellow globe-shaped flowers.

Trollius chinensis is an Asiatic species with deep golden flowers growing 24 inches tall.

Trollius ledebouris, 24 to 36 inches tall, has deep golden flowers which bloom much later than the other kinds.

Trollius pumulus has large golden flower-like buttercups. It grows 9 to 12 inches high and is also suitable for the rock garden in shady places.

Trollius patulus is one of the Asiatic species with handome wide-open buttercup-like flowers of rich gold, 9 to 12 inches high. This is also a good plant for the rock garden.

Then, of course, there is a fine race of hybrids ranging from palest yellow to deep orange; growing from 18 inches to 36 inches tall.

The trollius is truly a beautiful perennial and is to be recommended highly.

PENTSTEMON

We have growing in the foothills of Alberta and in the Canadian Rockies, several species of pentstemon. For the hardy border, the pentstemon (or beard's tongue) are most satisfactory plants. The great number of showy species allows much latitude in choice of color and habit. All are perennial but some of them bloom the first year from seed.

In a dry and hot sandy place, they are likely to be short-lived, although nearly all the species thrive best in full exposure to the sun. They are not particular as to type of soil as long as it is fairly rich and not sandy. Pentstemon are propagated by division and by seed.

Although many of the pentstemon (five stamens) family are native to the USA and Canada, many kinds of the 60 or more European hybrids which are known, also do grow well here in Alberta. An excellent garden race has been produced here, designated as pentstemon gloxinioides. These seem to be the product of hybridization and selection.

Pentstemon gloxinioides can be raised from seed by sowing them in the greenhouse early in the season and flowering them successfully during the growing season. These come in various shades and colors and make a very showy and colorful display in the garden.

Among a few of the types to be recommended for Alberta are:

Pentstemon menziesii are to be found in the Rocky Mountains. They are of a shrubby nature and grow about 15 inches tall. These are free bloomers and come in two colors — white and blue.

Pentstemon grandiflorus grows about 24 inches tall; the flowers are 2 inches long in shades of lilac or blue.

Pentstemon humilus is a low-growing plant not more than 6 inches tall with rather narrow, deep-blue flowers sometimes ranging to white, the lower lip bearded within. This plant may be found in our Rocky Mountains and is most suitable for the rock garden.

Pentstemon secundiflorus is about 24 inches tall. The leaves are narrow and somewhat glaucous, and it makes a splendid cut flower because of its showy habit.

Pentstemon campanulatus has a branching habit from the base, about 18 inches tall. The flowers are long and narrow and of a rose-purple color.

The pentstemon hybrids are a showy group of plants. They must be started in the greenhouse very early in the spring, and should be well grown. The pentstemon requires a light rich soil in a sunny sheltered spot in your garden.

In growing pentstemon from seed, the seedlings should be pricked off when the third or natural leaf appears. This is not only good sense, but common sense, too. The third leaf, being sturdier and stronger, is much easier to handle. The only time they should be pricked off in the cotyledon stage is when you see signs of the seedlings damping off.

DODECATHEON

Another lovely and showy plant which is native to Canada and Alberta is the dodecatheon, perhaps not too well known. The dodecatheon, sometimes called the shooting star or American cowslip, is a hardy herbaceous plant with flowers that are hard to forget after seeing them for the first time.

The flowers have been compared to a diminutive cyclamen, for they are pendulous and seem to be full of motion.

The stamens in dodecatheon media, which is an Eastern species, come to a sharp point and seem to be shooting ahead while the petals stream behind like the tail of a comet.

The flowers represent every shade from pure white through lilac and rose to purple, and they all have a yellow circle in the middle, that is, at the mouth of the corolla.

Dodecatheons belong to the same order with primula and cyclamen, but in a different tribe from the latter, while its reflexed corolla lobes distinguish it from the 10 other genera of its own tribe. The native dodecatheon of the Rocky Mountains is known as jefferyii and by its introduction into cultivation has improved immensely both in height and size of bloom.

There are 17 known species growing throughout the North American continent. Several of these are growing here in Calgary in the Reader Rock Garden. They seem to grow in any well-cultivated soil in sun or part shade. Although some kinds grow from 9 inches to 15 inches tall, they all seem to show off at their best in the rock garden.

Dodecatheon alpinum is the smallest of the group with flowers twice as large as some of the taller kinds and of a rich dark purple. There is a white species (dodecatheon alpinum alba) which is most attractive when growing among the other kinds.

In the culture of these dodecatheon plants, all they require is an open, well-drained soil, not too dry, and moderately rich, and a shady or part-shady position. In too sunny a border, the flowers are of short duration. The rockery with a northern or eastern aspect suits them best.

They are propagated by division of the crown or by seeds, the latter method being rather slow. The leaves of the dodecatheon disappear after flowering and do not appear again until the next spring. It is their rest period.

PRIMULA

One class of plants which do exceedingly well in our climate is the primula family. The home gardener should become better acquainted with these hardy and sweet-smelling plants, among the loveliest of our early flowers.

The primula auricula, which is a European perennial, sends up short spikes bearing flowers of many colors. It is one of the well-known European flowers, but has never received the attention in this country it has across the ocean.

Here, it has to be planted in a partly shaded spot and in an acid soil.

Auriculas may be propagated by seed for several purposes and for the production of new varieties, but to perpetuate choice varieties it is necessary to propagate either by offsets or division of the plant.

Seeds should be sown indoors in shallow boxes or small 3- to 4-inch pots early in March so that the seedlings may be well developed before warm weather sets in. The soil used in the seed pots must be very light and sandy, the surface made smooth and the seed then sown and pressed lightly into the soil. After this, a light covering of sand can be given. The flats or pots then are watered, covered with paper, and placed in a temperature of 60 degrees until they have germinated, which usually takes from 3 to 4 weeks.

They may then be moved to a fairly light indoors position and shaded from direct sunlight in a rather lower temperature to induce a stocky growth.

As soon as the seedlings are large enough to handle conveniently, prick them off into flats 2 to 3 inches deep containing a mixture of 2 parts peat moss, 1 part screened loam, and 1 part sharp clean sand.

Watering should be carefully attended to, and everything done to promote active growth so that, if possible, the plants may be large enough after June 1 to require a second shift into larger boxes or out into the garden.

Auricula seedlings go through the hottest months much better in boxes or in the garden than in pots, as they are not large enough to set out in their permanent location in the garden. They may be placed in coldframes in a partly shaded place on the north side of a wall or hedge, or almost any position where they will be shaded from the sun and still receive plenty of light.

The frame should be provided with a sash which may be kept over the plants most of the time, giving air in abundance in favorable weather. During the warmest weather, the whole sash should be raised by placing a piece of wood under each corner to allow the circulation of air among the plants.

At freeze-up, the young auricula seedlings should be covered with strawy litter, after which they may be left in the coldframes all winter. They will even survive the winter without a covering, but it is better to cover them. It is this hardiness which makes them an ideal flower for our cold spring climate.

In the spring, they may be bedded out in the garden in a partly shaded location.

The auriculas will not bloom the first year after bedding out, but will the second year if they were well grown the first year, and they are at their best the third and fourth years.

When these plants are so established, you will have a lovely bed of auriculas for many years to come. Any time or effort spent in the raising of these lovely early-blooming plants will be well-rewarded and worthwhile. The primula auriculas are splendid plants for rock garden and edging, or for solid beds in part shade.

Some of the many species of primulas which may be grown here with wonderful success are the following:

Primula cortusoides, growing in part shade in the rock garden, and bearing showy carmine rose-colored blooms.

Primula sikkimensis, a charming hardy plant suitable for cultivation in a shady or partly shaded border in deep moist soil. It bears light yellow blooms.

Primula ameones, one of the most attractive hardy primulas. The blooms are of violet-lilac shade.

Primula polyanthus (or bunch-flowered primrose), if massed in a garden or among shrubs, furnish a delightful display of blooms early in the spring.

Primula microdonta alpicola, suitable for planting in borders where the soil is rich and moist. It bears drooping, fragrant, cream or pale sulphur-colored flowers in May or June.

Primula cashmeriana, an easily-grown plant which has rounded heads of lilac or mauve blooms in early spring. This primula is the first to bloom.

Primula veitchii, a showy, hardy plant suitable for a cool place in the garden. It bears rich rose-colored flowers.

Primula pedemontana has pink, white-eyed flowers and thrives in a moist, gritty soil compost in the rock garden.

Yellow-flowered primula florindae, one of the most striking of all the hardy primulas. It is vigorous and easily managed in moist soil or around a pool in part shade.

Primulas are mostly hardy perennials native to Europe and other temperature zones. One type which is native to Alberta is known as primula farinosa.

Primulas give a wide range of extremely beautiful plants for the rock garden, flower beds, the wild garden, the greenhouse, and even window boxes, and thus we can enjoy the blossoms of the many showy species in spring and summer and all through the winter.

Some of the earliest primulas to bloom outside are primula cashmeriana primula veris (the English Cowslip), primula longiflora, primula vulgaris (the English common primrose) and primula auricula.

HOLLYHOCK

The hollyhock, known botanically as althaea rosea, is an old garden favorite full of sentiment and association with the distant past, and only the ravages of a dire rust disease have robbed it of the proud position it held among garden flowers during the beginning of the present century.

Hollyhocks are plants of strong, vigorous growth, noble aspect, and of the most ornamental character. This plant must not be neglected or ignored, for we can ill dispense with its stately beauty.

Before the ravages of disease, there were in existence large collections of named varieties, and the hollyhock was then one of the most important of flowers.

Within recent years, the disease having been somewhat controlled, either from loss of its virulence or through preventive measures, collections of named varieties are again being formed.

In the light of my own experience, I believe one can get the best and surest results by raising plants from seed of good strain. The seed may be sown at any time during the early months of the year in a greenhouse, and outside after the middle of May.

Sow the seeds in flats or pots and place them in a warm house to assist germination.

Pot the plants singly as they develop, and keep them growing freely and sturdily in a cool, airy temperature, removing them to the open garden as summer advances.

If well grown, plants should be in 6-inch pots in early April. Later on in the season, about the first of June, they should be planted out where they are to bloom.

As hollyhocks demand liberal feeding, their permanent location should be well prepared by deep digging, at the same time working in a good quantity of rotted manure. A scattering of lime will benefit them.

Plant 36 inches apart and firmly, and should the fall months be dry, give water frequently, as drought disposes the plants to attack by disease.

The following spring, the plants will grow vigorously, and the only attention needed is copious watering during dry spells. The flowers will appear from July onwards.

The hollyhock is a hardy perennial and biennial. It should, however, be covered in the fall with peat moss or strawy litter after the first severe frost, removing the covering in April the following year.

Should rust appear, however, root out the plants and destroy by fire, and make the next planting on a new site some distance away. Thorough spraying with fungicides may be expected to hold the disease in check if applications are made early and to the undersides of the leaves. But if Bordeaux mixture is used, the plants will look rather peculiar with the deposits of Bordeaux on the foliage. Use 8 to 10 tablespoonsful of Bordeaux mixture to 1 gallon of water. This may have to be done once or twice during the growing season.

Hollyhocks grow to a height of from 6 to 10 feet and must be staked and tied to keep the stems from damage by wind.

A few fine named varieties are: Appolon, rose; Brennus, crimson; Ettie Beale, flesh pink; Diadem, rich yellow; Venus, white; Enchantress, yellow; and Mrs. Barron, rose pink.

The hollyhock plants love a sunny border where the soil has good drainage.

SUNFLOWER

The genus helianthus includes the common annual sunflower, and about 15 hardy herbaceous perennial plants rather coarse in habit with yellow flowers which are usually large, numerous, and bloom in August and September.

The sunflower family is of easiest culture, and is adapted to a variety of soils. It is seen to best advantage when planted in masses, rather than as solitary specimens and should be given plenty of room, being a gross feeder.

Most sunflowers, especially helianthus annuus, are too coarse to be harmonious near the house, but find an effective setting in the background against against the shrubbery border or the back of the perennial border.

Sunflowers grow readily in many soils, but best results are obtained upon light, rich, calcareous soil, well supplied with moisture and unshaded by trees. Preparation of the soil should be thorough, deep fall-digging being preferred to spring preparation.

There are a few lovely perennial kinds which are to be recommended, including:

Helianthus orgyalis, 8 feet tall with numerous lemon yellow flowers, very leafy stems which make the plants most attractive.

Helianthus divarcatus, 2 to 3 feet high, and found wild in the gravelly ditches of Alberta. It is most satisfactory when brought into cultivation where the proper conditions exist.

Helianthus pumilus, native to the eastern slopes of the Rockies and dwarf, and suitable for the front of the border. These are native to this continent.

There are, also, quite a few kinds that have been improved and cultivated in gardens. These include:

Helianthus multiflorus and its double variety, Soleil d'Or, growing 4 to 5 feet high and most attractive.

19

Miss Mellish and helianthus multiflorus maxims, all tall with yellow, bronze or orange blossoms.

Propagation is by seeds sown in a light, sandy soil in a greenhouse or cold frame when the weather is favorable. It must be remembered that the helianthus family must be planted in a sunny place because they are essentially sun-loving. The smaller ones are suitable for the rock garden or sunny banks.

The dwarf or alpine kinds bloom in May to July;

A few varieties suitable for the rock garden are:

The Bride, white with silvery foliage; Fireball, scarlet red; Sudbury Gem, crimson; Rubens, yellow; Rose Queen and Ben More, flame; and Ben Nevis, Chrome-yellow.

The dwarf kinds have what is known as persistent foliage, and must be covered in the late fall after the first hard frost with peat moss, and the mulch is removed about the middle of April the following spring.

Growing from Seed

One of the first questions the new gardener is going to ask is: "How do I start growing any of these perennials?"

Most are grown from seed sown in the greenhouse or indoors under protection.

But if you haven't got a greenhouse, how do you go about growing perennials from seed?

The best way is to reserve a corner of the back garden for this purpose.

This ground should be dug to a depth of 10 inches with well-rotted manure placed in the bottom. Afterwards the soil should be raked to a fine tilth, and made level.

When all frost has come out of the ground (usually after May 24) sow the outdoor perennial seeds, generally to a depth of about quarter of an inch in rows about 15 inches apart. The seed should not be sown too thickly.

This seed must be watered regularly with a fine spray. After rooting, it is not necessary to water so often.

When the seedlings are 2 to 3 inches high they may be transplanted to their permanent positions in the flower beds, or borders, for blooming the next spring.

Seedlings may be transplanted from their back garden seed bed nursery the second year after planting the seed, but it is better to transplant them to their permanent locations the first year, because then they will bloom the second year.

General Notes

STAKING PERENNIALS

All tall and intermediate perennials need staking when they begin to put on growth.

Where there are large clumps, three or four stakes may be needed. The first tie should be made about half way up the stems.

Tying of perennials at the right time is of the utmost importance. If this necessary work is neglected, plants may be broken or bent by wind and rain, and the whole appearance of the perennial garden border will be spoiled for the entire season.

It has often been said that the little things are so important in gardening. This is true, and if you consistently care for the little details, you will find your larger gardening problems are fewer.

Those who have wide beds or borders will find they are quite trodden down after staking plants is completed. This should be immediately remedied by cultivation. Do not cultivate in spots, but cultivate the whole area. The benefit of cultivation cannot be over-estimated and should be done at least once a week and especially a day or two after heavy watering. Cultivation keeps the weeds down and lets the air into the plants.

True cultivation is just lightly and evenly breaking the top crust of the soil. Some people go too deep and thereby break and injure the roots of the plants.

DIVIDING PERENNIALS

When dividing perennials for transplanting, always use the young parts of the old plant. You will find them on the outside of the perennial. It is better, if at all possible, not to use the centre or older part of the plant.

PERSISTENT FOLIAGE

I would like to mention, in passing, plants having persistent foliage. By this I mean plants that retain a green crown of foliage above ground all winter. All perennials should be covered, but varieties of this type *must* be covered if they are to survive the alternate thawing and freezing of this climate.

Sweet William, Canterbury bells, pinks, carnations, saxifrages, sweet rocket, and auriculas, are often lost, because they have persistent foliage and are not covered in the fall.

Mr. Munro in Memorial Park, Calgary

21

Perennials by Heights

(And by colors, with planting hints and blooming times)

Note:

Numbers in first column after flower's name indicate:

(1) — These perennials should be planted in sun
(2) — These perennials should be planted in shade
(3) — These perennials may be planted in sun or in shade
(4) — These perennials should be planted in part shade

UNDER 12 INCHES

NAME (Generally, common name) *Number: in Sun or in Shade*	COLOR	HEIGHT *(in inches)*	DISTANCE BETWEEN PLANTINGS *(in inches)*	NORMAL BLOOMING TIME
Anemone (1)	Blue, Mauve, White	8	8 to 9	April, May
Ameone Primula (4)	Reddish Purple	6	8 to 9	April, May
Begonia, Fibrous-root or Ornamental (2)	Various	10	8	June to September
Blue Flax (1)	Blue	9	8 to 9	June
Bunch Polyantha (4)	Various	6	8 to 9	May
Buttercup (2)	Yellow	3 to 4	3 to 4	April, May, June
Candytuft (1)	White, Pink	8	8 to 9	May
Cashmere Primrose (4)	Mauve	6	8 to 9	April
Cat Mint (1)	Blue	9	8 to 9	June
Cowslip (4)	Pale Yellow	9	8 to 9	April
Crocus (1)	Mauve, Yellow, White	3 to 4	3 to 4	March, April
Dutch Hyacinth (1)	Blue	9	9	April, May
Dianthus Plumarius Casius (1)	Pink	9	8 to 9	June
Dianthus Superbus (1)	Mauve	9	10 to 11	July
Dwarf Iris (1)	Various	3 to 4	3 to 4	May, June

22

English Daisy (4)	Pink, White, Red	3	6	August
English Primrose (4)	Pale Yellow	6	6	April
Forget-Me-Not (4)	Blue, Pink, White	9	6 to 8	May
Fritillaria (2)	Yellow, Mottled	9 to 10	6	April, May
German Catchfly (1)	Rose	9	9	May
Grape Hyacinth (1)	Blue	6	6	April
Golden Flax (1)	Golden	9	9 to 10	June
Hyacinth (1)	Blue, Pink, White, Mauve	9	8	April, May
Lily of the Valley (4)	White, Pink	3	6	May
Ox Lip (4)	Yellow	9	8 to 9	May
Perennial Flax (1)	Blue	9	8 to 9	May, June
Pinks (1)	Various	6	6 to 8	June
Primula Cortusioides (4)	Rose	9	8 to 9	July
Rock Cress (1)	White, Mauve	6	6	April
Scilla (3)	Blue, White	3	3	March, April
Snowdrop (1)	White	3 to 4	3 to 4	April
Snow-in-Summer (1)	White Leaves and White Flowers	9	8 to 9	May, June
Sweet William (1)	Various	9	8 to 9	June
Winter Aconite (1)	Yellow	2 to 3	3	March

FROM 12 TO 23 INCHES

Aster (1)	Blue, White	12	10 to 12	July, August
Balloon Flower (1)	Blue, White	18	12 to 14	July, August
Beard's Tongue (3)	Blue	18	12 to 14	July, August
Begonia, Tuberous-root (2)	Various	15	10 to 12	June, July, August
Bluebell (1)	Blue, White	12	10 to 12	May, July
Blue Lobelia (1)	Blue	12	12	August
Campanula Sarmatica (1)	Light Blue	18	16 to 18	July

FROM 12 TO 23 INCHES

NAME (Generally, common name) Number: in Sun or in Shade	COLOR	HEIGHT (in inches)	DISTANCE BETWEEN PLANTLINGS (in inches)	NORMAL BLOOMING TIME
Campanula Tetham Beauty (1)	Blue, White	18	16 to 18	July, August
Canterbury Bell (1) (Campanula Medium-biennial)	White, Pink, Blue	18	16 to 18	July, August
Cardinal Flower (4)	Red	15	12 to 14	July, August
Carnation (1)	Various	15	12 to 14	August
Chinese Lantern (Physalis Franchettii) (1)	Orange	18	16 to 18	August, September
Cinquefoil (4)	Red	18	12 to 14	July
Columbine (4)	Various	12 to 15	10 to 12	May, June
Common Peony (3)	White	18	24	June, July
Coral Lily (4)	Coral	18	6	July
Daffodil (1)	Yellow	12	10	April
Dianthus Barbatus (1) (carnation or pink family)	Various	18	15	July, August
Dwarf Dahlia (1)	Various	15 to 18	15 to 18	July, August, September
Dwarf Dragon Head (3)	Mauve	18	12	July
Elegant Lily (3)	Scarlet	18	6 to 8	June
Florindae Primula (4)	Yellow	12	12	July, August
Flower of Job (1)	Pink	18	15 to 16	July
Foxglove (Perennial) (3)	Yellow	18	10 to 12	July, August
Globe Flower (4)	Yellow	18	18	April, May
Hound's Tongue (1) (Pentstemon)	Blue	18	18	May, June
Hybrid Campion (1)	Red	12	12	July
Iceland Poppy (1)	Various	12	8 to 9	April, August
Japanese Peony (3)	Red	18	18	April, May

Name	Color			Blooming
Lupine (prairie-type) (3)	Blue	18	12	July
Lychnis Haegeana (3)	Scarlet	12	10	July
Musk Mallow (1)	Blue, White	18	10	June
Polyantus Roses (1)	Various	12 to 18	12 to 18	June, July, August
Phlox Canadensis (1)	Blue	18	12	May
Primulinus Gladiolus (1)	Various	15 to 18	6 to 8	August, September
Pyrethrum Queen Alexandra (3)	Pink	18	18	July
Russell Lupine (1)	Various	18 to 24	18 to 24	August
Scabiosa Caucasica (4)	Mauve	18	18	June
Shasta Daisy (3)	White	18	18	June, July, August
Sweet William (biennial) (4)	Various	18	15	July, August
Tulip (1)	Various	12 to 15	6 to 8	May, June
Virginia Bluebell (4)	Blue	18	8	August
White Lobelia (1)	White	12	12	August

FROM 24 TO 35 INCHES

Name	Color			Blooming
Baby's Breath (1)	White, Pink	24	24	July, August
Bee Balm (Monarda) (1)	Mauve	24	18 to 20	July, August
Campanula Phyctldocaly (1)	Light Blue	30	24	July, August
Campion (4)	Scarlet	24	18 to 20	July
Candlestick Lily (4)	Yellow	30	10 to 12	July
Chrysanthemum (1)	Various	24	10 to 12	August, September
Columbine (3)	Various	24 to 36	24 to 30	June, July, August
Columbine Coerulea (4)	Blue, White	24	24 to 30	July
Columbine, Crimson Star and Rose Queen (4)	Scarlet, White	30	24 to 30	July, August
Coreopsis (1)	Yellow, Brown	24 to 36	24 to 30	July
Day Lily (3)	Yellow, Orange	24	24	June, July, August
Dragon Head (1)	Mauve	24	15 to 16	July
Foxglove (Biennial) (4)	Various	30	18 to 24	July, August

NAME (Generally, common name) Number: in Sun or in Shade	COLOR	HEIGHT (in inches)	DISTANCE BETWEEN PLANTLINGS (in inches)	NORMAL BLOOMING TIME
Gaillardia (1)	Yellow, Bronze	24	16 to 18	July, August
Gladiolus (1)	Various	30 to 36	9 to 10	August, September
Gypsophila Paniculata (1)	White	30	24	July, August
Hanson's Lily (4)	Mauve	24	8 to 9	July
Helenium (1)	Yellow	24	24	July, August
Honesty (biennial) (4)	Mauve	24	24	August
Iris (Flag) Barbatus (1)	Various	24 to 30	18	June, July
Jacob's Ladder (1)	White, Light Blue	24 to 36	24	August
Japanese Iris (2)	Various	30	18	June, July, August
Leopard's Lily (1)	Yellow	24	8 to 9	July
Mullen's Pink (Biennial) (4)	Pink	24	24	August
Oriental Poppy (1)	Scarlet	30	24	July, August
Painted Ladies (3)	Various	24	12 to 18	June, July
Pentstemon Heterphyllus (1)	Blue	24	18	June, July
Peony (1)	Various	30	24	June
Phlox (1)	Various	30	18 to 24	July, August, September
Plume Poppy (4)	White	30	24	July, August
Pyrethrum James Kelway (1)	Scarlet	24	18 to 20	June, July
Pyrethrum Robinson (1)	White	24	20 to 22	June, July
Scarlet Bee Balm (1)	Scarlet	24	18 to 24	August
Snake Weed (4)	White	24	18 to 20	July, August
Trollius Ledebouri (4)	Dark Yellow	24	24	July, August
Veronica (1)	Blue, White	24	24	July, August

26

FROM 36 TO 47 INCHES

Plant	Color			Bloom
American Turk's Cap Lily (4)	Red	36	10	July
Anchusa (1)	China Blue	36	24	June, July
Aquilegia McKana Giant (4)	Mixed	36	30	July
Campanula Latiloba (4)	Dark Blue	36	30	June, July
Campanula Spicata (1)	Blue, White	36	30	June, July
Dahlia, Cactus and Show (1)	Various	36 to 48	36 to 48	July, August, September
Delphinium (1)	Various	36 to 48	36	July, August
Globe Thistle (3)	Blue	36	36	August
Golden Glow (1)	Yellow	36	36	August, September
Henry's Lily (4)	Yellow	36	10	July, August
Lythrum Morden's Pink (3)	Pink	36	36	August, September
Maltese Cross (1)	Red, Pink	36	30	June, July
Meadow Rue (1)	White	36	30	June, July
Purple Loosestrife (4)	Mauve	36	30	July, August
Rose Alpina	Pink	36	36	June, July
Shrub Roses (1)	Various	36 to 72	36 to 72	June, July, August
Thalictrum Dipterocarpum (3)	Mauve	36	20 to 24	August
Tea Roses (1)	Various	36 to 48	36 to 48	June, July, August
Veronica Spicata (1)	Blue, White	36	30	August, September

FROM 48 INCHES AND MORE

Plant	Color			Bloom
Delphinium Pacific Giant (1)	Various	48	36 to 48	June, July, August
Hollyhock (1)	Various	48	18	July, August, September
Monkshood (aconite) (3)	Blue and White bicolor	48	36	June, July, August
Rose Hugonis (1)	Yellow	72 to 96	36 to 72	June, July
Rose Rubrifolia	Red	60 to 72	36 to 72	June, July
Thalictrum Aquifolium (3)	Mauve	48	36	July, August
Tiger Lily (1)	Yellow	48	9	August, September

BORDERS

Practically every home in Calgary has a flower border, by far the most popular type of floral gardening in this city.

In summer they beautify the fronts and sides of the homes like a priceless necklace glorifies a beautiful woman.

There are actually three distinct types of borders, any of which can either be herbaceous (that is, perennial) borders; annual borders; a mixture of perennials and annuals; and/or shrubbery borders.

The three types are:

1.   The shrubbery border in which various forms of garden shrubs of flowering habit are blended so as to make the harmony whole.

2.   Now almost obsolete, is the narrow ribbon border in which plants of dwarf habit and bright coloring were used to produce geometrical designs on the green sward. This form of gardening was common in the British Isles around large establishments and public places until recent years, but public taste has now been educated to see and to like the newer, curving border.

3.   The border proper, the one that was used when gardening had to be done without the aid of lawns, all the plant occupants being hardy by nature whether of biennial or perennial duration.

It may be said that our borders today are much improved along artistic lines. Much has been added to them and the greater possibilities we have are due largely to our greater wealth in plants.

To have a good flower border is by no means an expensive undertaking if a few essentials are regarded. The first and most important requisite is a good depth of soil; it matters little what the kind of soil, if good. But it is better, if possible, to vary the texture and be able to control the quantity of moisture.

Lilies are among the most beautiful flowers. They like a soil that is light, cool and moist, hence decayed humus or peat moss is valuable.

Many other subjects, such as annuals from warmer climates, like a soil that absorbs heat rapidly and retains it, such as a soil of a sandy texture.

But the great majority of perennial plants require a retentive compost that will not dry out readily in hot weather, and it must be made rich enough to grow plants successfully. One cannot starve the plants and expect good flowers and foliage.

If the natural soil is not really good or suitable, make it so. If it is not possible to do it all at once, begin well, and add to it as time goes on as the plants need the space, for it will be found that in a mixed border of plants, which practically take care of themselves, there will always be plenty for one's own use and a quantity of roots to spare.

The location of such a border is an important consideration so far as general effect and efficiency are concerned. Along the line of a fence or boundary, near the margin of a wall or driveway, or next to the house are good locations.

The front line may be a straight, curved or irregular in outline, according to the situation or fancy of the gardener. The plants will lend themselves to one or all forms, oftentimes forming a line of their own by outgrowing their allotted space.

Many plants are suitable for this kind of work.

Begin with the old-fashioned flowers such as larkspurs, monkshood, holly-hocks, peonies, loosestrife, painted ladies, iris, oriental poppies, day lilies, bleeding heart, baby's breath, bell flowers, true lilies and a host of other perennials. The perennial garden phlox should be added, with their various bright and colorful blooms.

One of the best uses of a perennial border is to make it a catch-all for all hardy plants. Here you may plant wild asters, golden rod, wild lilies, buttercups, brown-eyed susans, fireweed, and anything and everything which will interest you in woods or fields, where these plants may be dug up as soon as they finish blooming.

Cut off the tops, leaving all the leaves just above the ground, plant them firmly, water them well, and most of them will live.

The border reflects the personality of its maker. One caution must be given—never spade up or fork over such a border when newly-planted. Let all enrichment be given as a top dressing in fall, allowing the plants to come up through it as they will.

The best time to plant is in the month of April in this part of the country. The available material is so rich and plentiful for the making of a perennial border that there need never be duplication. Nor is the best hardy border an expensive luxury; it requires no rare exotics, and its chief members may be the common plants of the neighborhood brought together under conditions which give each a chance for development.

A perennial border is in its chief glory in June, July and August, and shows enormous amounts of blooms. Visitors who exclaim at its beauty do not recognize the roadside flowers that are planted in the perennial border because of their improved condition under cultivation.

No two days are alike in a well-planned perennial border. No two days show the same blooms. Often a visit in the afternoon gives a totally different impression from the morning. This can go on from early spring until late fall when cold and frost lay those beautiful plants low.

To create an individual hardy border, the horticulturist must divest himself of any prejudice and cheerfully start a flowering rhubarb where its large foliage is needed, backed up by the not-so-large foliage of the hollyhock. He should estimate plants for their beauty, their individuality and their season of bloom as members of his general plant. He should be prepared to consider any plant a prize if it fits and any plant a weed if it is inharmonious.

Now, to get down to greater detail in planning a perennial border. Use an effective placement which gets away from too severe or geometric an arrangement.

Some of the taller-growing and loveliest perennials suitable for planting in the background are delphiniums, monkshood, hollyhocks, golden glow, meadow rue, loosestrife, perennial zinnia, globe thistle, bugbane, and the perennial mallow. You will find these more impressive when planted in groups of threes.

Monkshood (or aconitum) come in shades of blue and a bicolor of blue and white, with one in off-white.

Differing from the delphinium, which likes to grow in a sunny spot, aconitum will do well in either shade or sun. The foliage of this hardy, herbaceous perennial is most showy. The plant grows from 3 to 5 feet tall, and bears helmet-shaped flowers in summer and early autumn.

It belongs to the buttercup family, ranunculaceae.

It does well in ordinary soil and is suitable for the back of the herbaceous border.

Some of the best species include aconitum napellus, 4 to 5 feet tall, with dull blue flowers in July and August; the blue and white variety named Bicolor; and the white species, alba.

Another species named wilsonii grows about 5 feet high, and bears violet-blue flowers in August and maybe September. Fischerii is another recommended monkshood species, and this averages about 3 feet tall.

All parts of the monkshood plant are poisonous, so care must be taken wherever they are grown.

The annual straw flower, or helichrysum, is a showy plant which makes a fine display in any border or bed. The blooms may also be dried for winter bouquets.

The althaea, which is so well known by its common name, the hollyhock, comes under three classifications, perennials, biennials, and annuals. The single hollyhock is a perennial, the double is a biennial—perhaps the most beautiful—and the annual hollyhock, a single, grows only to a height of about 2 feet.

The rudbeckia, possessing the charming common name of golden glow, will do well in either sun or shade. The variety known as Laciniata, in its double form, is the best of these. Golden glow require an abundant supply of water during the growing season, and will indeed bring a golden glow to a garden.

Meadow rue (or thalictrum), is perhaps one of the daintiest of perennials, both in flower and foliage. Admirers go into ecstasies over it. Three species which I would advise you to buy are glaucum, aquilegifolium, and dipterocarpum. The glaucum is yellow, the aquilegifolium purplish-mauve, and the dipterocarpum mauve. Dipterocarpum is the most delightful of the three, and in fact is my favorite among all perennials in Calgary. All these meadow rue do well in sun or shade.

The purple loosestrife (lythrum), grows to a height of 3 or 4 feet, and will thrive best in a sunny spot. It should be given plenty of water. There is a variety known as Morden's Pink, which is most showy in the border. The lythrums bloom a little later than most of the other perennials, and are of a very erect habit.

This hardy perennial plant, fine for the border or beside a pool, belongs to the lythraceae family. The blooms are reddish-purple or rose colored.

Among the finest species for the perennial border are lythrum virgatum and the rose queen. Once loosestrife is established, it blooms freely.

The perennial zinnias (heleopsis) belong to the same family as the sunflower, and they, too, have the yellow flowers with brown centres. They like a hot, sunny location, and bear semi-double blossoms.

The echinops ritro is commonly called the globe thistle because of its likeness to a thistle. It is rather odd in appearance, and is a coarse-growing plant of easy culture.

The bugbane (cimicifuga) is an impressive perennial with fluffy, creamy-white flowers. This is another plant which is not too difficult to grow, and will thrive in either sun or shade. The best species to buy is racemosa which has beautiful foliage.

The mallow (lavitera) is another charming perennial which, when in bloom, is clustered with rose-colored blossoms. The species I would recommend is cretica.

The tiger lily (lilium tigrinum) is an all-time favorite, with its vivid orange lily, spotted with brown. The bulbs should be planted about 9 inches deep and 8 to 9 inches apart in the row. If planted in groups of 3 to 5, a much better effect results when they are in bloom, rather late in the season. They make a colorful cut-flower.

The lupine or lupinus is another decorative perennial and annual belonging to the pea family leguminosae. But the chief favorites are the herbaceous perennials which make a magnificent display in any such border.

Their tall spires or blooms have a distinctive appearance. The perennials reach a height here of 2 feet, though they may grow higher under exceptional cultivation. The flowers have a wide range of coloring, from white through lavender and pale blue to deep blue and purple, and from pale yellow through salmon pink and apricot buff to crimson.

All lupines will thrive in ordinary garden soil that has been dug deeply and enriched with decayed manure. They flourish in full sunshine or in part shade.

Bleeding heart (or dicentra spectabilis) is suitable for planting in a herbaceous border, and also thrives in ordinary, well-cultivated soil. It reaches a height of 20 to 24 inches.

Another advantage is that the bleeding heart, which grows wild in Japan and China and belongs to the fumareaceae family, can be potted in the fall and taken indoors.

The forget-me-not, another old-fashioned and well-loved plant, is a lovely little flower, most suitable for border or rockeries located in shade.

The botanical name of the little annual is myosotis, and it belongs to a family which also includes annuals, perennials and biennials.

Phlox come in many lovely colors and these flowers are a prime favorite as well as one of the most important groups of garden plants.

They are invaluable in the herbaceous border, in the rock garden or in summer beds.

The giant species tetra phlox grows up to 20 inches high, while dwarf phlox, ideal for bedding, grow only 6 to 8 inches tall.

Phlox also come both as annuals and perennials.

The border carnation has long been a favorite. It will grow in well-drained soil, and an open, sunny position should be chosen.

The hardy border pink also is invaluable for grouping towards the front of a perennial border, or for filling small beds. It blooms early in June.

All tall-growing plants should be planted about 2½ to 3 feet apart, to allow ample room for development, and it is also important that they be staked and tied up at the proper time. When the plants are approximately one foot high, stakes measuring 5 to 6 feet in length should be driven well into the

31

ground, to a depth of about 1 foot. They should be placed behind the plants, and this is one of the secrets of a neat and well-kept border. Without stakes, your tall plants may be broken down and bent by winds or heavy rains.

I would like now to offer a few ideas on various color schemes you might use with different kinds of annuals.

A bed of geraniums and white marguerites with an edging of two rows of blue lobelia is effective. Or then again, you might want to edge it with white alyssum.

A border of stocks in red, white and blue, and an edging of German catchfly (viscaria), alternating with red, white and blue, is also nice. The stocks grow 15 inches high while viscaria will only reach about 9 inches.

A bed of red salvias or geraniums with yellow snaps spotted throughout will be enjoyed immensely.

The ordinary butterfly flower when grouped in various pastel shades and edged with the dainty forget-me-nots becomes a thing of entrancing beauty.

ANNUALS

Annuals, in all their brillance, can be considered the accessories, the finishing touches to your garden.

Annuals carry out the color scheme where perennials leave off.

Calgary is famous for the colorful beauty of its gardens, and it is the annuals which add the special touch of splendor to glorify the midsummer blaze.

I would like to give you a few hints on purchasing annuals, and also on planting them.

Don't jump to buy a basket of flowers that you see in full bloom, because the chances are that the cycle of bloom has been pretty well reached in the basket and you will not receive the full benefit of the plants.

This applies to most basket plants: soak well your baskets an hour or two before planting and make sure that the flower bed or border soil is well pulverized. It is best to plant on a dull day or in the evening.

When planting out annuals, a good guide is to leave as much space between the plants as they themselves are tall. This is one of the reasons why I have mentioned the various heights throughout this article. For example, the intermediate snap which grows 12 to 15 inches high would be planted 12 to 15 inches apart. This does not hold true in all cases, but is a fairly reliable guide.

The first week in June is the time to set out annuals. Over-enthusiasm leads many people to get out and do it in late May, but the risk of a late frost is great and the advantage to be gained, if any, is not worth the risk.

Annuals come in three general sizes, tall, intermediate and small or dwarf. At the end of this chapter there is an appendix listing them by the sizes to which they normally grow.

Among the tall-growing annuals is the larkspur, a member of the delphinium family. It is one of the most beautiful and desirable early annuals for your garden, and is available in shades of light azure blue, intense Oxford blue, lilac, salmon rose, ruby red, white and mixed colors. These are extremely well-suited for grouping at the back of a border, or in the centre of a flower bed. They are of an erect habit; and should be placed 15 inches apart.

An attractive bed of flowers is a mixture of intermediate snapdragons, edged with pink and blue German catchfly (viscaria). If the bed is a large one, you could have two rows of German catchfly. As these are low-growing plants, they should be placed approximately 9 inches apart.

Viscaria oculata, an attractive annual, comes in three colors — soft pink, pale blue and rich red. It is mostly used for edging borders but can be used in solid beds, too. I suggest that wherever possible you collect the seeds from the smallest of these plant. In this way, you will probably get fairly dwarf-sized plants that are similar to the parent plants.

Nemesia has a great variety of colors and it is interesting to note that although it is a native of the African desert, it grows extremely well here and around Banff and Lake Louise. Two of the best species are nemesia compacta and nemesia strimosa, both of which grow to 9 or 10 inches tall and like well-drained, light, sandy soil.

Nemesia compacta, which can be purchased in mixed or straight colors. makes a delicately attractive bed with its great variety of pastel shades. Nemesia also makes an excellent edging for a bed of tall-growing flowers. Space the plants 9 inches apart.

This annual requires a sunny location in the garden. Compacta and another species, suttonii, will not thrive in old, heavy soil.

It is wise to improve the soil every two or three years by introducing virgin soil and sand into the bed and borders. In this way, nemesia, one of the most colorful annuals when given proper treatment, will grow well and reward the gardener with many lovely hues.

Giant zinnias may be purchased in a large selection of mixed or straight colors, and should be planted 16 to 18 inches apart in a very sunny spot in the garden. These, too, should not be set out until all danger of frost is past.

There is a dwarf zinnia variety known as Cupid zinnia, which makes an excellent edging for a bed of larger ones, should you desire a complete bed of the same flowers. Having a complete bed of one kind of flower has its own particular attractiveness.

Asters and stocks, old-fashioned but popular annuals, are most attractive when grouped. They make a good addition to the perennial border, and can be bought in mixed or straight colors. The aster, being the taller, should be planted 15 inches apart, the stocks 10 inches apart. A most appealing bed or border is one composed of stocks in red, white and blue colors. To complete this border, and still retain the red-white-and-blue color scheme, edge this with white and blue lobelia.

Everyone is familiar with the sweet perfume of stocks, especially in the evening. In our dry atmospheric condition, flowers do not perfume the air as potently as they do in more humid climates. Because of this fact, an effort should be made to have as many as possible of the more strongly perfumed plants in the gardens.

Strangely, when stocks are in the seedling stage and grown in the greenhouse, they resent too much water. The opposite is true when they are grown outside in the garden.

Dwarf dahlias, which are grown from seed in the greenhouse, are most suitable for borders and large flower beds. They grow to a height of 18 inches to 24 inches, in many shades and colors. They also must not be set out until all danger of frost is past.

The annual phlox is a popular flower and can be purchased in numerous lovely and vivid colors. There are two kinds procurable — the tall, which grows 15 inches high; and the dwarf, which grows 9 inches high. The dwarf is especially dainty and sweet for edging.

The schizanthus, which is also appropriately called the butterfly flower makes a lovely and extremely dainty bed. The flowers of this plant resemble the wings of a butterfly, and come in very pastel shades.

The toadflax (linaria) is another suitable flower for edging, especially the species known as fairy bouquet. This would make a good edging for a bed of schizanthus. Another suggestion for a color scheme is a bed of red geraniums with yellow snapdragons. Both stand out vividly, and an edging of yellow marigolds would be effective with such a combination.

Another sweetly perfumed flower is the verbena, which comes in lovely colors, with white spots in the centre of each flower. This flower seems to catch the eye, and as it more or less has a trailing habit, it quickly carpets the flower bed. The verbena comes in tall and dwarf varieties, and is half-hardy.

For steep, dry banks, and rockeries, I would recommend the following: portulaca, or moss rose; the mesembryanthemum, or ice plant; the dimorphotheca, or African daisy; and the annual dianthus, or pinks.

The antirrhinum or snapdragon is a general favorite as a summer flowering plant. It belongs to the foxglove family scrophulariaceae, and is found growing wild in South America and in Europe. The name antirrhinum is from the Greek language meaning snout flower, which is a reference to the shape of the flower.

Although they are actually a perennial, snaps are treated and grown here as annuals. The most popular type of snap is the intermediate, which grows about 12 to 15 inches high. The tall type, growing about 36 to 48 inches high, is the most useful in grouping at the back of a border. The tom thumb varieties are splendid for edging around beds or along borders. You can obtain all these kinds in a goodly number of mixed shades or straight colors. The snaps will grow in any good garden soil, but need lots of sun.

The tall kinds should be planted 15 to 18 inches apart, the intermediates 10 to 12 inches apart, and the small or tom thumb types 6 to 7 inches apart. Snaps should be raised from seed every year, and the plants destroyed after flowering.

The seeds are started early in March in a heated greenhouse at a temperature of 60 degrees Fahrenheit. Drain the flats, and then fill them with a sifted compost of two parts loam and one part peat moss, with a little sharp sand added.

Scatter the seeds thinly, covering them with just a sprinkling of the sifted soil. If covered with glass or paper and kept moist, the seeds will soon germinate.

When the seedlings are an inch high, transplant them, two inches apart, in other flats filled with similar compost. The seedlings must then be hardened off in coldframes during May before being planted outside at the beginning of June.

One of the newest snapdragon varieties is the Double Hybrid in mixed colors, with spectacular flowers. The blooms are 1¾ inches across and 1½ inches deep, and they make a wonderful display. The plants are from 20 to 30 inches high.

Another most attractive snap is the Ruffled Tetraploid, which is extremely large. The central spike grows 24 inches or more in height, surrounded by lateral, smaller spikes. The plants are exceptionally strong, with dark green foliage, and provide long-stemmed flowers for cutting because they are base branching.

The tom-thumb varieties provide all kinds of colors suitable for edging.

The rock hybrids are small, compact and bushy, about 6 inches high, and especially suited for rock gardens. They bloom earlier than most snaps, and have a trailing habit.

Alyssum is a most popular plant for edging and for rock work. It blooms profusely all summer, in fact right up to freeze-up. It comes in white and purple, and I especially recommend a sweet alyssum of a pink shade, called Pink Heather.

Other varities to be recommended include: Carpet of Snow, Magic Carpet and Violet Queen (which holds its color throughout the season).

Then there is the floss flower (ageratum), a half-hardy annual especially adapted to edge beds of geraniums, scarlet sage (salvias), cannas or such.

Ageratum varieties include Blue Mink, Blue Bedder, Dwarf and Midget Blue, the latter being a lovely little edging plant 2 to 3 inches high, with true ageratum blue flowers.

The callistephus or common aster is a favorite annual which is in its full beauty during August and September. There are numerous single and double varieties in attractive forms and colorings.

Incidentally, all present-day asters are descended from the Chinese aster.

Here are a few of the best common asters: Ostrich Plume, 18 inches high, and in my opinion, the most graceful of all; Victoria, also 18 inches high and possessing stiff upright growth; and the Comet, approximately the same size and somewhat similar to the Ostrich Plume. The Comet is obtainable in a greater variety of colors among which are red, lavender, white, pink and pale yellow.

The asters are versatile and will grow in part shade or in the sun. They furnish a beautiful display of bloom when planted among flowering early perennials such as the peony, 'and this is because they carry on the color scheme when the earlier perennials have passed. The aster can be obtained in either single or double kinds.

The cornflower is a dainty little flower which is represented by single or double species in blue, rose or white. It is particularly valuable as a cut flower for decorative purposes indoors. The seed can be sown outside as soon as the soil is warm enough. It grows 9 to 12 inches tall.

The sweet sultan, or centurea moschata, is a hardy annual which grows about 18 inches high. In this plant you can find some of the loveliest shades imaginable, and they will add considerable beauty to a garden.

The clarkia is native to North America and is another attractive annual growing 12 to 24 inches high, and is extremely free flowering. Another desirable feature about it is that it will remain in bloom over a considerable period of time. The clarkia can be sown from seed out-of-doors and requires no care other than good garden soil and an ordinary amount of water.

The clarkia elegens, native of California, is the best known species of this plant and you can recognize it by the loose sprays of vivid crimson flowers.

A great deal of improvement has been made on other varieties, and some of the colors obtainable are: salmon, scarlet, firefly, double salmon, double pink and snowball white.

The cosmos is an annual with beautiful foliage and is found to be invaluable for table decoration. It should be grown in a sunny location where it will be sheltered from high winds. Any good garden soil will serve it, but if the soil is too rich, the foliage will make growth at the expense of the flowers.

Crimson flax, as its name implies, is a brilliantly-colored flower that can be grown from seed out-of-doors. It grows about 9 inches high and is splendid for edging.

Japanese pinks, known to most gardeners as dianthus heddewigii, bear a profusion of large, fringed flowers in various colors. If the roots are left in the fall, they will continue to blossom the second year only. They, too, like the antirrhinum, are really perennials although treated as annuals.

If you have a sandy spot in your garden and are not quite sure what to put in there, the California poppies with their saucer-shaped flowers are delightful. They will grow 12 to 15 inches high and can be obtained in large assortment of shades, among which you will certainly find something suitable.

There is also a miniature variety of these, 6 inches high and suitable for sowing around the edge of the bed, or adding a touch of color to your rockery. Once they are sown, they will seed themselves thereafter.

The coltass gem dahlia can be set in a sunny position where it will, if the flowers are picked off as soon as they fade, bloom gaily all summer until the frost comes. The chief color is red. I should mention here for some of you who might be wondering what a dahlia is doing among annuals, that it is again one that can, even though it is a perennial, be treated like an annual.

Then there is the French marigold, a dwarf that makes a charming edging. The blooms are usually yellow and may be sometimes marked with crimson. The Scotch marigold is distinctive in several handsome shades of golden yellow and orange yellow varieties.

The African marigold is a sturdy, colorful flower, and comes in shades of bronze, red, gold, canary yellow, and near-white. If you have left space in the perennial border for a few annuals, the African marigold is fine for this purpose. Group them fairly well back in the border.

They are also lovely for beds which could be edged with the dwarf French marigolds or dwarf zinnias, or any other suitable dwarf plants which you might choose. They should be planted 16 inches apart, as they are rank growers. The dwarf zinnias and dwarf marigolds are placed 9 inches apart.

Another marigold, the bur marigold or bidens, is a hardy summer-flowering annual from Mexico belonging more to the daisy family. It grows 24 to 36 inches high, has divided leaves and daisy-like flowers with yellow centres and white or yellow ray florets. It will grow in ordinary garden soil but requires lots of sun. Plant outside after June 1, seedlings 12 inches apart.

The night-scented stock has pale purplish flowers and is, as it name implies, most fragrant in the evening. It is very pleasant when sown near a bedroom or living room window.

The salvia or scarlet sage is perhaps one of the most colorful and decorative bedding-out plants that can be grown here.

It is also popular for borders, edgings and pot culture, and may be used as a cut flower. It is really a perennial but can be treated as an annual in this climate.

But annual or perennial, this flower — possibly the most brilliantly colored to be found in our Calgary gardens during the summer — must not be set out until all danger of frost is past. It is most delicate, and very susceptible to frost. When chilled, it drops its blooms and leaves, and is rendered almost useless for the remainder of the flowering season.

Never set out this tender plant until all danger of frost is past, possibly not until about June 10. Scarlet sage needs warm, muggy weather.

It is advisable to choose the early-flowering dwarf varieties such as St. John Fire and Blaze of Fire, from among the various types available for different purposes.

St. John Fire is the earliest and smallest-growing scarlet sage that you will find listed, and grows only 10 inches tall. Blaze of Fire, also dwarf, and used in City of Calgary gardens, reaches a height of about 15 inches. Both bear brilliant scarlet flowers which bring a gay blaze of color into a garden.

The salvia splendens is the tallest-growing variety with the largest flowers. It is not suited for outdoor planting here in Alberta, but can be grown as pot plants as you would grow geraniums in the greenhouse.

The lovely scarlet of the salvias is well set off by an edging of white alyssum or two rows of lobelia. A combination of all three could also be used effectively.

The name salvia stems from salvare — to save — and results from the medicinal value the plant was supposed to possess. It belongs to the libiateae family, and many varieties also are found in South Europe, North Africa and South America.

Petunias are among the most popular of bedding plants, most elegant and showy with their trumpet-like flowers in a wide variety colors. And, believe it or not, they belong to the potato family.

They are versatile, being useful in full beds, as edging plants, and also for cultivation in pots in the sun-porch or greenhouse.

Petunias are half-hardy perennial plants, and the modern varieties have large double or single blooms. They are usually treated as annuals, and the improvement in color is very marked in the modern varieties. A generation ago they were chiefly of unattractive, crude magenta and purplish shades, but today the range of colors includes rose, pink, crimson, pale blue, violet, purple and white.

The flowers of some varieties are attractively fringed, others are striped with colors which contrast with the ground color, and altogether the petunia is a flower far more worthy of cultivation now than it was a few years ago. It is strongly recommend to those who can give it the conditions which are essential to successful blooming: well-drained, warm, rather light soil, and a position fully exposed to the sun.

Petunias are essentially sun-loving plants and are useless if planted in shady spots. In shade they will grow, but will not bloom. They are very suitable for sunny window boxes or planters.

Petunias used for the decoration of window boxes should be planted there towards the end of May or early June—either single or double flowered varieties may be used for this purpose. When grown out-of-doors, they are seen at their best in a hot, dry summer, when they become smothered in large handsome blooms.

Petunias have what might be described as a rather weak rooting system; the roots are very fine and short. Before transplanting, petunias should be watered

37

well about two hours before you move them. This helps to retain the soil around the short, fine roots, making transplanting a safer operation.

Petunias are very soft, and wilt readily. Therefore, to water them before transplanting is more necessary than in the case of many plants, although all plants should be watered an hour or two before transplanting them into the garden.

The sweet pea, which is so aptly named, is one of our old-time and all-time favorites. The fragrance of the sweet pea matches the delicacy of its blooms, and the multiple colors in which it is grown would be too lengthy to name. It is botanically known as lathyrus odoratus, which is no less descriptive than the common name sweet pea.

The sweet pea is a flower which there can be no substitute for any more than there could be for other sweet-smelling flowers such as lily-of-the-valley and mignonette.

One great obstacle to the successful growing of sweet peas is a hot, dry climate, particularly one in which really hot weather with drying winds is likely to strike suddenly after a nice cool spring.

Sweet peas love cool, moist weather. The old small-flowered varieties such as were used many years ago, were more capable of surviving in an unfavorable climate than the much-flowered ones which succeeded them.

One thinks of the sweet pea primarily as flowers for cutting and for this purpose it is indeed indispensable. Its attractive form and extremely wide range of lovely colors are equalled by those of very few other flowers. In places where sweet peas grow well, they make an attractive light screen in addition to providing flowers for cutting for weeks on end.

The requisites of success with sweet peas are an early start, a deep root run, and an abundance of moisture. Not one of these three will, by themselves, assure strong vines, long-stemmed flowers, and a long continued season of bloom.

The lack of any one of them, however, may prevent you achieving the much desired results.

Most instructions for growing sweet peas suggest that they should be planted in a trench. Too often it is left at that.

A trench in this connection, is not merely a v-shaped furrow scraped out with a hoe just before planting. It means digging out a real trench 18 inches to 24 inches deep and 24 inches wide, to be especially prepared for the job it has to do.

The old-fashioned and elaborate directions in the making of a sweet pea trench still hold good. The traditional old cow manure, alternated with layers of soil and bonemeal, is placed in 6-inch layers, finishing off with a layer of soil on the top.

Preferably the trench should be prepared in the fall. There is more time to do the work in the fall and the soil will have a chance to settle during winter. Furthermore, and even of greater importance, it will be ready for planting at the first opportunity in the spring.

If the trench cannot be prepared until just before planting, it is well to settle the bottom layer of the refill with a very thorough watering before the second layer is added.

Such thorough preparation is really not so much work as it sounds. It will supply the foundation for a splendid crop of sweet peas. A well-dug and well-prepared trench is the first step to success.

Sweet peas can be sown or planted in the garden, although it is best to start them inside and plant them out about May 24 or the beginning of June. The greenhouse plants should be placed 9 or 10 inches apart in the middle of the trench. Three weeks before setting out sweet pea plants, the young stem which has grown from the seed an inch above the soil, should be cut off. In this way, new and stronger shoots will appear.

When these new shoots appear, the weaker ones should again be cut off, retaining one strong shoot. Single bamboo canes or stakes made from 1 inch by 1 inch and 8 feet or 10 feet in length are generally placed behind each plant.

The plant is tied to the stake by wrapping raffia or string twice around the stake and once around the vine. In this manner, the string will not slip down. Clips are now available for tying, which save a great deal of time and work. They simply slip down over the stake and vine.

If you want to grow sweet peas from seed outdoors, sow the seed thinly in the trench, about 2 inches deep, toward the end of April, depending on whether it is an early or late spring.

Water immediately you sow the seed outside, and continue to irrigate through the germination period. When the seedlings are about 2 inches high, thin to about 9 inches between plants.

Then use the same procedure as suggested for seedlings started in the greenhouse.

Sweet peas are plants which, if well grown, demand daily attention. All lateral or side shoots should be removed each day. In the first stages of growth, these young shoots can be brushed off with your fingers, leaving one strong vine.

To grow prize sweet peas, the tendrils as well as the surplus shoots should be removed. This entails daily tying, as the tendrils are that portion of the vine which encircle and grip the stake.

This all seems like a lot of work, but the results are well worth it—to have best success, the work must be consistently carried out.

When they receive such attention, you will have sweet peas with stems 15 to 18 inches long, with 4 to 6 blooms on each stem.

Sweet peas like a very rich soil; this means they must be fed frequently, about every 10 days, with a liquid manure.

A top-dressing of soot is beneficial in bringing out the color of the blooms.

Sweet peas, like green peas, are subject to mildew. They should always be irrigated; and not watered on cool days or chilly evenings. Do not be afraid to cut your sweet peas; the more the blooms are cut, the more profuse they become.

The common cause of a short flowering season with sweet peas, even when weather and other conditions are favorable, is neglecting to prevent the forming of seed pods. In growing sweet peas, this is very important, for once a crop of seeds have set, the plants will have accomplished their purpose and have no further interest in continuing to produce flowers. Moreover, stems that are cut as soon as the buds break, provide blooms which will last much longer indoors.

Be sure to keep your sweet pea blooms cut all season long.

Even with our short growing season, there are many hardy annuals which may be grown from seed outdoors. But those which can be grown from seed outdoors, also can be grown in the greenhouse from seed (See list of annuals at the end of this section).

After the ground has been dug over and raked finely, the seeds are scattered, broadcast or in rows, whichever you prefer, in the way you wish them to grow, and rake the soil lightly over them. They must, of course, be kept moist during the germination period.

When sowing seeds, care should be taken to see that the tall, intermediate, and dwarf varieties are sown where they will show to best advantage. This is an economical way of getting a fine display of bloom in a garden at a low cost. To the amateur gardener, it also presents a challenge which is not found in the bedding out of greenhouse plants.

The following are some of these outdoor-sown annuals which may be safely recommended:

The flower of Adonis, commonly known as pheasant's eye, has fern-like leaves with deep red flowers. The best of these annuals are adonis aestivalis, which grow to a height of 9 to 10 inches, with deep red flowers; and adonis autumnalis, growing to the same height as the former, with bright red blooms. They require a bright, sunny spot in the garden for best results.

The godetia is a beautiful hardy annual of which there are many varieties. Among these are found tall and dwarf kinds growing from 9 inches in the dwarf varieties, to 18 inches in the tall varieties.

The godetias come in many lovely colors, mixed or in straight colors of white, pink, salmon, rose, deep crimson, and pale lilac. They, too, like a sunny location. The dwarf varieties make a lively edging and bloom profusely throughout the summer.

Baby's breath (gypsophila elegans) is a dainty little white-flowered hardy annual, 12 to 15 inches high, which is so useful for cutting and lending elegance to bouquets of sweet peas or other flowers. Baby's breath likes a limey soil.

The calendula, or Scotch marigold, is a showy annual from Southern Europe, belonging to the daisy family. It grows 15 to 18 inches tall, bearing large heads of yellow and orange flowers, which are in full beauty during the summer. The Scotch marigolds will seed themselves after they become established in a garden, coming up every year by self-sown seed.

Annual toadflax (linaria maroccana), is an annual with whorled, narrow leaves. It grows from 9 to 12 inches tall. The species known as fairy bouquet is most dainty. Linaria grows in many lovely colors and reaches a height of 8 to 9 inches tall.

Red flax, which is a native of North Africa, is an extremely beautiful and handsome hardy annual. It grows to a height of 15 to 18 inches tall and is much branched at the base. It blooms from July to freeze-up and the large flowers of the best variety, Rubrum, are of a fine blood-red color with a beautiful satin sheen on the petals. This lovely plant is invaluable in the flower border where it may be sown in May.

Rose mallow (lavatera) is an erect, beautiful, hardy annual which bears large trumpet-like flowers of rose or crimson coloring. There is also a white variety. This is one of the most attractive of all the hardy annuals. It reaches a height of 18 inches to 24 inches or more, and also blooms throughout the summer from seeds sown out-of-doors in May.

Night-scented stock (matthiola bicornis) is another fragrant, hardy annual. It grows to a height of 9 to 10 inches, has rather slender stems, and bears small purplish-white flowers which are inconspicuous during the day, but open in the evening, when it is also most fragrant.

To obtain full benefit of their fragrance, it is usual to grow these stocks near the house so that the air, scented by their perfume, is wafted through the open windows.

California bluebell (Nemophila) is a hardy annual from California, and bears chiefly blue flowers with white centres. The only kind that is commonly grown is nemophila insignis which reaches a height of 6 inches, and in June bears blue, white-centred flowers. It is one of the most attractive of the dwarf hardy annuals, and the flowers are showy. A place fully exposed to the sunshine must be chosen, and well-drained, rather light soil, is likely to give the best results.

The nemophila is also suitable for sowing in the rock garden in a sunny location.

The Shirley poppy is another colorful annual. Seeds of several strains of Shirley poppies are sold by seedsmen, including the variety with double flowers (which seem to lack the charm of the single ones), in rose, bluish, pink, and allied shades.

Then there is the opium poppy, of which there are many varieties, with large, double, brilliantly-colored flowers in many shades. It grows to 24 inches tall. It is a deep, lovely red, with a black spot on each petal.

Mignonette (Reseda), which grows wild in North Africa, is an old garden plant, deliciously scented, which was introduced into Britain 200 years ago. The favorite kind is reseda odorata. It is grown for the fragrance of its flowers, which, in the wild type, are small and greenish-yellow, though considerable color variation is shown in the modern varieties which have been raised by continued selection throughout many years.

Mignonette is one of the most delightful and much-loved of all the hardy annuals. It must be grown in a sunny place in well-drained soil which is not deficient in lime.

All the annuals sown out of doors must be thinned out if they are seeded too thickly. The thinning should be done when the plants are 2 inches tall and the soil moist.

There are very few annuals which will do well in too shady a location, but a few exceptions are the following:

The English daisy, botanically known as bellis perennis; the annual forget-me-not (or myosotis); the nimulus, commonly called the monkey musk; pansies; and the nicotiana, or tobacco plant.

But there are many old-time favorites, including petunias, phlox, violas, and the above, which do well in part shade.

The delightful English daisy may be removed as a plant even when blooming, and set out in the garden any time after June 1.

Another flower with a daisy-like bloom is the black-eyed susan, or rudbeckia. This is a showy plant, easily grown outdoors from seed in any soil, in sun or shade.

A member of the daisy family, compositae, is the blanket flower, or gaillardia, a popular and hardy annual. It bears large, brilliantly-colored flowers, fine for cutting. A recommended variety is Indian Chief.

A favorite is the little viola, generally treated as an annual here.

Two evening-opening anuals are the evening primrose (oenothera) and the tobacco plant or nicotiana. Another attraction about the tobacco plant is its sweet smell. Crimson Bedder is an excellent variety of the tobacco plant.

One of the real old-time favorites is the nasturtium, easily grown from seed sown outdoors after May 24, and germinating in about four days. Nasturtiums belong to the wallflower family, cruciferae. There are two principal types, climbing and dwarf.

A lovely annual, with gorgeously colored, trumpet-shaped blooms, is the velvet flower, or salpiglossis.

The hollyhock is grown here as an annual because the plants will flower the first season, even from seed. It makes a splendid background.

Annual carnations are another excellent flowering plant for garden beds and borders. These annuals have been greatly improved in recent years, and the best varieties produce large, double, fragrant blooms in a great range of coloring.

Beautiul Burns Rock Gardens, Calgary

Annuals by Heights

Number after plant's name indicates:
(1)—These annuals should be planted in sun
(2) — These annuals should be planted in shade
(3) — These annuals may be planted in sun or shade
(4) — These annuals should be planted in part shade

UNDER 12 INCHES

NAME (Generally, common name) *Number: in Sun or in Shade*	COLOR	HEIGHT *(in inches)*	HOW TO PLANT: *By Seed Outdoors* (S) *By Transplant* *from Greenhouse* *(T)*	NORMAL BLOOMING TIME
African Daisy (1)	Yellow	6	T	July, August
Alyssum (1)	White, Purple	6	T	June, August
Butterfly Flower (4)	Various	9 to 12	T	July, August
Bowallia (3)	Blue	6	S or T	July, August
California Blue bell (1)	Blue	4 to 6	S or T	June, July, August
California Poppy (1)	Various	10	S or T	July, August
Candytuft (1)	Pink, White	9	T	June, July
Dwarf Nasturtium (1)	Yellow, Red	6 to 8	S or T	June, July, August
Dwarf Zinnia (1)	Various	10 to 11	T	June, July
English Daisy (4)	White, Pink, Red	6	T	June, July
Evening Primrose (1)	Yellow	6	T	June, July
Flax (4)	Various	9	S or T	June, July, August
Forget-Me-Not (2)	Blue, White, Pink	6 to 8	S or T	April, June

43

UNDER 12 INCHES

NAME (Generally, common name) Number: in Sun or in Shade	COLOR	HEIGHT (in inches)	HOW TO PLANT: By Seed Outdoors (S) By Transplant from Greenhouse (T)	NORMAL BLOOMING TIME
Four-O'Clock (1)	Scarlet	6 to 8	S or T	June, July
Gerbera (4)	Yellow	5 to 6	T	July, August
Godetia (1)	Various	8 to 9	S or T	July, August
Golden Feather (1)	Yellow	6 to 8	T	July, August
French Marigold (1)	Brown, Yellow	6 to 8	T	July, August
Heliotrope (1)	Various	10	T	July, August
Ice Plant (1)	Various	3	T	June, July, August
Linaria (Fairy Bouquet) (1)	Various	9	S or T	June, July, August
Layia (4)	Brown, Yellow	8 to 10	S or T	June, July, August
Lobelia (1)	Mauve, Blue, White	3 to 4	T	June, July, August
Love-Lies-Bleeding (1)	Red	9 to 10	S or T	June, July, August
Love-in-the-Mist (4)	Blue	10	S or T	June, July, August
Lupine (1)	Various	10 to 12	T	June, July, August
Matricaria (1)	Green, Yellow	8 to 9	T	June, July, August
Monkey Musk (2)	Bronze, Yellow	10	S or T	June, July, August
Moss Rose (1)	Various	6	T	June, July, August
Nasturtium (1)	Yellow, Red	6 to 8	S	June, July, August
Nemesia (4)	Various	9	T	June, July, August
Nierembergia (1)	Blue	6 to 8	S or T	June, July, August
Night-Scented Stock (4)	Mauve	8 to 9	S or T	June, July, August

44

	Color	S or T	No.	Blooming time
Pansy (4)	Various	T	4 to 5	May to September
Pheasant's Eye (1)	Red	T	9	June, July, August
Phlox (1)	Various	T	9 to 10	June, July, August
Pinks (1)	Pink	T	9	June, July, August
Prince's Feather (1)	Yellow, Red	T	9 to 10	June, July, August
Scarlet Sage (4)	Scarlet	T	9 to 10	June, July, August
Snapdragon (1)	Various	T	6 to 48	June, July, August
Stock (1)	Various	T	9 to 10	June, July, August
Swan River Daisy (1)	Blue	S or T	3 to 4	June, July, August
Verbena (4)	Various	T	10 to 12	June, July, August
Viola (4)	Various	S or T	6 to 7	May to August
Virginian Stock (1)	Various	S or T	4 to 5	June, July, August
Viscaria (1)	Blue, Red, Pink	T	7 to 9	June, July, August

12 TO 23 INCHES

	Color	S or T	No.	Blooming time
Aster (1)	Various	T	12 to 15	July, August, September
Arctotis (1)	Mauve	S or T	12 to 15	July, August
Alonsoa (1)	Red	S or T	15	June, July, August
Baby's Breath (1)	White	S	18	July, August
Bachelor's Button (1) (cornflower)	Blue, White	T	12 to 15	July, August
Balsam (4)	Pinkish	T	12 to 15	July, August
California Bluebell	Mauve	T	15	June, July, August
Calendula (1)	Yellow, Orange	S	15	June, July, August
Clarkia (1)	Various	S or T	15	July, August
Campanula (1)	Various	S or T	15 to 18	July, August

NAME (Generally, common name) Number: in Sun or in Shade	COLOR	HEIGHT (in inches)	HOW TO PLANT: By Seed Outdoors (S) By Transplant from Greenhouse (T)	NORMAL BLOOMING TIME
Centaurea (1)	Pink	15 to 18	T	July, August
Chelone (4)	Pink	18	S or T	July, August
Chrysanthemum (1)	Various	15 to 16	T	August, September
Cockscomb (1)	Red	15 to 18	T	July, August, September
Dianthus (1)	Various	15 to 16	T	June, July, August
Felicia (4)	Mauve	18	S or T	July, August
Flax (1)	Red, Blue	15	S or T	July, August
Floss Flower (4)	Blue, White	12	T	June, July, August
Gaillardia (1)	Bronze	18	T	July, August
Giant Zinnia (1)	Various	15 to 16	T	July, August, September
Heliopsis (1)	Yellow	18	T	July, August, September
Jacaranda (4)	Blue	15 to 18	S	July, August, September
Kochia (3)	Red	18 to 24	S or T	July, August, September
Larkspur (1)	Blue, Pink, White	18 to 24	T	July, August, September
Love-Lies-Bleeding (4)	Red	15	S or T	June, July, August
Lychnis (1)	Red	15 to 18	T	July, August, September
Mallow (1)	Purplish	18 to 24	S or T	July, August, September
Mignonette (4)	Green, Red	15	S or T	June, July, August
Petunia (1)	Various	12	S or T	June, July, August

	Color	Height		Bloom
Poppies (1) (Opium and Shirley)	Various	18 to 24	S or T	June, July, August
Scabious (1)	Various	15 to 18	T	June, July, August
Sweet Sultan (1)	Pink	12	T	June, July, August
Salpiglossia (1)	Various	18 to 24	T	June, July, August
Strawflower (1)	Various	18 to 24	T	June, July, August
Sunflower (1)	Yellow	18 to 24	S or T	June, July, August
Sweet Woodruff (4)	Blue	15	S or T	July, August, September
Tobacco Plant (4)	Various	18 to 24	T	June, July, August

24 INCHES TO 35 INCHES

	Color	Height		Bloom
Castor Oil Plant (3)	Green Foliage	24	T	No bloom

36 INCHES TO 48 INCHES

	Color	Height		Bloom
Hollyhock (1)	Various	36 to 48	T	June to September
Jewel Weed (2)	Pink	36 to 48	S or T	June, July, August
Snapdragon (1)	Various	48	T	June, July, August

MORE THAN 48 INCHES

	Color	Height		Bloom
Climbing Nasturtium (1)	Yellow, Red	6 to 8 ft.	S or T	July, August, September
Moon Flower (1)	Blue	6 to 8 ft.	S or T	July, August
Sweet Pea (1)	Various	6 to 8 ft.	S or T	June, July, August

BULBS

A bulb is a thickened, fleshy and usually underground bud, generally growing roots from its underside.

The function of the bulb is to carry the plant over an unfavorable season, as over winter, or a dry summer.

The bulbs are either formed in rings or layers like those of the hyacinths and onions, or scaly like those of liliums.

The term bulb, as properly understood, applies to a large class of flowering and ornamental bulbous plants in their dormant condition. During this period, they are collected, dug, stored, shipped, sold, and planted.

This class includes, in addition to the true bulbs, many that are botanically known as corms — which are solid, as crocus and gladiolus; or tubers — which are succulent and have the buds or eyes near the surface, as the dahlia and potato; or rhizomes — which are fleshy, creeping, underground stems, like certain kinds of iris and many wild plants and pips; or the flowering crowns of the lily-of-the-valley; or certain other dormant, fleshy roots, like those of peonies and ranunculas.

The true, or feeding roots, grow generally from the base of the bulbs; the stems, flowers and foliage, from the crown of the bulbs. There is an exception to this in certain lilies which throw out roots above the bulb.

The bulb is a storehouse for the plant in which new stems, leaves, and flowers are formed after flowering. In fact, the bulb contains a new plant which is protected and fed within the bulb by the reserve food and energy collected during one season, for the plant's successor.

After the flowering period, the plant above the bulb, and the roots beneath, are ripened off and die away. The bulb is then in its dormant condition. It is during this state of rest, lasting approximately three months in the western prairies, that bulbs are taken out of the ground and safely transplanted from place to place as desired.

There is particular charm and interest in growing bulbs. This is because they produce flowers of remarkable beauty. Many of them are very fragrant. They make up an endless variety in habit, form, size, and color.

They are adaptable for many purposes, and many of them flower equally well under either garden, greenhouse or·house culture.

When the thermometer stands at some below-zero mark in early spring, how these lovely bulbs, growing indoors, cheer our hearts. We can surely feel that spring is not far away . . . that it is around the proverbial corner.

Among bulbous plants are many that are sufficiently hardy to stand the severity of our Calgary climate. The kinds that are suitable are nearly all dormant in the fall, which is the proper time for planting them so they will flower the coming season.

Late in April, spring is ushered in here with blooming of the blue and white scillas, snowdrops, crocuses, winter aconites, grape hyacinths, and daffodils.

They are followed at the end of May by the Dutch hyacinth, tulips, and fritillaries, and many others.

Gardeners usually think of bulbs as divided into two classes, hardy and tender, or those which stand freezing or those which don't.

The proper depth to plant bulbs varies according to the kinds. It is a common fault to plant them too deeply or too near the surface.

Hyacinths, tulips, and daffodils, and similar large bulbs should be planted from 4 to 6 inches deep, and about 9 inches apart; smaller bulbs, somewhat shallower and closer. Hardy bulbs root during the early fall, September being the right time to plant them. The ground, being still warm, gives them the start they require.

If planted too near the surface, the freezing, thawing, and heaving of the upper crust of the soil in mild winters could cause the bulbs to break from their roots.

When cold weather has set in and the frost has penetrated 6 inches into the ground, then cover the bulb beds with a strawy litter to a depth of 4 to 6 inches. This protects not only from severe freezing, but from equally injurious thaws. Do not put the covering on too early; generally October is early enough.

Gradually remove the covering in the spring, say about the middle of April, providing the weather is favorable.

The general run of bulbous plants thrive in a loamy soil inclining to sandy. This soil attracts moisture, gives drainage, and admits air. If the soil is clayey and stiff, a liberal mixture of peat moss and sand with the addition of manure will be beneficial.

The texture of the soil should be such that stagnant water will not remain around the bulbs, as it tends to rot them.

The sooner bulbs are put in the ground in September after they are ripe, the better for the bulbs. No matter how long they may keep, they do not improve when out of the ground, as they have a tendency to dry out and lose vitality.

But hardy spring flowering bulbs should be planted in the open ground in the fall, not earlier than six weeks before regular frosty and freezing nights are expected. Cool weather is necessary to deter top growth which if a bulb is planted too early in the fall is likely to start after four to six weeks of root development.

More detailed descriptions of some of the favorite Calgary bulb-like flowers follow.

BEGONIA

One of our most popular bulb plants, whether for the greenhouse or for filling summer flower beds, is the begonia. Both the flowers and the leaves of this attractive plant are ornamental. Some types are grown for their ornamental leaves, others for their flowers. Some bloom in summer, others in winter, while a few flower more or less all year round.

Begonias are found in a wild state chiefly in South America, though some are native plants of India and other Far Eastern countries.

They can be grouped into three sections: (1) tuberous rooted, raised from seed, (2) fibrous rooted, (3) those valued for their ornamental foliage, which may be either tuberous or fibrous.

The tuberous rooted begonias are those most commonly grown here both indoors and for bedding out during the summer, the latter usually accomplished by plunging the pots outside in the garden early in June.

These have large tubers and have been evolved by crossbreeding between several South American species or wild types of begonias, and by further crossbreeding between those so raised.

There are innumerable varieties with single, semi-double, or double flowers in almost every color except blue.

In some varieties, the edges of the petals are frilled, while in others the petals are crested. The plants have stout, fleshy stems about 15 inches in height and large, deep green glossy leaves.

It is really worth while selecting named varieties from a catalogue for cultivation in pots. Those who plant to raise the tuberous rooted begonias either from seed or tubers, should start them towards the end of February or the beginning of March in the greenhouse.

The tubers are started by setting them in shallow boxes. Place an inch of peat moss in the bottom of the boxes, and set the tubers on this about half an inch apart with more peat moss sprinkled between them, the top being left uncovered.

The boxes are kept in a warm place at a temperature of about 60 degrees, and the peat is kept moist. Soon fresh shoots and roots will develop. When these are about half an inch long, the tubers are potted separately in 4-, 5-, or 6-inch pots, according to size.

The best compost in which to pot tubers should be three parts fibrous loam, two parts peat moss, one part sharp sand, and one-half part well-rotted manure. To every bushel of this compost, add one pint of bone meal.

Begonia plants must be potted firmly — the operation being carried out with the finger and the thumb. The roots and tubers are fleshy and are easily damaged, and for this reason it should be done by hand and not with a potting stick.

When the roots reach the sides of the pots, the plants are finally repotted, 6-, 7-, or 8-inch pots being selected according to the vigor of the plants.

A temperature of between 55 to 60 degrees is sufficient for tuberous-rooted begonias after the tubers have been potted, as too much heat produces weaker growths. They should be kept in a rather humid atmosphere and shaded from hot sunshine during the day.

When they are planted outside, about 10 to 12 inches apart, they must also be placed in part shade. This is important, because the flower petals are easily scorched by strong sunshine. It may be wise to remove the first set of buds which appear on the begonia plants. By so doing, much larger blooms will appear later.

Weak liquid manure is then applied twice a week to increase the size of the blooms.

After flowering is over, less water is given and when the leaves have ripened, the plants are dried off entirely, generally about the end of September. The dead stems are cut off just above the tuber, the tubers taken from the soil, allowed to dry in the air for an hour or so, and then stored in boxes of dry sand or soil. Store them at a temperature of 40 degrees.

Sometimes they are in full bloom when an early frost threatens. When this occurs you can, of course, lift the pots containing the begonias and take them indoors. This is one reason why it is preferable to put begonias in pots and why it is better to plunge them into the garden in pots at the time of bedding out.

For flower beds outside in the garden, the tuberous begonias which are not going to be potted are started in the same way. When the new shoots are several inches long, the plants are gradually hardened off and are placed in a coldframe about the middle of May.

The frame must be kept closed for a day or two and then gradually opened to give free ventilation to the plants, as this hardens them thoroughly. About the beginning of June, weather permitting, you may bed out begonias. They should be planted in the shade of trees, by preference, about 10 to 12 inches apart.

After they are planted, the surface of the begonia bed should be top-dressed with a layer of peat moss or rotted manure. During the dry, hot weather, they must be kept well watered. They will continue to bloom until freeze-up.

There are many varieties of tuberous begonias which are of a drooping habit of growth. These are ideal plants for cultivation in suspended baskets or window boxes. Their long, slender shoots hang down over the sides of the baskets or boxes, and produce lovely blooms.

Wire baskets should be lined with peat and filled with the compost already advised. The sprouting tubers may then be placed 6 inches apart in baskets, with the tops of the tubers being just covered with soil.

Begonia Rex and similar varieties are the chief types grown entirely for the beauty of their foliage. They have short fleshy rhizomes or root stocks from which long stalked, oval, or wrinkled leaves grow. These leaves average 6 inches or more in diameter.

The leaf stalks, veins, and in some cases the upper surface of the leaves are covered with fine hairs. The leaves are beautifully marked with silver and green, light and dark green, red and green, purple and green, in the different varieties.

These are only grown indoors and make very decorative plants for the home or greenhouse.

Both the fibrous-rooted begonias and the ornamental-leaved begonias are easily increased by means of cuttings. Those who spend time and care in raising begonias will be richly rewarded with a wealth of glorious color.

The fibrous-rooted begonias differ from the tuberous species in that they are grown from cuttings or from the fibers which develop from cuttings, and they are also, generally speaking, smaller plants. The fibrous types are mostly about 10 inches high, compared with an average of 15 inches for tuberous types.

The fibrous begonias are mostly red and pink, and the blossoms also are smaller than those from tuberous begonias but generally more numerous.

The tuberous root will generally give better results, however.

A good, healthy tuber should be about 3 inches in diameter and up to about 2 inches long, and free from brown blemishes. If you buy fibrous begonias, get a plant which is blooming. A good fibrous begonia should be continually blooming during the season.

51

The begonias belong to the begoniaceae family, the name commemorating Frenchman Michel Begon.

DAFFODIL

Daffodils, which grow in such lovely profusion in more temperate climates, could, I believe, be grown here to a much greater extent than they are.

Though many varieties of daffodils have been experimented with here, there are still many others which could be tried out.

A good number of Calgarians, however, are still under the impression that daffodils cannot be grown in our difficult climate.

They can be grown here IF they are planted outdoors early in the fall (generally in September), so as to build up their rooting system while the soil is still warm.

A variety which I know grows here, and which in my opinion does best in our climate, is that known as the King Alfred. Maybe, there are others, too, which will do as well or maybe better. I hope gardeners will do more experimenting here with different new varieties. But the King Alfred daffodil has been tried out in Calgary, and it is proved suitable.

In preparation for the planting of daffodil bulbs, the soil should be prepared in the same manner as for tulips.

The daffodil thrives in ordinary, well-tilled garden soil, but is at its best in well-drained, loamy ground. If your soil is heavy or heavily clayed, sharp sand ought to be added freely and really well-rotted manure may also be dug in with advantage.

There is no better artificial manure for daffodils than bone meal. This should be scattered on the ground at the rate of 2 oz. a square yard, and forked in before the bulbs are planted.

The best time to plant these bulbs is early September and an endeavor should be made to get the planting completed by the end of September.

The depth at which the bulbs are set must depend on their size, for some are very much larger than others. Large bulbs of the trumpet daffodils should have a soil covering of not less than 4 to 5 inches and some at a depth of 7 or 8 inches, and the medium-sized bulbs should be covered with 3 to 4 inches of soil.

Daffodils can be left undisturbed for many years, in fact until they become so crowded that they fail to bloom freely. But, generally, it will be found that daffodils planted in beds or borders need to be lifted at the end of four years.

Some people may want to grow daffodils in pots. They are one of the easiest of all bulbs to grow in pots for the decoration of the house or greenhouse in early spring. By potting bulbs at intervals of a week or two from September until the end of October, it is possible to have house plants in bloom from February until the middle of March, or even longer.

The way to achieve success in the home or in the greenhouse is to use a compost of old turf with which a little decayed manure and a good sprinkling of sharp sand have been mixed. They will do far better in such a mixture than if soil from the garden is used.

The bulbs should be set at such a depth that the greater part of each one is covered with soil. The smaller bulbs may be wholly buried. The number of bulbs that can be set in a pot must, of course, depend on their size. Four bulbs of moderate size, or three large bulbs, can be placed in a 6-inch pot.

Daffodils belong to the narcissus family and are favorites for cultivation here in greenhouse or out of doors. Nowadays the word narcissus and daffodil are commonly used indiscriminately, though daffodil is correctly applied to flowers which have trumpets and narcissus to those with cups or crowns.

When buying daffodil bulbs get those which are at least 1½ to 2 inches in diameter and firm. Don't buy bulbs which are too long or thin, and avoid also those which have blemishes.

DAHLIA

The dahlia, which grows so well in our climate, was so named after Professor Andreas Dahl, a Swedish botanist.

The dahlia is a tender, tuberous-rooted summer and autumn flowering plant which is found wild in Mexico. It belongs to the daisy family.

During recent years, remarkable results have been achieved in raising new types of dahlias and in improving the older types. As a result, this plant is now of far more value for the decoration of the garden during the summer and autumn than it was.

The new cactus and decorative types of dahlias are a tremendous improvement over the older varieties.

Dahlias will thrive in full exposure to the sun, and in any ordinary garden soil which has been well dug and enriched with well-rotted manure.

Planting living tubers outside should be done during the first week of June, when all danger of frost is past. It is most important to allow the plants ample room for development — at least 3 or 4 feet between tubers. If crowded, they will bloom sparsely and the blooms will be of poor quality.

Dead blooms must be picked off as they fade, or the flowering period, particularly in the single-flowered varieties, will be shortened.

Staking and tying must be done as soon as the taller dahlias are planted. Unless adequately supported, the stems will suffer during windy weather, as they are very brittle. However, the long-growing types need little or no support.

It is necessary to thin out the side shoots, because they are usually so numerous that if left, the growth will be so crowded that many of the blooms will be hidden.

The dahlia plants should be inspected frequently during the summer, so that any shoots for which there is no room can be removed.

If dahlias are planted in reasonably good soil, in a position fully exposed to the sun, with ample room for their development, they will do well.

When the first sharp frost has cut down the plants, the tubers should be lifted without delay, because if left in the ground longer and exposed to severe frosts, they may be damaged. The tubers should be stored in sand in a frost-proof building.

When replanting in the spring, the old dormant tubers should be planted out around the middle of May.

However, the way to get best results is to grow them from cuttings. To obtain cuttings, the old tubers should be removed from storage in February or March and placed in boxes in a greenhouse. The tubers should then be partly

Plants in flat and coldframe

Above:
Weeping
Caragana

Left:
Author in
Reader Rock
Gardens, Calgary

Below: Van Houtti

Below: Flowering Currant

covered with peat moss or loam, and kept watered. If kept at a temperature of 55 to 60 degrees, they will soon start new growth.

When the young shoots are about three inches long, they should be cut off, with a piece of tuber attached. The cuttings should then be inserted into pots filled with light, sandy loam. In three to four weeks' time, the cuttings should be well rooted and can be hardened off in a coldframe. The new plants should be set out in the garden in June.

I would like to mention a few of the different types of dahlias. Resembling the single type, the "collarette" has an inner ring or collar of florets, often an entirely different shade from the rest of the bloom.

Another, the small-flowered and decorative cactus, is one of the most beautiful.

The tall peony-flowered, the dwarf peony-flowered, the star dahlia and the double or show dahlia are among the best double or semi-double varieties.

These varieties all range from 2½ to 5 feet in height.

Also a favorite with a great many people is the pompom which reaches a height of 2 to 3 feet. This dainty little dahlia is a small brother of the show type. It has the same colors and form, but the flowers are smaller and more abundant.

As a rule, the smaller the flowers, the prettier they are. The larger pompoms suffer by comparison with the best pompom show type which are very small. At our own flower show, the pompom have, on several occasions, been selected as "best in the show."

The coltness hybrids, which are a dwarf type of dahlia producing vari-colored flowers, are easily raised from seed in the home or greenhouse.

Seed sown in April will germinate in a matter of days, and will grow rapidly. When the seedlings are 3 inches tall, they should be potted in 3-inch pots. After a few weeks in the 3-inch pots, they will require re-potting in 4-inch pots.

In this manner, you will be growing sturdy plants, which will have their first set of blooms before they are planted outside in the garden, which time should be about the first week in June.

From then on, plants will bloom very freely, provided they are given proper cultivation and an ample supply of water.

Dwarf hybrids are obtainable in straight or mixed colors, and grow to a height of 18 inches.

Both the large and small-flowered, decorative cactus dahlia come in many soft and pastel shades, as well as in deep, rich, dark shades. It is a common sight to see many perfect blossoms out at one time on each of these plants.

Insects which usually attack the dahlia are aphids or aster beetles. If this occurs during the growing season, spray plants with Black Leaf-40, using 2 teaspoonsful to a gallon of water, and adding a melted 1-inch cube of soap to the solution. Spray once a week, until the insects are gone. They will usually be found just below the blooms, and on the undersides of the foliage.

The aster beetle attacks the roots as well.

The dahlia is a heavy feeder, and the soil should be fertilized constantly, at least every ten days during the growing season. Artificial manure can be used, one large tablespoonful for each plant, cultivating it into the soil and watering well afterwards.

Be careful when purchasing dahlia tubers. Try and get only those with a well-pointed, firm root; and be sure it has eyes in the tuber (and not in the stem).

GLADIOLUS

The gladiolus is one of the most popular perennials, and one which grows extremely well in Alberta.

The Calgary Gladiolus Society has, for many years, held a special show to give growers an opportunity to show their outstanding blooms. To see the gladiolus thus displayed, in all its delicate, enchanting beauty, one would scarcely believe that it could be grown to such perfection out of doors in our rigorous climate.

It has the appearance almost of some hothouse plant. But the gladiolus is not nearly as delicate as it appears to be.

The lovely new pastel colors and tints in which the plants are now grown create this illusion of delicacy. Few flowering plants have been so greatly improved in recent years as the gladiolus, or sword plant, as it is sometimes called.

The gladiolus belongs to the iris family, the name being derived from the Latin gladius — a sword — in allusion to its sword-shaped leaves.

The original species or wild types are mostly native to North Africa, although some grow wild in Southern Europe. Very few of these are now grown, preference being given to the new and vastly improved varieties, their present perfection having been attained by crossbreeding and hybridizing.

It was the introduction of the pale yellow gladiolus primulinus, from the Zambesi Falls early in the present century, that helped greatly in the production of the remarkable range of color in today's varieties.

The primulinus is a plant of slender growth, bearing small, hooded flowers of varying shades, the upper petals curving inwards, forming a hold over the stamens and pistil. This plant had been used in the development of a new race of gladiolus, which is known as the primulinus or small-flowered type.

The prims, as they are usually called, are charming for table decoration, and will last a considerable length of time in the house. Another feature in their favor is that they are fairly easy to grow.

Planting outside should be carried out as soon as the ground is warm enough, maybe about the end of April or the first week in May. These plants will thrive in any good garden soil, which has been prepared in the fall by digging into it a liberal quantity of manure. Glads are gross feeders and also need a lot of water.

If your soil is heavy or largely clay, thoroughly decayed manure and sharp sand should be mixed into the garden.

When planted, the corms should be placed on a layer of sharp sand, the larger varieties 11 or 12 inches apart and the primulinus corms 6 to 8 inches apart, and all at a depth that they can be covered with 3 inches of soil.

When planting glads in groups in the perennial border, it is wise to allow sufficient room for each plant to develop properly.

Another good plan in planting a bed of glads is to place all corms on the surface of the flower bed, before planting, at the correct distance apart.

If this rule is not followed, it is easy to become confused by planting a few corms, and then not remembering where each was planted, resulting in a poor design when the plants grow.

By planting corms of gladiolus at intervals of ten days from the end of April or early May, a succession of bloom is assured until freeze-up.

During the summer, especially in hot, dry weather, the gladiolus requires an abundance of water. Also the soil must be cultivated frequently. The large-flowered varieties will need to be supported by stakes to keep them upright in windy weather, but the prims do not, as a rule, need staking.

To improve the size and color of the blooms, an application of soot and hardwood ashes to the soil, at the rate for both of one large handful a square yard, is valuable before the plants bloom. This of course should be cultivated thoroughly into the ground.

The size of the blooms is improved by the application of artificial fertilizer every 10 days or so, from the time buds are seen until the flowers begin to open, and a top dressing of dry wood ash is beneficial at the same time.

There is no difficulty in growing this flower from seed in the green-house. Most of the seedlings will bloom the third year. It is possible that a few of them will bear small flowers the second year if the seeds are sown early enough.

Sowing may be done in February or March in a heated greenhouse with a temperature of 55 to 60 degrees.

A box 8 inches deep should be drained by boring a few holes in the bottom and this filled with a compost of two-thirds loam and one-third peat moss with a good scattering of sand.

Before this is put into the box, a layer of rough turf should be placed in the bottom. The seeds are placed 1 inch apart and covered with ¼ of an inch of the compost. If the soil is kept moderately moist the seedlings will show through in a few weeks.

These seedlings are not disturbed until the autumn after the leaves have died down. The corms are then taken out and stored for the winter in a frost-proof place.

All glads outside should be dug up after the first frost, the tops cut off ½-inch above the corm, and stored away for the winter. Never should they be left in the ground all winter.

When lifting corms, choose a dry day. Dig them up and leave them on the ground until quite dry. If you have a number of varieties, lift each separately and place in trays or boxes, making certain that each variety is correctly labelled.

In its best form, the gladiolus is a truly lovely flower. The beauty of the spikes, its lasting properties as a cut flower, render it increasingly popular. Planted in beds, lines or groups, glads produce a surprisingly lovely effect in the garden and the cheapness of the corms enables them to be largely used for garden decoration.

Spikes grown for house decoration should be cut in the cool of the evening when the lowest three florets show color, placing them in water immediately so that they can take up as much moisture as possible. Never allow the ends to dry off, or the flowers will not open in water. When cutting spikes, leave at least four sets of leaves on the plant, so that the new corm can be built up another year.

Gladiolus grown for garden display should have the faded spike cut off immediately after the last flower fades, to prevent seed from forming, cutting below the lowest weathered flower so that the corms can develop and ripen before being lifted in the fall.

The many growers of gladioli in the City of Calgary deserve great praise for the high quality of blooms which they have raised. Many have not only raised excellent blooms but have exhibited them throughout the Dominion, bringing back championship prizes to our city.

The following varieties have been recommended by the Calgary Gladiolus Society, and have been found to be most suitable for Alberta's short-growing season:

White — Snow Princess and Maid of Orleans; and in the lovely pink shades with white is Mrs. L. W. Angus. Royal Gold is attainable in light yellow; and for a magnificent deep yellow Gate of Heaven is unsurpassed.

For the softer shades of apricot and buff, Greta Garbo is recommended.

For the deeper shades of salmon, there is Aladdin.

Tip-Top is a lovely scarlet, and will add dash to your border, as will Red Charm. Incidentally, red blossoms will attract that elusive little bird, the humming bird. Black Opal is a sultry velvety maroon, and is distinctive in appearance.

Among the delicate mauves is Elizabeth the Queen, and among the purples, King Lear is popular.

Although similar to the purples, the medium and deep violets can be used to further enhance the beauty of your garden, and will be found listed under such names as Blue Admiral and Atlas. Ranging from smoky ash to bronze and copper are Zuni and Chief Multnomah.

Lastly, if you like the varieties with blotchy leaves, they can be obtained in white, light and medium colors with conspicuous blotches on the blossoms, and these are indeed striking in appearance.

Other varieties which I can also recommend in the large class are:

White: Florence Nightingale, Prof. Gourdriau and Snow Drift. Cream: Lief Ericsson, Salmon's Glory and Lorelie. Yellow: Gold Bank, Gold and Spotlight. Buff: Peach Glow, Regina and Potrol. Orange: Atlantic Circe. Salmon: Salmon Queen and Boldface. Light Pink: Pink Harmony. Medium Pink: Friendship. Deep Pink: Spic and Span. Scarlet: Dieppe and Sans Souci. Red: Red Charm. Black Red: Ace of Spades, Ruffled Ebony and Negus. Rose: Burma, Rose Spire and Rose Charm. Lavender: Huntress and Lavender Joy. Purple: The Rajah and King David. Violet: Violet Charm. Smoky: The Owl, Storm Cloud and Dusty Miller.

It must be remembered that gladiolus bulbs must be lifted from the garden in the fall and stored inside, generally in the basement, in a minimum temperature of 40 degrees. A good way to store is to place the bulbs in paper bags, with holes torn in the bag so that air may get into them. Or they can be stored in shallow boxes.

A healthy corm should have high shoulders (like a top) and be about 1½ inches to 2 inches in diameter and maybe 2 inches long. It should not be too squat, and it should be firm-fleshed.

Watch out for and avoid brown blemishes or soft spots, and also make sure it isn't attacked by thrips.

IRIS

The perennial iris is, in my opinion, one of the most beautiful flowers grown. When one sees 30 or 40 different varieties growing together in a profusion of bloom, one really does appreciate the iris. A reason for this is that each individual shade sets off the other.

The iris, sometimes called the flag, can be obtained in a great many varieties, and it has perennial rootstocks, rhizomes or bulbs. It is native of Europe, although several kinds do grow wild in North America, especially around the Lake Superior region. Incidentally, the rhizome is the fleshy rootstock at the base of the plant and the actual roots are attached to the rhizome.

Irises are divided into two main classes — those which have the thick rootstocks or rhizomes, and those which are grown from bulbs. All those growing from rhizomes have sword-shaped leaves.

The irises possessing a thick underground rhizome are divided into three different types — tall bearded, dwarf bearded, and beardless.

The bearded kinds, sometimes called the poor man's orchid, are so named because the outer petals or falls have a thick line of fine hairs stretching down the lower half of them.

The beardless kinds are, of course, without these hairs.

Irises vary in height from the dwarf cushion type, 6 inches high, to the tall beardless kinds, three feet high. A great many irises bloom in May or June, but a few will flower throughout the greater part of the summer.

The structure of the iris differs from that of most plants inasmuch as the three outer petals grow downwards and are known as falls, and the other three stand erect and are called standards.

The flowers of the tall bearded iris will appear in May and June and are about 5 inches in diameter. There are several lovely shades, among which are rose-pink, blue, yellow and crimson.

Owing to the gorgeous coloring and easy cultivation, these irises are prime favorites. They are extremely hardy and will grow in ordinary garden soil, although intensive cultivation is necessary to produce the best results.

The soil should be dug deeply and some well-rotted manure worked into it.

A sunny, well-drained position suits them best, however, though they will also grow and flower in semi-shade.

A good many gardeners make the mistake of planting iris too deeply. This must not be done, as it is necessary for the rhizomes to be sun-baked to produce the maximum amount of blossoms. If they are planted too deeply they will just rot away and eventually die. The proper depth is when the rhizomes are placed flat and only half covered, with all the roots, however, under the ground.

They are planted one foot apart, with the tips of the rhizomes pointing towards the outside. If the outside clumps of soil are dry, they should be thoroughly watered. An annual dressing of lime is good, and should be applied in the fall.

The best time to propagate or divide iris is in July or August. It may be done in April, but the disadvantage of this lies in the fact the flower will not be so good the first year from spring planting.

When the flowers deteriorate in size and number, the plants should be lifted and divided and then re-planted in July, preferably on a new site. If they are to occupy the same position as formerly, the ground should be treated as recommended for the initial planting.

The dwarf bearded iris is treated essentially the same as the tall bearded iris. A few of the colors include white, azure, sky blue, yellow and purple.

With the beardless iris, although the spikes reach a height of approximately 3 feet, the foliage grows only to about 2 feet. This foliage is similar to the bearded iris, resembling sword-like leaves.

The Siberian iris is a graceful plant with narrow grass-like foliage and slender flower stems 2 to 3 feet in height. The flowers are much smaller than those of the bearded iris, but they are produced in far greater quantities.

These are found to be especially suitable for a big garden or along water courses. A sunny, moist position, ordinary garden soil with peat moss added, and abundance of water are their chief requirements.

They are very hardy and planting outdoors may be done in autumn or spring. Once they are planted, they should be left undisturbed until they fail to bloom satisfactorily.

The Japanese iris is a very distinct type with large, flat clematis-type flowers. If, too, grows 2 to 3 feet high and will also do well in a moist, sunny place.

For those desirous of introducing some dwarf varieties of irises into a rockery, here is a list which will certainly enhance a garden and add to its general charm; iris arenarium, the sand iris, 8 inches high and possessing canary yellow blooms; and iris azurea; iris cristata; iris lacustris; iris pumila and iris cuprea, all of which are different shades of blue.

The sand iris grows best in very sandy soil and a sunny location. It bears yellow blooms.

Iris crustata has pale blue flowers and grows 6 inches tall. The crustata will do well in part shade and ordinary soil.

Iris ruthenica has grass-like foliage with orchid-like flowers in two shades of blue. It has great elegance and will thrive in part shade or sun in any good garden soil.

Irises, as a rule, are not too susceptible to the diseases that attack other plants, but can be seriously injured by iris rust, or leaf spot as it is sometime called. The symptoms of the disease are at first yellow-brown spots, oblong in shape and later bearing dark brown spores which rapidly spread.

The spots are pale in dry weather. In moist weather the disease spreads rapidly and the plant, including the flower, may become diseased.

The disease is caused either from planting infected bulbs or rhizomes or from diseased materials decaying in the soil.

It can be controlled by care in cleaning the land and by lifting the rhizomes every other year.

Unfortunately, there is no means of detecting infected bulbs and a very small number can produce an epidemic. When the disease appears, spray the infected parts or places with Bordeaux mixture. Use eight tablespoonsful to a gallon of water. This will help check the disease, but will not give it adequate control in severe cases.

The most efficient method is to cut off the diseased parts of the leaves and burn them. This may have to be done two or three times, but if you delay at all, the disease will have probably spread too far.

A good, healthy rhizome should be about 3 inches long and about 1½ inches in diameter. The foliage should be green when the rhizome is purchased.

PEONY

The peony (paeonia) is one of our best-loved perennials.

In delicacy of tint and fragrance, the peony more nearly approaches the rose than any other flower. It is a hardy herbaceous or a shrub-like perennial, but in this part of the world the herbaceous peonies are the favorites.

The peonies bloom in May or June and come in single or double varieties.

The name paeonia is said to commemorate à French physician, Dr. Paeon, and peonies belong to the buttercup family ranunculaceae.

Comparatively few species of wild types of peony, which are natives chiefly of Europe and Asia, are grown now in private homes. The Calgary parks department, however, has a few wild species growing. The blooms of these are much smaller than the ordinary cultivated peony, although they are quite profuse.

Peonies must be planted outside either in April or toward the end of September in a deep rich soil. They take some time to become established and they should be planted where they can remain undisturbed for years.

The site should be prepared by digging the ground about 2 feet deep and mixing bone meal with the soil, using one-half handful to each plant. Never work manure into the soil where peonies are to be grown, as they resent manure, but they love bone meal.

Peonies do well in a sunny place, but the colors do not stand up as well as when they are planted in a partly shaded place.

Peonies should not be disturbed as long as they are healthy and producing good flowers. The only time a peony should be moved is when you see signs of deterioration. Then move them to a new location.

It is not wise to place peonies in a too prominent place in the herbaceous border, for they usually finish blooming earlier then most flowers, and then will take up a good deal of room without adding to the beauty of the border after blooming.

Peonies are really at their best when planted in a bed by themselves. Tall annuals can, of course, be planted in between the peony plants to bloom later in the season, giving you a fairly long blooming period.

Peonies may be planted in open spaces among shrubs or in other informal parts of the garden where they have room to develop and are not likely to be disturbed. The should not be planted in deep shade or in places where the soil has become impoverished by roots of neighboring trees and shrubs.

During hot, dry weather, they should be watered thoroughly. They will not flourish if they are allowed to become dry at the roots.

Peonies should be planted so that the crowns or pips are just 2 to 3 inches below the level of the ground — this is very important.

They should be spaced 30 to 36 inches apart.

If healthy peonies fail to bloom satisfactorily, the trouble more than likely lies in wrong planting.

When buying peonies, choose firm, plump crowns with young fibrous roots and having 3 to 5 pips or (buds) on the crowns.

Three kinds which are recommended for early blooming are peony tenuifolium (a single, or double), peony tenuifolium flora plena (a double), and peony officinalis (a single). These three species do not grow very tall, only about 15 to 18 inches high.

The peony tenuifolium is blood red with fern-like foliage and comes in both single and double varieties. The flora plena is also red. Peony officinalis is a deep pink with single blooms, and is a profuse bloomer when well grown.

If you wish to propagate peonies to increase the stock, you should lift and separate the clumps toward the end of September. This will give them a better chance of getting established outdoors before a freeze.

Double varieties only are propagated. Single varieties are raised from seed in the greenhouse.

The first year after planting, peonies should be mulched around the roots with a strawy litter after the first frost. It is not necessary to mulch them after they are established.

Here are some recommended double varieties:

Alberta Crousse, a light rose-pink; Baroness Schroeder, flesh white; Bunker Hill, light red; Edulis Superba, brilliant pink; Germaine Bigot, a lovely pink; Grace Loomis, pure white; James Kelway, rose white; Karl Rosenfield, dark crimson; Lady Alexander Duff, soft blush pink; La Lorraine, creamy-white; Mad Cabot, pinkish; Marie Crousse, pale lilac rose; Mrs. Edw. Harding, large pure pink; Sarah Bernhardt, deep rose-pink, silver tipped.

TULIP

Tulips, a large group of hardy bulbs, provide some of the most brilliant flowers of spring and early summer. They are natives of various parts of Europe, Western Asia and North Africa and the name is said to be derived from the Turkish word tulbend, a turban, referring to the shape of the flower.

For gardening purposes, tulips may be separated into three chief classes. The early or May flowering, June flowering, and the species of wild types. There are innumerable species of both the May and June flowering tulips, the latter comprising the darwin and cottage tulips, which bear large, handsome blooms on tall stems.

Tulips thrive best in well-drained, loamy soil. They do well for one season in ordinary garden soil, but may prove disappointing the following season unless given special treatment, or unless the soil is made more suitable.

If tulips are planted in formal beds or borders to provide a spring show of bloom, and later on are to be replaced by summer bedding plants, care must be exercised in their management, or they will prove useless another year.

In such circumstances, it is necessary to lift them, in this climate before the leaves have turned yellow, and replant them in a trench or a reserve border. They must be taken up with as little damage to the roots as possible, and replanted about 4 inches deep. They ought to be well watered after the transplanting.

After such treatment, the leaves are likely to die down earlier than they would have done if the bulbs had not been disturbed. When the leaves have died down, the bulbs should be lifted, set out to dry under cover for a few days, and then stored until planting time in early September.

A better way of managing tulip bulbs, and one that can be carried out when they are not to be replaced by summer flowering plants, is to leave them undisturbed until the leaves have died down, and then to lift, dry and store them until planting time in autumn.

This better method is much to be preferred to that of leaving them throughout winter in the ground, particularly in respect to the May and June flowering varieties. Tulips may, if necessary, be left undisturbed for two years, but afterwards, unless they are lifted and replanted, dried and stored, they will become over-crowded and deteriorate rapidly.

In gardens where the soil consists of well-drained, rich, sandy loam, tulips are likely to prove more successful than in places where the ground is heavy and largely clay.

The best time to plant the May and June flowering bulbs is September, that is the darwin and cottage tulips. Bulbs should be set at a depth of 4 inches, or where the soil is heavy, at a depth of 3 inches.

I would suggest that you put a layer of sharp sand under the base of all bulbs, as this encourages roots and at the same time gives good drainage.

It is a mistake to plant tulip bulbs in too rich a soil, and it is unwise to use fresh manure unless it is really well decayed. Bone meal is best for tulip bulbs. It should be scattered on the surface of the ground, before planting, at the rate of 2 ozs. a square yard, and be turned in with the garden fork.

When growth shows in spring, the soil between the tulips should be cultivated frequently with a small hoe.

One of the secrets of success in growing tulips is to get them planted early enough while the soil is still warm, so that they may be able to produce their rooting system before cold weather sets in. October and November is too late, because by that time the ground will be much too cold and they will just rot in the ground.

After the first hard frost, the bed should be covered with a layer of strawy litter about three inches deep if the tulips are to be left out all winter. In April, the litter is removed from the bed.

Here are the names and colors of a few of the best kinds of tulips for our climate:

The cottage tulips—Amber Crown, yellow, flushed with rose; Don Pedro, deep brown; Ellen Willmott, primrose yellow; Inglescombe Pink, salmon rose; Inglescombe Scarlet, bright red; Inglescombe Yellow, yellow; Orange King, reddish orange; and Velvet King, violet-purple.

The darwins—Bartagon, bright red; Canada, pure white; Clara Butt, rose; The Bishop, purplish blue; Isis, red; Zulu, deep purple; Donders, crimson; and Margaret, light rose.

For those who like the doubles, there are several handsome varieties: El Toreador, scarlet and buff; Blue Flag, purplish; Murillo, rose and white; Yellow Rose, yellow; Corydon, lilac purple; Pride of Harlem, rose red; William Pitt, red.

There are, of course, several kinds of tulips to choose from, although the darwins are to be recommended first. Some of the others are the Rembrandt tulip, parrot tulip, and species of wild types such as tulip kaufmanniana, sylvestris, cluisiana, and persica. The last four are suitable for the rock garden.

How do you recognize good healthy bulbs when you go to purchase them?

A tulip bulb should be well-rounded, measuring at least 1½ inches through at its widest point. The outside of the bulb should be a clear, clean brown with the white fleshy part underneath having no blemishes. Tulip bulbs with flat sides should be avoided.

Before planting tulip bulbs, you should dig the bed over to a depth of 10 to 12 inches, working in a liberal supply of bone meal and decayed manure. Plant the bulbs at a depth of 6 inches and 9 to 10 inches apart. To be sure that you have them evenly spaced. It is a good plan to spot them over the bed before planting. In this way, you know exactly where each tulip bulb is to be placed.

OTHER BULBOUS PLANTS

There are several other bulbous plants to be recommended, including the fritillaria pallediflora and fritillaria mealiagris, plants with a drooping habit. The flowers of these rather unusual plants are bell-shaped in yellow, white, and mottled effect.

The bells are fairly large and hang over in a peculiar drooping habit. This species, being bulbs, must be planted in September. Also plant them 4 inches deep and 6 to 7 inches apart.

Another charming little flower which may be grown here is the snowdrop (galanthus). In the British Isles it is one of the best loved flowers, being one of the first harbingers of spring, and it is sometimes called the "Fair Maid of February" for this is the month in which it blooms there.

Snowdrops are ideal plants for the rock garden, naturalizing in the grass, edging beds of spring-flowering plants, or for cultivating in pots. They grow from 6 to 9 inches in height, have narrow strap-shaped leaves and white flowers, produced singly on slender stems.

The name galanthus is derived from gala (milk) and anthos (a flower). For naturalizing in the lawn, the bulbs are planted in September, 3 to 4 inches deep. To produce a natural effect, they are scattered thickly on the surface and each bulb is planted where it falls. Once planted they are not disturbed, as they increase year by year.

In the rock garden, they are planted in pockets of light soil at 2 or 3 inches apart in irregular clusters. They should not be disturbed until they show signs of deterioration, when they are lifted in August and replanted in fresh soil.

The scilla siberica, which is similar to the snowdrop, is another beautiful little flowering plant. It is the first flower to bloom here in the spring. It is extremely hardy and makes a lovely edging or is also most suitable for naturalizing in grass.

The crocus is a hardy bulb which blooms early in spring, and belongs to the amaryllis family of amaryllidoceae. There are more than 75 species and many varieties.

The early spring-flowering crocus adds much to the charm of a garden, in a rock garden or on grassy slopes. Many think informal groups in grass look best.

It grows well in ordinary garden soil which has been well cultivated. It should be planted in a sunny position.

In the rock garden and flower border, bulbs should be covered with 2 to 3 inches of soil.

Lilium or true lilies are among the most beautiful of bulbs for cultivation in the greenhouse or out in the garden. The majority are hardy and thrive best in light, well-drained soil. Most also grow best in part shade.

It is best to plant lily bulbs outdoors in April. When planting, surround the bulbs with coarse sand. You can leave them undisturbed for several years as long as they grow vigorously and flower freely.

Recommended species include lilium martagon, terrifolium, tangofolium, elegans, henryii, sulphureum, hansonii, and croceum.

Grape hyacinth is the general name for a number of popular bulbs most of which bear grape-like clusters of flowers in spring.

This hardy, beautiful bulb, whose botanical name is muscaria, belongs to the lily family, liliaceae. It grows 6 to 12 inches high, is mostly blue, and thrives in ordinary, well-cultivated soil. When planting grape hyacinth, sand should be mixed in freely.

It, too, is splendid for the grassy bank or for the rock garden. Plant grape hyacinth bulbs outdoors early in September.

The Roman (or Dutch) hyacinth is a favorite species grown in pots or bowls indoors. It is not recommended for out of doors.

The supply of hyacinth bulbs for cultivation comes almost entirely from Holland, and because of this all are frequently known as Dutch hyacinths.

The winter aconite (eranthis) is a hardy, low-growing, early-flowering tuberous rooted plant valuable for planting in rock gardens. It grows wild in Britain and belongs to the buttercup family.

A favorite is eranthis hyemalis, growing only 3 or 4 inches high and bearing yellow flowers (resembling the buttercup), surrounded by a leafy frill which adds greatly to its beauty.

It is one of the earliest flowers of the year, and in this part of the world blooms in April, provided the weather has been favorable.

Plant the tubers outdoors in August if possible, so that they may become well-rooted before the cold weather sets in. Set them about 3 inches deep and several inches apart, for this tiny plant is seen at its best only when massed. A large group, the flowers wide open to the early spring sunshine, makes a charming picture.

Winter aconite will also grow quite well below large trees in open places.

The plants must not be allowed to dry out, for they require a fair amount of moisture.

Hyacinth

ROSES

The rose, which is fittingly called the queen of flowers, is surely loved by all. There is no flower more popular or better known than the rose. It was probably the first flower known and cultivated in a double state.

It is the double-flowered hybrid garden species which most persons immediately think of when the name rose is mentioned.

Much less attention has been given the wild and single-flowered or semi-double species. But these single-flowered or semi-double shrub roses have a quaint charm and ornamental value of their own, though it is not so generally appreciated.

And the shrub roses are especially valuable in this part of the world because the double hybrids, also called tea roses, do not winter well in our climate, while most of the shrub roses are hardy.

But because the name rose means to most people those exquisite blooms purchased (at considerable cost) from the florist, or the crowning glory of beauty, fragrance and elegance in a bowl in the home, or remembered as reigning supreme in the garden of more temperate parts of the world, let's discuss first (though briefly) the hybrid tea roses.

These hybrid tea roses can be grown here, but it is most difficult to do so.

There are a few varieties of these double roses which, with a lot of care, can be cultivated in Calgary. But I must again emphasize that it is generally a losing battle to try to grow tea roses here, simply because they just are not hardy enough to survive our winters.

You can of course buy a rose in the spring, plant it, tend it with loving care, and bring joy to your heart by producing the queen of flowers. But you'll be very lucky if you can protect it through our winter.

On the other hand, the rose lover can take heart — it has been done.

There are a few varieties of the more hardy of these tender roses which have been cultivated by Calgary gardeners with success. But it takes a lot of care.

My experience has been that the best way in Calgary to protect a rose tree through our winter is to bend the stem over (before the first frost) on a cushion of mulch, then place about 3 inches of mulch over this bent bush, and then 6 inches of soil on this second layer of mulch.

In this manner, you may get your hybrid rose through the winter.

Another way, maybe safer for our coldest winters but involving a lot more work, is to take up the rose tree, root and all, before the first frost, and bury the whole plant at least 3 feet down in the soil during the winter.

In either case, of course, you disinter or exhume the rose in the spring— and hope for the best.

So, because not many tea roses are grown in Calgary, except in greenhouses, let's look at the many hardy shrub roses which are grown successfully here.

There are numerous varieties of the single and semi-double shrub roses which, beside being very hardy and vigorous growers, are of definite value in a local garden, particularly in a shrub border.

They are, I think, seen in their full beauty only when allowed to grow naturally with little restrictive pruning. Some will flower in early summer, others will blossom again in the fall. These can be used attractively also if grouped in a bed on the lawn, and need little care apart from an occasional thinning-out of weak and dead branches.

These shrub roses withstand, very well, the rigorous Western Canada climate, and do not need to be covered during the winter.

Here are a few of these varieties:

Rose Hugonis: this forms a lovely bush 6 to 8 feet high with gracefully arching branches covered with small leaves and yellow single blossoms which measure about 2 inches across. It begins to bloom about the middle of June.

Next, the Austrian Briar, called rose lutea, bears a deep rich yellow single flower.

Another variety, a bicolor, is the Austrian Copper Briar, with striking orange-scarlet single flowers — 2½ inches across.

The Persian Yellow is a semi-double flowered variety of the Austrian briar.

The Harrison's Yellow is a semi-double with deep yellow petals and stamens. It blooms freely, and reaches a height of 3 to 4 feet.

Rose rubrifolia is appropriately named because its flower, foliage and stems are of a pleasing reddish color throughout the season. During the winter it is covered with red berries which are attractive against the white of our winter snow. This single-flowering shrub grows from 5 to 6 feet tall.

Rose setigera is our own prairie rose, and our provincial emblem, and has slender stems often of considerable length. This is especially true when the plant is brought under cultivation. It bears deep rose-colored flowers from 2 to 2½ inches in diameter, usually appearing in July and August. The flowers are extremely fragrant.

Rose altaicea, which bears large single white blossoms in July, is a splendid species and deserves a place in any flower garden.

Rose Hansa is a semi-double red variety and is suitable for massing in beds.

Rosa Rugosa is perhaps one of the most ornamental varieties of the shrub roses, with very dark green lavish foliage and large semi-double red flowers.

Rosa alpina is a shrub which grows to about 3 feet and has delicately arched branches, with single pink blossoms about 1½ inches in diameter. In the fall, the seed pods on this species are striking in themselves. They measure about 1½ inches in length and remain for a long period on the bush.

Many stores of all kinds have thousands of rose bushes to tempt garden-lovers during the early spring, and these beautiful flowers are just sitting and waiting for you, at most reasonable prices.

When you go to buy your rose bushes, I suggest you look for sturdy, well branched plants free from blemishes, full budded but with the buds not too far advanced. You should make sure it is hardy, that is, that it will grow in our climate. The nurserymen or florists should be able to tell you if it will grow and bloom here. Unfortunately many varieties offered for sale here will winter-kill in Calgary.

In the culture of roses, the preparation of the soil is a matter of great importance. Shrub roses should be regarded as a permanent fixture in a garden, especially if you choose the single-flowering kind which do not need to be disturbed for many years.

Hardy roses will flourish in any garden provided the ground is well prepared. The best·time to plant roses of any variety is April or May. They should be planted in a sunny location. When your roses arrive from the nursery, they should be unpacked with the least possible delay and planted. But before planting roses, it is a good idea to soak or "puddle" the roots in a thick mixture of soil and water.

Any pruning necessary should be done about the end of May, with the weak and dead branches being removed. At the first pruning after planting, the branches should be cut back to within three or four buds of the base of the previous year's growth.

In future years, pruning need not be so severe. It is sufficient then to cut out the dead and weak branches, and to prune back the remaining branches about half or two-thirds. This strengthens the rose bush.

The chief objective in pruning is to ensure a shapely bush, and to cut out dead, diseased, and weak shoots. The remaining branches are then fully exposed to the beneficial action of sun and air.

Rose bushes which are overcrowded with shoots are certain to prove unsatisfactory. They will yield poor blooms and probably fall prey to certain pests and plant diseases. It is a mistake to prune roses too early in the spring, however, because should late spring frosts be experienced in early May, the young growths are likely to be damaged.

The rose, like the potato and tomato, is attacked by a remarkably large number of pests and fungus diseases. According to outstanding authorities who specialize in rose-growing, more than 60 diseases have been recognized in different parts of the world. A few of the more serious ones which are to be found in our climate include: rose blackspot, rose mildew, rose grey-mould, greenfly and aphid.

The most effective fungicide for the control of diseases is Bordeaux-mixture used in quantities of eight to ten tablespoons to one gallon of water.

For insects, use Black Leaf-40, 2 teaspoons to 1 gallon of water. Melt a one-inch cube of soap, and add it to the gallon of water.

Flour of sulphur is effective against mildew. First wet the foliage, and then dust the sulphur on the plants, particularly on the undersides of the leaves. Pests and diseases usually attack the reverse side of leaves first.

RAISING FLOWERS FROM SEED

A seed is that part of the plant which is the outcome of flowering and which is used to propagate the species.

In the technical or botanical sense, however, the seed is the ripened ovule. The seed contains an embryo which is a miniature plant. The embryo has a seed coat or testa, one or more leaves known as cotyledons, a bud or a growing point called a plumule and a short descending axis known as the caulicle. From the caulicle, or stemlet, the radicle, or root, develops.

This embryo is a minute, dormant plant. Each embryo is a distinct process of fertlization in which the pollen of the same flower or that of another flower of the same family has taken part.

The ovule or seed is contained in the ovary. The ripened ovary is the seed case, or pericarp. The pericarp with the parts that are amalgamated with it is technically known as the fruit. In many instances there is only one seed in the fruit, and the seed and its case may adhere.

Many of the so-called seeds of horticulturists are really fruits and contain one, a few, or many seeds. As examples, the seeds of beet and lettuce are really the fruits. Grains of corn, wheat, and the seed of strawberry are also fruits. Beans and peas are true seeds, the fruit part is the pod in which they are borne.

Seed of apples and pears are also true seeds, the fruit being the fleshy part which surrounds them.

Germination is the unfolding and the growing of the dormant or embryo plants. The first visible stage in germination is the swelling of the seed. Afterwards, the integument or husk is ruptured and the caulicle appears. When the caulicle protrudes the seed has sprouted. We may all watch this miracle in the spring.

Seed that has sufficient life to sprout may still be too weak to carry the process to complete germination.

The ideal test for the vitality of seeds is to plant them in soil in conditions that are somewhat similar to that in which they are finally to be planted. This test eliminates the seeds which are weak and not able to grow under ordinary conditions, and to push themselves through the soil.

The greater the sprouting success, the greater the germinating power, but one must not expect actual germination will always be as great as the percentage of sprouting.

In order that seeds may germinate, they must be supplied with moisture and air and be given a definite temperature. The necessary temperatures vary with the different kinds of seeds, and they are really determined only by experience. As a rule, seeds germinate best when they are fresh, that is, less than one year old.

The quality of seed cannot be told by a mere casual inspection, but is ascertained only by a careful test. This should include three steps — an examination for purity, vitality, and trueness to name.

Unless seeds possess a high requirement in all these respects, their use will entail great loss to the horticulturist.

In spite of our very short growing season here, we can successfully ripen hundreds of different varieties of seeds.

Most grass seed requires special treatment both in purity and germination tests. Before sowing your lawns, you should test your grass seed.

You can make this test by sowing a hundred seeds in a small flat 3 inches by 9 inches and about 2 inches deep. The soil test is advisable, and care must be taken not to plant the seed too deeply. Grass seed should be sown on the surface and the lightest covering of soil and sand put over the seeds.

Before planting, the soil should be thoroughly watered, and after sowing a fine rose spray should be used to avoid disturbing the seed.

The seed should germinate in approximately ten days and an 80 per cent germination is considered good. If the germination is below 80 per cent then the seed is of an inferior quality.

Not all flower seeds germinate as rapidly as does grass seed, although some germinate even more quickly.

Nasturiums, zinnias and dahlias germinate in three to four days, while perennial phlox takes from three to six months. Some varieties of primulas take a year to germinate.

Following is a list of flowers best grown from seeds:

Antirrhinum (snapdragon), aster, balsam, bearded tongue (pentstemon), calendula (Scotch marigold), cockscomb, chrysanthemum (annuals), Drummond phlox, floss flower (ageratum), German catchfly, heliotrope, larkspur (annuals), lobelia, lupine (annuals), love-lies-bleeding (amaranthus), marigold (French and African), moss rose (single and double), nemesia, nicotiana (sweet-scented tobacco plant), nasturtium (dwarf and double); petunia, pinks, scarlet sage (salvia), salpiglossis, stocks, Virginia stocks, sweet pea, verbena and zinnia.

And the following should be grown from seed out of doors immediately the seed has ripened because they need to be stratified (this is, the thickening of the seel by layers caused by frost action):

Bleeding heart, calendula, California and Iceland poppy, some varieties of columbine, cotoneaster, English primrose, gaillardia, globeflower, lupine (perennials), monkshood (aconitum), and sunflower.

Fertilization is effected by pollen grains which, when they come in contact with the stigma, germinate and send down long tubes through the pistil into the ovary. These pollen tubes contain nuclei which fuse with the nuclei of the ovules and fertilization is effected. The ovules then develop into perfect seeds, capable of reproducing the parent plants.

At the end of one side of the seed coat is a scar (lilum) which indicates where the seed was attached to the pod. Near the lilum is a microscopic hole, the mycropyle. This is where the pollen tube enters to fertilize the ovule, and through which the root emerges when germination starts.

As soon as the seeds are placed under ideal conditions for germination, the moisture which enters through the seed coat and micropyle, dissolves the food materials contained in the seed leaves. Heat causes the embryo to become active, and the young shoots and roots, as they develop, emerge through the micropyle, and the seedling stage is reached.

Before the seedlings are capable of obtaining food from the soil, they derive their nourishment from the cotyledons.

To ensure that the seeds can get sufficient air, it is necessary to sow them at the correct depth in the soil, for if sown too deeply, sufficient oxygen is not available for them to breathe and they decay. Too much moisture also has the same effect, as it prevents air from reaching the seeds.

To obtain the maximum percentage of germination of the majority of seeds, it is necessary to exclude most of them from the light.

Investigations have proved, however, that the seed of some plants germinate better when exposed to the light. The principal of these are fire weed, loosestrife, gloxinia, and tuberous begonia seeds.

When saving seeds it must be remembered that many hybrids which have been obtained by inter-crossing one kind with another, do not breed true to type, so that it is necessary to continue that cross by vegetative means — that is by division of the root or cutting of the specifically desirable plant.

Most of the original species or wild types of plants breed true, however, providing the flowers are prevented from being cross-pollinated. To prevent cross-pollination, the flowers are enclosed in cotton bags and artificially pollinated with pollen from flowers of the same plant or the same species of plant. Unless the flowers are protected in this way, there is no guarantee that the flowers will not become cross-fertilized by insects or bees.

As soon as seed is ripe it should be gathered into paper bags, identified and hung up to dry in a well-ventilated room or shed.

To hasten the drying of berried fruits, the seed is washed out of the pulp. The larger seeds are rubbed in a handful of sand before spreading them out to dry. When thoroughly ripened they are packeted and stored in a dry cool place.

Except with rare and choice or especially good strains, it is generally not worth the trouble of saving seeds, because they can be purchased so cheaply. However, home-saved seeds are often much superior to those obtained from the seedsman because you know they are fresh.

The general rule is that seeds should be planted at a depth equal to four times their diameter. Seed of the average size are therefore lightly covered with fine soil and sand mixed together. Very fine, dust-like seed is not covered with soil but is left on the surface and falls in among the soil particles.

The best way to obtain the maximum percentage of germination is to keep the soil uniformly moist. This is accomplished by placing flats in water and irrigating them from underneath, and covering them over with a sheet of glass and paper to prevent rapid evaporation of moisture from the soil, thus reducing necessity for too frequent waterings.

Glass covers, when used in this manner, should be removed for 15 minutes daily and the condensation which gathers on them should be wiped off before the glass is replaced.

Newspaper should be placed over the glass until the seed germinates, when both the glass and paper are removed. But care has to be taken that seedlings, under this protection, do not become blanched, drawn or spindly.

It should be emphasized that watering is the most important operation in raising plants from seed. I might add that careful watering is also most important in cultivation of all pot plants, particularly with very small seeds which have little or practically no covering of soil.

A good plan, and one that can easily be practised where only a few plants are being raised, is to place the pot, or flat, in a hand-bath or bucket in sufficient water to come just under the surface of the soil, and allow the soil to be watered from underneath. Small seeds like saxifrages should always be watered from underneath.

Careless or too heavy watering on the other hand has a tendency to make the surface of the soil hard. It is important, too, that pots or flats be set perfectly level.

When a watering can is used, the finest rose obtainable is to be preferred, and the water applied in a fine spray, but never in such quantity to permit water collecting on the surface of the soil. A syringe may also be used for this operation.

Just a few words about the type of water to use. The best is rain water, if you can collect it. Next best is tap water kept fresh in a barrel and at the same temperature as the greenhouse. I don't recommend water straight from the tap to the plants, if you can get either of the alternatives.

As soon as the seedlings appear above the surface, they must have more light and air. The glass and paper is lifted off and the seedlings are then gradually brought to the light. When they are large enough to handle they are pricked off or potted separately in flats or pots according to their size and vigor.

The seeds of a number of rock plants are best sown as soon as they are ripe. Some — especially certain kinds of perennials (alyssums, rock (or wall) cress, aethionema, potentilla, dianthus, silene, and trollius acaulis) — germinate within five to seven days. Whereas the asters, campanulas, oenothera, and veronicas take from two to three weeks.

Some of the primulas, gentians, dwarf phlox, ranunculus and aquilegias may remain dormant for may months.

These seeds are sown in small flats which are covered in the bottom with peat moss and filled with a compost of loam, peat moss and sand, in equal proportions. This is passed through a small mesh screen and is made firm and smooth with a small piece of board.

The compost is moistened by immersing the seed flats to their rims in a pan of water until the moisture is seen to ooze through the surface. Then they are set aside to drain for half an hour.

Seeds are now scattered thinly on the surface and generally covered with a light sprinkling of finely sifted soil.

Seeds that have not germinated by fall should be exposed to frost (that is, they should be stratified) during the winter and if taken into a greenhouse in spring, most of them will germinate quickly.

The question is often asked of me, "How long will seeds remain sound when stored or kept over for another year?" Seed such as alyssum, ageratum, anchus, antirrhinum, aster, aubrietia, begonia, coleus, nicotiana, schizanthus, sweet william, violas and lilies are good for two years.

Aquilegia poppies, delphiniums, sunflowers, lupines and sweet peas are good for three, four, five, and ten years if they are kept in a cool dry place.

Vegetable seed will keep anywhere from one to three, three to four, and some from eight to ten years depending on the kinds.

Pots or flats containing seeds of choice high alpine plants like androsace, wahlenbergia, primula, linum, saxifrage, and certain kinds of trollius should not be thrown out until at least two years after sowing.

The fungi liverwort is frequently troublesome on the top of these slow-germinating seeds. The best prevention for this is to thoroughly scald the soil before using it. Even then, a sharp lookout should be kept for liverwort and the first little piece that happens to appear should be removed with a sharp point of a knife.

However, I recommend that you obtain fresh seeds, as they will germinate more readily and will be of more sturdy growth.

Where seed is to be sown in rows, a row in the garden should correspond to a row as planned on paper, that is, at the proper distance from another, according to the scale adopted. A garden line should be used to keep the rows straight and parallel.

With a hoe, if a seeder is not being used, open the furrow to the desired depth advised on the seed packet, being guided by the line or a mark. Sow the seed along the bottom of the furrow, fill in with the soil and firm with the hoe blade.

If a rain follows the sowing, the resulting crust should be lightly puverized so that the young seedlings will have little difficulty in pushing their way to the surface.

When watering young seedlings, use a very fine spray and never let the seeds dry out too much during the germination period. When the third or true leaf has formed on flower or vegetable plants, they must be thinned out for best results.

A few seeds for perennials for borders and rock gardens which should be sown indoors within the first two or three weeks of February are as follows:

The pentstemon in variety, sempervivums, primulas in variety, alyssum (known as cloth of gold), aubrietia, arabis, cerastium, saxifrages in variety, and gentians.

With the exception of the primulas, saxifrages and gentians, these are all sown in a compost of two parts fibrous loam and one part peat moss, one part sharp sand well screened.

The primulas, saxifrages, and gentians require two parts peat moss, two parts loam, and one part sharp sand. All of these germinate within a period of from 10 to 20 days.

They are pricked out into flats when they are about an inch high and have produced their second set of leaves.

When the pentstemons, sempervivums, aubrietia, arabis, cerastium and alyssum are well-rooted in the flats, they should then be placed in a sunny spot in the greenhouse near the glass. All these latter mentioned plants are sun-loving. Although these are very hardy perennials, they must be hardened off before being set out in a sunny location when eventually planted outside.

Primulas, gentians and the saxifrages need different treatment. When they are pricked out, instead of a bright sunny spot in the greenhouse, they need part shade. This can be attained by white-washing the glass under which they are to be placed. They too, like all plants which are grown indoors, have to be hardened off. They also like a partly shaded place in the garden.

From the middle to the end of March is generally the correct time for the sowing of seeds indoors for those who possess a greenhouse, large or small, or even a sunporch. Generally speaking, all annuals and biennials are easily raised from seed indoors.

The more tender species require considerably more care in watering, shading, and general management, to prevent damping off when the seedlings are in a young and delicate state. Too much heat, a sudden change in temperature, too much or too little moisture, may have disastrous effects.

The exact requirements needed for these delicate kinds can only be learned by experience which, after all, is the best teacher, but a greenhouse temperature of 55 to 60 degrees is generally recommended.

Seeds of perennial plants, propagated indoors, particularly alpines, present more difficulty than is the case for most annuals and biennials. Work with perennial seeds requires considerable knowledge of different species. I recommend raising alpine seedlings in pots and flats. Great care should be taken with the compost in which the seeds are to be sown, also to see that the drainage is as perfect as possible.

A general compost which will suit most varieties of perennials in the greenhouse consists of two parts fibrous loam put through a one-quarter mesh screen, one part peat moss and one part sharp sand with the addition of some crushed brick.

For lime-loving plants, such as carnations, pentstemons, gypsophila, and sedums, lime rubble could take the place of crushed brick.

For peat-loving plants like the primula family, lady slippers, lily of the valley, forget-me-nots, ferns, and gentians, one added part of peat may be substituted for the one of loam.

Where space for flats in the coldframe is limited, it is possible to pile the flats upon one another, 2 or 3 deep. When the seedlings are well up, the flats may be taken from the closed frame and placed in the greenhouse or sunporch in a shaded place for a few days to green up and harden off before the seedlings are pricked off.

Pricking off should be done when the natural or rough leaves have formed. Never leave seedlings in the flats or pots long enough to become drawn and spindly. Some seedlings are very slow in making growth after first germinating, and it will be generally found that carefully pricking them off will give them a fresh lease in life and influence good growth.

In transplanting seedlings there is always a tendency to select the largest and finest, and if there are more than are wanted, destroy the smaller and weaker ones. If this is done when dealing with seedlings raised from seeds of the double-flowered petunias, it will be found that most of them will produce single blooms. It is the same with stocks.

The largest percentage of double flowers is produced from the smallest seedlings. This detail is of less importance in the cultivation of petunias for planting out of doors than of those to be grown in pots under glass, for the single-flowered varieties are to be preferred for filling beds and borders, the double ones for the greenhouse or sunporch.

Nevertheless, the smallest seedlings, even of the single petunias, often bear the most brilliantly colored blooms, so they should not be discarded in favour of the larger, vigorous ones.

As soon as the seedling petunias have become well rooted in the pots of soil to which they were moved, they should be placed in a coldframe, providing the weather is mild. There they will remain until the end of May or early in June when they are to bloom.

Named varieties of petunia or particularly good double varieties may be propagated by means of cuttings which are taken in August and inserted round the edges of pots filled with a sifted compost of peat moss, sand, and

74

loam. They will form roots in a few weeks. When well-rooted the cuttings must be potted separately in small pots.

For pricking off seedlings, shallow boxes or flats should be prepared, 2 to 3 inches deep. Drainage holes must be provided and some rough fibrous loam or peat moss should be placed at the bottom of the flat, which is then filled with a mixture of loam, sand, and peat moss.

Having filled the flats up to the level of the flats and the soil being made smooth and fairly firm, the seedlings should be taken from the seed flat, gently separated and then planted (or pricked out) into another flat.

They may be planted in the flat anywhere from 1 inch apart to 2 inches according to the vigor and size of growth.

For pricking out, a dibber should be used — a bluntly-pointed piece of rounded hardwood is usually what I use, about three times thicker than a lead pencil. For small seedlings a piece of wood just the thickness of a lead pencil with a blunt end will do.

Use the dibber to gently loosen the soil under the seedling, take this seedling out ever so carefully with your hand, from the first flat in which you sowed the seed, make a hole in the soil in the second flat to which you are transferring the seedlings, and put the seedling in the hole you have just made, directing the roots evenly with the dibber.

Then the dibber is used to press the soil around the seedling roots, after which the soil is smoothed and arranged so as to settle the seedlings firmly into position.

Arrange the seedlings at equal distances apart in neat rows across the flat.

Lastly give a thorough watering with a fine rose and place the flats or pots in a coldframe, provided the weather is favorable. If the weather is unfavorable, you will have to carry the plants on in the flat in the home or greenhouse until such time as they can be placed outside in the frame. Later, the plants may either be potted or planted outdoors in their permanent location.

Plants which have become well established in pots are most reliable for planting, as they go out with their roots intact and without disturbance, and if well watered in, they may safely be planted even in the hot summer weather.

Now, let's deal with the propagation of seeds and plants especially suitable for rock gardens.

A large number of desirable alpine and rock plants may be raised from seed. The keen horticulturist should keep a sharp lookout for seeds in his own rock garden and should gather such as he thinks he may require.

It is better to sow the seeds of most alpine plants as soon after gathering as possible. Many kinds, if kept until the following spring and sown then, will take a long time to germinate, and will germinate irregularly, coming up in threes and fours over a considerable period of time.

If such seeds are sown as soon as they are ripe, they will usually come up quickly and evenly.

Seed may be gathered in small bags or envelopes, care being taken to have bags and envelopes of a type suitable for the purpose — those which do not leak at the corners. Use of ordinary envelopes which are not gummed securely right up to the corners will result in small seed being lost. Suitable envelopes may be bought cheaply at a stationery store.

The interested seed collector will be wise in always having about him a few of these envelopes for use not only in his own garden, but when visiting the garden of his generous-minded friends — and most gardeners are generous.

On gathering and packeting seeds, it is important to write the name of the kind clearly and at once on the envelope, adding the date, name of the donor, and if thought necessary, brief notes as to height, color, or cultural requirements.

If the seeds are not absolutely ripe and dry when gathered, and sometimes this cannot be helped, they should be kept in a dry, airy place to finish ripening. They may be spread out to air, though they should not be dried rapidly in the sun. Care must be taken not to put them where sudden gusts of wind will blow them away. Many a valuable pinch of seed has been lost in this way.

Many seeds are extremely small and therefore difficult to distribute evenly on the soil in the flat or pots without special precautions. A good plan in such a case is to mix the tiny seeds with a small quantity of fine, dry sand, and then scatter the mixture.

Larger seeds are comparatively easy to sow evenly by exercising a little ingenuity, either sprinkling from between the fingers and thumb or by dropping them carefully from the edge of a piece of paper folded trough-wise or V-shaped.

Large seeds may even be placed singly by hand at regular intervals. Though this may seem a laborious process, it often saves the even slower job of pricking off seedlings which would be necessary later if the seeds had been sown too thickly in the first place.

Sowing seeds thinly cannot be insisted upon too strongly. It is a great mistake to sow the whole packet just because one happens to have it, for this may result in the seedlings coming up so thickly that they will interfere with one another before they are large enough to be pricked off and separated.

A comparatively thin crop of seedlings will grow and develop far better than a crowded mass, and few people require seedlings by the thousand. It is surprising, when seeds are really small, how many there are in the merest pinch.

The larger, heavier seeds often tend to become exposed after a few waterings, through not having been covered with sufficient depth of soil. However, it is better to cover with too little soil at sowing, than too much.

The exposed seeds are easily noticed by the careful horticulturist, and it is then an easy matter to cover them with a little more soil. Whereas, if they have been covered too deeply at first, they may fail to germinate.

Many people have asked me if they could take cuttings of certain trees, shrubs, and plants.

To take cuttings is the practice of growing plants from severed parts of grown plants. A cutting is the horticulturist's name for a piece of stem, root, rootstock, or leaf, which, if cut off and planted under suitable conditions, will form new roots and buds, reproducing the parent plant.

The term cutting is usually given to parts of the stem. A part or whole of a leaf, when so used, is called leaf cutting. A piece of root or rootstock is called a root cutting. The scales of some bulbous plants such as the lily can also be used as cuttings. These will form bulbs in one year.

Plants obtained by layering are provided with roots before they are detached from the parent plant, and therefore are not really cuttings.

76

Propagation by cuttings is an inexpensive and easy method of obtaining plants as it is a form of bud propagation. All plants cannot be profitably increased in this way, but the gardener learns by experience what species yield a good percentage of healthy plants from cuttings, and plans accordingly.

Here are some of the flowers from which cuttings may be obtained:

Calendula, candy-tuft, chrysanthemum, coreopsis, dahlia, English daisy, English primrose, flag, forget-me-nots (perennials), gaillardia, golden glow, larkspur (perennials), lily of the valley, marguerite, carnation, pansy, peony, petunia, phlox (perennials), pink (dianthus), pyrethrum, sweet william, veronica, and violet.

Cuttings of growing wood are made either off the soft-growing tips, as in geraniums, coleus, fuchsias and petunias, or off the same wood in more mature condition.

It is generally true that cuttings of too-hardened wood will rot. Even if they may not rot, they require more time to root and may not make the best plants. Sometimes cuttings of young wood will also rot if they are not grown under the proper conditions.

The treatment of cuttings taken in hard or soft wood is the same. They should be planted in sharp sand under glass. Large greenhouses have one or more houses set aside for this purpose.

In smaller places, a propagating bench can be made at the warmest end of the greenhouse.

The wood for cuttings should be fresh, and precautions should be taken to prevent wilting during the making and planting. The average length of cuttings should be from 2 to 3 inches, but they can be made longer or shorter. Much depends upon the nature of the plant. Many growers prefer short cuttings. The advantage of a long piece to begin with is more than offset by greater danger of wilting.

In making cuttings, the proper procedure is to cut immediately below a bud or joint, removing the lower leaves, and leaving three to four leaves on the top. A well-sharpened knife or even a razor blade should be used. It is important that clean cuts be made at the node or joint.

Cuttings of plants with a milky sap, such as the euphorbia, should be dipped in ground charcoal before being planted. It is then well to allow them to dry for an hour or two, the tops being protected against wilting.

In planting cuttings, use a dibble or open a v-shaped trench. Never thrust the cuttings directly into the soil. Plant deeply enough to hold the cuttings upright, but no deeper, making due allowance for the settling of the sand.

The distance between plants should be just enough to keep them from pressing against each other. It must be remembered that they stay in this bed only until they are rooted.

As soon as growth begins, they should be potted into 3-inch pots into which a compost of two parts loam, one part peat moss, and one part of sharp sand has been placed. When the cuttings are planted, the moistened sand should be firmly pressed around them, and they should then be watered with a fine spray.

Give shade immediately, using newspapers to cover them for a few days. You may remove the covers in the evening or during dull days. Replace the paper during the heat of the day, while gradually making the plants accustomed to the full light of day.

Cuttings should never be allowed to suffer dryness. They should always be kept moist, but not too wet, however. Proper ventilation should be given, but all exposure to draughts must be avoided. A good temperature for propagating is 60 to 65 degrees Fahrenheit.

Sand is still the medium commonly employed for cuttings, although some now use a combination of peat moss and sand, and others formiculite. Brick dust and powdered charcoal are sometimes used for certain plants. Many plants can be struck in water, but this is not the professional way.

Large cuttings may be planted singly in 2- or 3-inch pots, the pots then being put in the cutting bed in the greenhouse propagating bench, if you have such a section set aside in the greenhouse.

The scales of bulbs, such as the lily, may be used in propagation. To do this, remove the scales intact, and plant them upright, like seeds, in soil consisting of two parts loam, one part sharp sand, and one part peat moss. This could be done during September or October with hardy lily bulbs.

After the lily bulbs have been rooted in the greenhouse, place them in flats, which should be left outside all winter, well mulched over. When growth starts in the spring, they may be planted out into their permanent place in the garden.

Many leaves are capable of producing roots. For most leaf-cuttings, the whole leaf is used with part of the stem on which it is grown. Choose the leaves which are fully matured and healthy. As a rule, no bud is developed from a leaf cutting sooner than in four to six months.

September is a favorable month for taking cuttings from soft-wooded plants such as geraniums, salvias, carnations, pinks, gypsophila, perennial phlox, double petunias, and many alpine plants. Hardwood cuttings may be taken in the fall after the leaves have fallen and then placed in a sand pit out of doors at a depth of 1 foot.

The propagation of alpine plants by means of root cuttings is not much resorted to, though it is useful in the case of plants of which seeds are not easily obtainable and which do not form suitable shoots for ordinary cuttings.

Phlox subulata is usually propagated by root cuttings. Other plants which lend themselves to this method are some of the dwarf rock garden geraniums, saxifrages (especially the choice kinds), the rock garden baby's breath and rosy veil, a double pink. Some of the primulas are propagated by means of root cuttings, especially those that do not set seeds.

The best time to take root cuttings is early summer or shortly after plants have finished blooming, and they will be ready to set out in the garden long before cold weather sets in, thus giving alpine plants a chance to get well-rooted before winter.

A great many people in the city raise their own vegetable and flower plants from seed. They do this not so much for the saving involved as for the sense of accomplishment and the thrill of growing their own.

78

GREENHOUSE PLANTS AND HOTBEDS

Greenhouses are for growing plants under glass.

The ordinary purpose of the greenhouse is to imitate the usual season and conditions under which plants normally grow.

It is an advanced stage of gardening, and with care it can produce some exciting and successful adventures in floral and vegetable gardening.

Here in Alberta where we have an outdoor season of only three to three-and-a-half months, the greenhouse is also much used for "forcing" growth.

Greenhouses can be big or small, and you can even get greenhouse results by growing plants in the basement or in your upstairs rooms, to varying limited extents, of course.

But if you're interested in greenhouse growing either for imitating the growing seasons (you can bring June to your greenhouse in January if you're careful and lucky), or for forcing, or for protecting tender seeds or tender young plants from our rather hard climate, I think you have to decide first how big or small you want the greenhouse to be, according to how much work you are willing and able to do.

For a greenhouse is a lot of work — besides being a lot of fun and satisfaction to the hard-working gardener.

Possibly the three most important details of the many required for the proper management of a greenhouse are ventilation, watering and the maintenance of a suitable temperature.

All this calls for experience in greenhouse culture. Attention to every small, as well as large, detail in the operation is of the utmost importance.

The temperature must be as steady as possible during the 24 hours of a day; it must not fluctuate widely. It rises in a greenhouse as the heat of the sun increases during the day, and of course falls as the day declines.

Therefore, if the correct minimum heat for the plants in the greenhouse is 50 degrees, the top ventilators ought to be opened when the thermometer registers from 55 to 60 degrees.

The greenhouse must not be allowed to become over-heated, or under-heated. Also care must be taken to prevent draughts, so remember this, too, when you open ventilators. Avoid draughts by selecting the ventilators to be opened.

In hot, sunny weather the floor and staging of a greenhouse must be moistened by damping down, that is, by watering the floor and syringing between the plants.

Naturally, as the heat of the day declines, later in the afternoon, the ventilation must be reduced by closing ventilators.

When a mixed collection of plants is grown in a greenhouse, with some plants in bloom and others not, it is difficult to maintain ideal conditions to suit all. In such cases, do the best you can to obtain an average temperature.

The secret of success in watering is not to moisten the soil until it is moderately dry. When watering, fill the pot to the brim.

Last, but not least, perfect cleanliness should be maintained by regular fumigation and spraying.

Now, briefly before explaining plant culture in greenhouses, let's consider how to obtain one. Of course you can build one, if you're handy that way, but nowadays it is easier maybe to buy one. They come of course in various sizes and are made in sections by builders.

It is a simple matter to bolt these ready-made sections together.

But when purchasing a greenhouse, it is wise to buy one made of sound, well-seasoned wood, and be sure you get the right kind of glass. I prefer the double diamond glass. Thinner glass may suffer severe losses during a hailstorm.

If the base of the greenhouse is of wood, it should be set on a concrete foundation, keeping the wood clear of the soil.

Large greenhouses and conservatories constructed to special designs also may be purchased from builders.

The cost of a greenhouse depends obviously on the size required, its quality, thickness of the glass, and the type of fixtures. Probably a small greenhouse could be purchased for $700 to $1,000.

Most greenhouses are heated by hot water or steam pipes running from the furnace, and the type of heating chosen will naturally affect the total price.

Now to get to work in the greenhouse.

The principal spring floral display in a greenhouse is provided from among the following:

Amaryllis, Begonias (tuberous and fibrous), Cape Cowslips (lachenalia), Carnations, Chimney Bellflowers (campanula pyramidalis), Chinese Primulas, Chrysanthemums, Daffodils, Dutch Irises, Freesias, Fuchsias, Geraniums, Gloxinias, Heliotropes, Hyacinths, Lilies, Lobelias, Narcissi, Pansies, Primulas in variety, Scarlet Sages (salvia) Tulips, and various other annuals raised from seed in the spring.

Among the first seeds to be sown in the greenhouse about the first of February, will be the pansy. The pansy is a familiar flower everywhere. There is much character in this flower, and it is often likened to a face. The word pansy is a corruption of the French word pensee, meaning thought; it signifies remembrance. Because of this, it is a favorite with many to plant on the graves of loved ones.

The pansy is one of the oldest garden flowers and has been mentioned as a flower-garden subject since early in the 16th Century. It has been found to be so distinct from wild species that its specific identity could not be told with accuracy, and in fact, this is the case to the present day.

It is generally considered, however, that it is descended from the viola tricolor, a small perennial violet, native to the cooler parts of Europe. It is found growing profusely in the British Isles.

The viola is a most interesting plant with three colors or shades, mostly blue, whitish, and yellow, but in the different variations one of the colors predominates.

Pansies are perennial, but are set out here as annuals. They may be set outdoors as early as the middle of May because they are very hardy. They delight in cool, moist weather and in this part of the country, particularly during a dry summer, require lots of water. They should always be planted in a partly shaded location in a rich, humus soil. The dead blooms should be removed daily, as this strengthens the plants, and they will then produce larger flowers. This is most desirable in the growing of pansies.

Today there are many improved pansies, which run in strains or families, rather than in definite varieties. These strains are maintained at a high grade by the best cultivation and the closest attention to selection of seed. The seed of the best strains is necessarily expensive, for it represents much work and care.

These fancy and high-bred strains, especially those grown for exhibition, require extra care in growing. Most of the best are of European origin. The chief points of merit in the high-bred pansy are the size of the flowers, brilliance of coloring, and arrangement of colors. The flowers may be self-colored, of only one color or partly colored.

The colors now found in pansies are pure white, purple black, pure yellow, different shades of blue, purple, violet and red purple. Pansy blooms are now grown three and four inches across.

Those who plan to grow their own pansies should sow the seeds in a mixture of two parts loam, one part peat moss, and one part sharp sand, thoroughly mixed together. The seeds take from two to three weeks to germinate, one reason why they need to be sown early. Pansies are of slow growth. The usual greenhouse procedure of pricking out, potting, and later hardening off is followed as with all indoor-grown plants.

Another flower, seed of which must be sown early in February, is the lobelia. It is widely used, and much liked for edging and for decorating window boxes. Of this species, there are the dwarf and trailing varieties.

There are two horticultural groups of lobelias — the annuals and perennials. The annuals are low and come in shades of blue, blue and white, mauvy pink, and pure white. These are suitable for bedding and edging.

The perennials again are of two types, the hardy lobelia syphilitica and the half-hardy or tender lobelia cardinalis.

The cardinalis are the more showy and splendid plants for spotting throughout a border, to which they lend color and gaiety. Whole beds of cardinalis are beautiful. In their native state, these grow in bogs and low, wet places, and the best results under cultivation are to be expected in moist and cool places.

The lobelia syphilitica is hardy enough to withstand our winters and may therefore be left outside, but the cardinalis must be dug up in the fall and stored in boxes of soil which should be placed in a cool but frost-proof basement.

The lobelia cardinalis is sometimes called the cardinal flower and grows to a height of from 2 to 3 feet. It is of straight, upright growth with smooth, glossy leaves, and bright intense cardinal flowers.

The syphilitica grows to a height of 2 feet and comes in colors of blue and white.

Another half-hardy perennial which is also grown successfully is the lobelia cardinalis fulgeus. It is not quite as showy as the cardinalis but still worth planting in any garden.

The soil for raising the seed of these lobelias must be fine and carefully screened. This is made necessary because the seeds are extremely fine, almost minute. When sowing them, merely sprinkle the seed over the flat and gently press them into the soil with a piece of board. Water them with a very fine spray and place a pane of glass over the flat, and then a piece of newspaper over the glass.

Whenever the slow-growing seeds of the lobelias germinate, the glass and paper should immediately be removed. They should then be gradually brought to the light. When you are pricking out lobelia plants, you may take two or three at a time on account of their smallness. For dainty and graceful window boxes, compact and pretty borders, grow lobelia in its different shades and colors.

The fuchsia is a genus of more than 50 species of deciduous shrubs, half-hardy and hardy in temperate climates such as the Pacific Coast and the British Isles, but it must definitely be classed as tender in our climate. It is native chiefly of Central and South America, though several kinds are found wild in New Zealand. It belongs to the evening primrose family onagasceae. Fuchsia was named in compliment to Leonard Fuchs, a German professor, back in 1878.

Fuchsias are easily cross-pollinated and produce good quality seed. The raising of new varieties by seed began with the cross-pollination of species with long-drooping flowers. At first, nursery men's selections included only flowers with red tubes and sepals and blue or purple corollas. Then a variety was raised having a white corolla. Subsequently, double-flowered varieties in various colors appeared. These all combined have produced the numerous varieties of the present day.

It is a pity only a few of the old species are cultivated today, and most of these are rarely seen outside botanical gardens.

The graceful and compact habit of growth renders fuchsias general favorites for hanging baskets, window boxes, pot plants, as well as for beds in the flower garden.

Propagation is by seed and by cuttings. The former method is usually employed for raising new varieties. The seed, when ripe in the fall, should be washed from the pulp in the berry, afterwards dried and sown at once, or kept to sow the following spring. The seed pots should be washed and dried, with clean pieces of crock placed in the bottom. They should be filled with a compost of equal parts light loam, peat moss and clean sharp sand, all passed through a fine-meshed sieve.

The surface should be made level then, and the compost watered. When partly dry, the seeds are sown (generally in October) very thinly and lightly covered. The pots should then be covered with a sheet of glass and paper. The even moisture causes germination which will take place in about 10 days if the temperature is kept about 60 degrees Fahrenheit during the night and allowed to rise slightly during the day.

After germination, when the seedlings are about 3 inches high, pot off the plants into 2½-inch pots, using the compost already mentioned. Pot lightly and place them in a light, airy position in the house or greenhouse, but guard against cold draughts and over-watering.

In January or February, the young plants are potted into 4-inch pots, using the same mixture. At this time, the plants will need an abundance of water.

When the pots are full of roots, the plants will be ready for their final potting in 6- or 8-inch pots, maybe in April. This can be ascertained by turning out one of the plants. For this potting, use the former compost, but add a little decayed farmyard manure or bone meal.

When flowering buds begin to appear, discard the inferior plants, retaining only the best for growing again the following year.

Fuchsias are easily increased by means of cuttings inserted in a sandy compost during April. When rooted they may be transferred singly to small pots and grown in an air-cool house or greenhouse.

Cuttings rooted in the spring will attain quite a height before the end of the season. They will bear pinching and stopping of the main shoots at a foot tall and will produce a number of side shoots which will form a base of the head.

During the winter, cutting plants are dried off and stored in a cool-frostproof place.

From their winter quarters these cutting plants, are placed, in March, in a warm room or greenhouse, the surface of the soil pricked with a pointed stick and then given a thorough soaking.

Syringe the plants daily and as soon as new shoots appear, prune back the laterals to two or three buds. After pruning the top, shake out the old balls of soil, prune the straggly roots and re-pot into similar-sized pots. Fuchsias trained in the form of standards and half-stands look charming in the conservatory or sun porch. Old specimens not required may be utilized to good purpose in the flower garden at the end of June.

In all cases it is advisable to retain fuchsias in their pots, plunging them to their rims in the soil or in the lawn, as the case may be. They would indeed look attractive at strategic points in a lawn, giving the appearance of growing in the grass.

The following are a few of the best varieties for general cultivation in the greenhouse or sun porch: Avalanche, with its carmine and violet flowers, is one of the best double flowered varieties; Charming has flowers with red sepals and dark corollas, making a pleasant contribution to a hanging basket; the flowers of the Earl of Beaconsfield are rosy carmine; those of Lena are mauve and white; White Madam Cerellsion and President Felix Faure are respectively double flowered scarlet and violet varieties.

The greenhouse cultivation of that lovely plant, the begonia, has already been described in the section on begonias, but I do strongly recommend begonias to the greenhouse gardener.

Another plant for the greenhouse is the lily of the valley (convallaria majalis).

Here, in November, single crowns or roots are placed an inch apart in 6-inch pots, working indoors, of course; the tips of the crowns level with the tops of the pots.

The best compost is equal parts of fibrous loam and peat moss. Shake this well among the roots, and then press moderately firm.

Place these potted plants in a coldframe and leave outside until January, well covered with a strawy litter.

At the end of January they must be brought into the greenhouse and kept at a temperature of 60 degrees. Water freely.

They may be planted outdoors after June 1.

The greenhouse tuberous-rooted flowering gloxinia plants are general favorites with most people. Their large tubular and rich blossoms together with their soft, velvety green leaves make a gorgeous display when in flower. Being natives of tropical Brazil, they require a warm temperature during their growing season. Though they may be grown so as to flower at almost any season of the year in the greenhouse, yet they naturally are summer flowering plants and do best when treated as such.

These plants are valuable for providing a display in the greenhouse, conservatory or in the home. They grow to a height of about 10 to 12 inches. From an underground tuber, rosettes of round-like hairy leaves are formed. These are deep green or flushed with red and about 3 inches in diameter. The funnel-shaped flowers are on stout stems 6 inches in length.

The original species gloxinia speciosa from which the beautiful modern varieties have been obtained, is purple. The greenhouse gloxinia is now obtainable in colors of white, rose, crimson, and purple. Some are self-colored, while others are edged or spotted with harmonizing or contrasting colors.

Although the best flowers are produced by two-year-old plants, raised from seeds or cuttings, the old tubers may be grown for several years. They require a minimum winter temperature of 50 or 60 degrees.

They are propagated in the greenhouse by seeds or by cuttings made of leaves or stems. Seed is preferable, however, unless one wishes to increase some choice colored varieties, then it is best to propagate by leaf cuttings, using partly matured, medium-sized leaves with a small portion of leaf stalk attached. These may be inserted in an ordinary propagating bed, where, if kept rather on the dry side, they will soon root, and form tubers. They may then be potted.

Seeds should be sown in a warm temperature early in February in flats containing a finely sifted mixture of peat or leaf mould, and clean sharp sand in about equal proportions.

The seedlings will begin to appear in about 10 to 12 days, when great care must be exercised in watering, or they will "damp off," as gardeners term it.

In fact, success with these plants throughout the year depends largely upon the care exercised in watering. Even in their most active growth, the water should always be given from the spout of the watering can, taking care not to wet the leaves although they like a warm, humid atmosphere during their growing season.

As soon as the seedlings can be conveniently handled, they should be potted singly into 2- or 3-inch pots and grown rapidly, using in subsequent shifts larger pots up to 6 or 7 inches, always in a mixture of two parts leaf mould or peat moss, one part good fibrous loam, and sand. The plants must be well shaded from sunlight and placed in a position free from draughts.

The seedlings should begin to flower by the middle of August when they should be given an abundance of air.

After flowering, the leaves will begin to mature, at which time water should be gradually withheld. Don't syringe the leaves. As soon as the leaves have all ripened off, the pots should be stored away in some convenient place for the winter in a temperature of about 40 degrees, giving just sufficient water to keep the tubers from shrivelling.

Toward the middle of February, the first-year tubers will show signs of starting into growth. A batch should be started at this time, choosing the tubers which appear most active; the remainder should be held back another month. This will give a much longer period of blossoming.

These tubers should have all the old soil shaken off and re-potted in clean, well-drained pots, using sizes just large enough to accommodate the tubers, the compost being the same mixture as recommended before. They should be given but little water until active root growth starts.

84

As soon as the pots are filled with roots, they should be shifted at once into the pots they are intended to flower in, as too frequent shifts would more or less damage their foliage which has a tendency to cling around the sides of the pots. The first lot of tubers should come into flower in June or July.

When carefully grown, gloxinias are particularly free from insect pests or fungus diseases, and the same tubers can be grown for several years. The greenhouse gloxinia is truly a beautiful plant and tubers can be obtained from any of our city florists or nursery men.

There is one thing which invariably makes November a brighter month than it otherwise would be here in Alberta. I refer to the wonderful display of glorious chrysanthemums in our florists' windows.

This lovely flower with its equally lovely name, which means golden flower, has been perhaps more written about than any other flower except the rose. As the rose is the flower of the West, so the chrysanthemum is the flower of the East. It is a native of Japan.

Unfortunately, we cannot grow chrysanthemums in variety here except indoors. The only varities which can be grown satisfactorily outside are the Korean hybrids and the cushion mums. But any of the other varieties can be cultivated indoors. In the British Isles and on the Pacific Coast, they bloom outside profusely throughout October, November and December. They are closely related to the pyrethrum family.

The common chrysanthemums of the florist, called large flowering and autumn mums, are blended from two species found growing wild in Japan and China.

Mums are propagated in four ways, by cuttings, division, seeds, and grafting. By far the most important way is the first.

The first step toward success is good, healthy cuttings. As they become established plants, they should receive generous culture throughout their entire growing season.

Plants of the preceding year afford stock from which to propagate the following season. Cuttings are generally taken from 2 to 2½ inches in length, the lower leaves removed and the cut made below a joint or node, then placed in a greenhouse propagating bed close together, where they are kept moist until rooted.

Cuttings should not be allowed to remain in the cutting bench. After the roots are half an inch in length, they will become hardened and this will check growth. As soon as they have rooted, they should be potted into 3-inch pots, using good mellow soil with a little rotted manure.

The chrysanthemum is a gross feeder, and therefore the fertility of the soil is important in the production of full blooms. Sods cut and piled for two years with a half or third of the bulk in half-decomposed manure, form an excellent compost.

A sufficient number of 4-inch pots are cleaned and well drained, and a compost of equal parts of turfy loam and peat moss with sand added freely is prepared.

The ingredients are passed through a ¼-inch sieve and allowed to stand in the greenhouse for a few days to get warm.

Everything is then prepared for the actual potting. The rooted cuttings are then potted firmly, well watered and placed on a shelf in a light position.

The small plants are next placed in 6-inch pots, and when they are well rooted they may be set in a coldframe.

By June, they should be ready for the final potting in 8- to 10-inch pots and they can then be put outside. The best compost now consists of three parts of fibrous loam, one part peat moss, one part decayed manure, bone meal and sharp sand. When the first frost hits, you must take back into the greenhouse any of the potted chrysanthemums you may have displayed outdoors.

Mums must at all times have lots of room for growth. They should never be crowded, indoors or outside. If they are over-crowded in pots, they become woody and hard, stunting their growth and giving poor development.

The Korean and cushion mums will stand quite a few degrees of frost. You may purchase the Korean hybrids and cushion mums in many different shades. Those who have very sheltered gardens with a southern exposure could have great success outdoors with these beautiful chrysanthemums.

To grow small chrysanthemums for table decoration, take cuttings in April from small plants, about 15 inches high, grown in the greenhouse in flower pots 5 or 6 inches in diameter. Commercially, a large number of these are grown. They are most useful for table and room decoration. Each new plant will bear from 4 to 6 blooms.

The cuttings are inserted in pots of sandy soil and placed beneath an electric light in a frame or greenhouse. When rooted, they should be potted in 5- or 6-inch pots, three rooted cuttings being placed in each pot. A suitable potting compost consists of fibrous loam with a little peat moss and decayed manure and a scattering of sand, charcoal and bone meal.

That colorful perennial favorite, the poinsettia, especially during the Christmas Season, will be found gracing many of our homes. The poinsettia is botanically known as euphorbia pulcherrima. The original plants were produced by a Dr. Poinsett who sold them to a famous Scottish nursery man by the name of Robert Buist, about the year 1833. Robert Buist developed the double varieties and sent both types to Europe. He never quite forgave the botanists for changing the name which he gave the plant, euphorbia poinsettiana, in honor of Dr. Poinsett, but the Frenchman did receive his reward from the public in general because his flower is known to most people as the poinsettia.

The family to which the euphorbia pulcherrima, or our greenhouse poinsettia belongs, is a large one consisting of hundreds of varieties. The family is known by the name of spurge. Within this family are found fine shrubs, evergreen or deciduous, according to the climates in which they are grown.

They are found at considerable elevations in Mexico, and sub-tropical conditions encourage their highest development. This explains why so many people have difficulty with them in the home after receiving them from a greenhouse. The change of temperature is hard on them, and they need to be kept in a warm and humid atmosphere for best results.

Under natural conditions, poinsettias form large bushes from 5 to 10 feet high and 10 to 12 feet in diameter with woody bases and hollow annual growths. The flower of the poinsettia is small and insignificant, of a yellow color.

Their beauty lies in the intense crimson leaves, or bracts as they are called.

There are some smaller varieties with creamy white bracts. They are found growing in parts of the Mediterranean, southern California, other tropical and most temperate regions. Although they are found growing at sea level in

86

those parts, they do not there reach the state of perfection which they reach in higher altitudes. In fact, they sometimes become deciduous and often stunted.

In the mountains of south India they reportedly reach a high state of development at elevations of 6,000 feet, where the temperature never falls below 50 degrees and does not rise over 75 degrees. They also experience a heavy rainfall in this region, so apparently these are the ideal conditions for the growing of poinsettias.

In Calgary they are good winter flowering greenhouse plants, and require special treatment. They succeed best in the warmest part of the greenhouse. They are propagated from cuttings taken in June when the old plants have started to grow, kept in a warm frame until rooted, and then kept growing with a minimum heat of 70 degrees. Any potting should be made with as little root disturbance as possible.

If stocky plants are wanted, several cuttings may be planted in one pot and checked two or three times during the summer by re-potting. Pinch back freely to obtain branches. They are best kept cooler when in flower, but are very sensitive to cold or sudden changes in temperatures. After flowering, water should gradually be withdrawn.

Cut sprays are best grown from cuttings each year. To obtain plants with large heads the same thing applies; they should be grown annually from cuttings but the old plants may be continued.

Old plants that have been resting may be introduced to heat and moisture in late spring, and will soon give a liberal supply of cuttings, which are usually taken from the young wood.

Successive sets of cuttings may be made at later periods if different sized plants are wanted. When well started, with all danger of frost past, the potted plants are plunged out of doors in a warm sunny place until the end of August, and then brought back indoors again.

Outside, they should be given plenty of water, light, and sunshine, plus good drainage. They do well in a good rich soil in 5- to 7-inch pots, but are apt to drop their leaves if exposed to cold or other unfavorable conditions.

In autumn, they are transferred to the greenhouse with a moderate temperature. When the bracts begin to appear, give more heat and some liquid manure to expand them.

When in flower, reduce the temperature to preserve them longer. After flowering, the plants may be stored away in a dry, warm place until spring. Before the buds begin to grow in the spring, prune them back to a healthy bud. Cut out any dead parts before potting them, when they will quickly start to grow again.

Sometimes mealy bugs get on the plant. They may be driven out by a moderate stream of water from a hose, supporting the heads with one hand to avoid breaking. They are quite brittle. Another remedy for mealy bugs is to lightly touch the bugs with alcohol applied with a small paint brush. Methylated spirits are usually used for this.

These plants contain a milky fluid which stains and is disagreeable. This milkiness, produced by cutting, may be got rid of by standing the stems in water. Dipping the ends in charcoal dust will also seal and stop the flow of this sticky fluid.

Greenhouses here are greatly used for forcing, by which is meant growing of plants outside their usual or normal season.

But there is some confusion about forcing and protecting in greenhouses. For example, begonias are not forced. We endeavor to protect them and to give them the season and the conditions under which they grow naturally.

Carnations and snaps, when flowered in the winter, are forced because we transpose their season. The chrysanthemums blooming in October and November are not forced, they are only protected.

Sometimes the word forcing is used in a special sense, to denote the production of flowers from bulbs or tubers in a very short time under the influence of a very high temperature.

Take for example the lily of the valley which could be placed in a temperature of 90 degrees and the large buds be forced to throw out their flowers before the plants obtain a firm rooting system.

The stable forced flowers are the rose, carnation, violets, lily of the valley, and various bulbs.

Of vegetables, the most important forcing kinds are lettuce, radishes, rhubarb, dwarf beans, and onions. Tomatoes and cucumbers, plus other vegetables, are of minor importance as forced products.

The growing of fruits under glass has received its share of attention too. Little of this fruit raising is really forcing, however, since the greenhouse is used chiefly to protect the plants and to enable better care to be given to them. The fruit does not ripen much ahead of its normal season. Greenhouse grapes, many of which are grown in the British Isles, are an example of this.

Much attention is given by florists to the forcing of hardy and tender plants, and this is one of the most interesting horticultural operations for the amateur gardener. The business of forcing is usually confined to imported stock of florists' plants.

There are hundreds of small privately-owned greenhouses in our city. In any of these, the vegetables which have been mentioned could be forced for table use. Skill in management and close attention to details are the requirements necessary to success.

Two fundamental elements, heat and light, however, are essential with such forced crops as lettuce, radish, and rhubarb in which only the vegetable part of the plant is wanted.

Bright sunlight is not absolutely necessary after the pollen has ripened with such crops as tomatoes. cucumbers, melons, and beans, in which the fruit is the aim.

Cool house plants as lettuce and radish, are well grown in solid beds, while heat-loving plants such as tomatoes, cucumbers, melons, etc., should be planted on benches built over the pipes.

The ideal soil for growing lettuce is a rich light soil. If you sow lettuce seed in September, you may have your first crop by the middle of November. It takes from 6 to 8 weeks (which is not long to wait for nice, freshly grown lettuce). It requires a temperature of from 55 to 60 degrees through the day, with a drop to 40 to 45 degrees at night. For head lettuce, you will require a higher temperature at the time of heading of about 5 to 10 degrees.

Radishes require the same general treatment as lettuce. As radishes mature in about half the time lettuce does, the radish seed may be sown in September between the rows of young lettuce plants and the product is out of the way when the lettuce begins to need the entire space.

Tomatoes, generally being a hothouse crop, require a temperature of 60 to 65 degrees by day with a drop of 5 to 10 degrees at night. This is one of the crops the pollen of which is dependent on the sun because the pollen must be dry and light in order to pollinate the pistils and produce fruit. The soil of the tomatoes may be on heavy order and contain a large proportion of fibrous loam with well-rotted manure.

To obtain a good yield of fruit through the winter months, it will be necessary to pollinate each flower. This may be done rapidly by hand. As spring approaches and the sun becomes stronger, a simple jarring of the plants is all that is required.

As to training, the single-stem method has been found to be the best, as the plants can be set much closer and still allow plenty of room to work around each plant.

This method consists in the pinching out of all lateral growths. Train the stems to a string or stake and support the heaviest cluster with soft strings. Plants from seeds sown in August will ripen fruits about the first of January, and should continue bearing until May.

Beans may be easily forced, using light, rich soil and strong bottom heat. They are usually grown in pots — three plants in a 6-inch pot. They make rapid growth and the green pods are fit to use in from 8 to 10 weeks from the time the seeds are sown, generally any time in the fall or early winter.

When growing, the plants should be sprayed with water frequently, as they are subject to attacks of red spider. The bean is self-fertile and need not be pollinated.

Asparagus and rhubarb are forced from old roots brought in from the garden after the first hard frost, and then subjected to a gentle heat. The crop develops from the material stored up in the old roots, few new roots growing through the forcing period.

Both these crops may be grown in out-of-the-way places in the greenhouse, under the benches, in corners of the potting shed, or in fact, anywhere heat and moisture may be had. One method for rhubarb is to grow it entirely in the dark. This produces a very tender stalk with little foliage.

For those with a green thumb, what a splendid hobby and pastime, the forcing of vegetables and plants could be during our long winters!

A secret of successful growing in the greenhouse is cleanliness, which means freedom from insects, pests, and diseases. There are two effective methods of keeping a greenhouse clean, and that is to either spray or fumigate. The importance of regular spraying and fumigation cannot be over-emphasized.

Fumigation consists of the killing of insect pests by means of various gases or vapors in closely confined spaces, such as a greenhouse or specially constructed frames to which a number of plants may be transferred to receive the treatment.

Various types of fumigant are employed. They may consist of some form of tobacco or nicotine compounds, and are simple to use. They are usually sold in the form of nicotine shreds or paper, and the directions of the makers may easily be followed.

The most efficient means of fumigation is calcium cyanide. Napthalene vaporized by means of heat is an excellent remedy for red spider. The materials required for fumigation by these recommended methods and the general conditions under which fumigation should be carried out, are as follows, but first a word of warning. *These gases are poisonous.* Therefore, it is important that I go into detail in this matter of fumigating.

Calcium cyanide — This compound is popular, as the gas is given off by material coming into contact with the atmospheric moisture. The gas is given off more slowly, and it is, therefore, less dangerous than an acid method, and on the whole, plants are less susceptible to injury.

Calcium cyanide is merely dusted down the walks of the greenhouse at the rate of one-eighth to one-quarter ounce per 1,000 cubic feet of space, and like all fumigants, is best used in the evenings.

Naphthalene Fumigation — One or two lamps are required for a greenhouse about 30 feet in length. The naphthalene is used at the rate of from 4 to 6 ounces per 1,000 cubic feet, it being essential to purchase only naphthalene guaranteed free from phenol.

The amount of gas is divided equally among the number of lamps to be used. The lamps are then lit, and the fumigation allowed to proceed for about 12 hours, again starting the fumigation in the evening.

Naphthalene has a tendency to taint such things as tomato fruits. This taint leaves the fruit after a few days, but the method is, on he whole, more suitable for such plants as carnations, cyclamen, and the smaller subjects in the greenhouse.

While any fumigation is in progress, it is wise to hang a notice on the door stating the nature of the fumigation. The door should be kept locked. All the methods of fumigation are safe so long as such simple precautions are taken.

In the case of naphthalene or calcium cyanide fumigation, the atmosphere in the greenhouse should be humid and the house well dampened down prior to carrying out of the operation.

During fumigation, the temperature should be kept as constant as possible. It is preferable for the temperature to rise rather than fall, and should be between 60 and 70 degrees. Fumigation must not be carried out in the daytime. After fumigation the house should be opened up as early as convenient, so as to prevent the early morning sun from shining into a gas filled house.

Small doses of the various fumigation should be employed in the first place. By the gradual increase of the quantities, the minimum amount for the killing of any particular pest can be ascertained; at the same time, the allowance required for any leaking of the house is also determined.

Several fumigations with smaller doses will often give better results than one fumigation with a stronger dose, and plants certainly suffer less ill effects. The intervals between fumigations should bear a definite rotation to the length of the life cycle of the pests. The best times to fumigate are just before pests are due to show up; or you could fumigate the greenhouse every three months.

For those who are not fortunate enough to own a greenhouse, a hotbed is the next best thing.

A hotbed should be started about the beginning of March. To provide heat for the bed, decomposing horse manure is generally used along with strawy litter. The strawy litter obtainable here is usually of a dry nature, and needs to be watered down.

The bed should be about 3 feet high and of such width and length that it will project about 12 inches beyond the frame to be placed on it. The hot bed should be trodden down as firmly as possible as it is placed in position. The hot bed should be turned over several times before placing the frame in its final location — this is important so that all portions of the bed will heat up.

When the frame is in position on the hot bed, a layer of soil 8 to 10 inches deep is placed on the manure inside the frame. The sash or top of the frame should be left slightly open for a few days to allow the escape of fumes from the manure.

When the heat of the bed has receded to a temperature of 65 degrees Fahrenheit, seed may be sown in the soil or in seed flats. The temperature of the hot bed is determined at all times by having a thermometer placed inside the frame.

The best location for a hot bed is some spot sloping to the south where it is protected by buildings or a board fence against the north and northwest winds.

The frames are made from either planks or boards, and may be portable or built in place; the former could be taken down and packed away except when needed. A high board fence, 6 feet high, is desirable to serve as a wind break. Also, it will serve as a support for the sashes and mats when they are removed from the bed. Portable frames are generally constructed of 2 by 4s and 1 by 6-inch boards (shiplap), the side pieces being from 9 to 12 feet and the ends 6 feet in length to receive either three or four ordinary sashes which are 3 by 6 feet.

The north side of the frame is made 18 inches high, while the south side is 12 inches, thus giving a slope to the south which will permit the water to run off and favor the passage of sun rays through the glass. The end pieces should be 6 feet in length, and should taper from 18 inches at one end to 12 inches at the other so as to fit the side boards.

The boards for portable hot bed frames may be held in place by means of stakes, iron rods, or bolts, and may be fastened to the ends of the side pieces so that they can pass through the holes in the ends of the frames which can then be fastened by nuts.

As supports for the sash, and to hold the sides of the frames in place, cross strips of board 3 inches wide, are sunk into the upper edge every 3 feet, and another strip with a width equal to the thickness of the sash is fastened on the edge to the centre of its side.

Frames of this size require a slightly deeper mass of heating materials than would be necessary for smaller frames.

For permanent frames, rough 1-inch boards may be used, although 2-inch planks will be found stronger. Stout stakes should be driven into the ground about 4 feet apart where the north end of the bed is to be located. These should project above the surface from 12 to 15 inches, and should be boarded up from a point just below the level of the ground, so that the stakes will be on the north side of the frame.

A second row of stakes should then be driven at a distance from the first row, equal to the length of the sash which is usually 6 feet, although other lengths are sometimes used. The south wall of the frame should then be boarded up so that it will be 5 or 6 inches lower than the north wall, after which the end should be closed and cross pieces should be fitted the same as for a portable sash.

To prevent frost from penetrating into the frames, straw should be banked against the boards outside so that it will reach two-thirds of the way to the top of the frame, and when the bed is ready for use, 3 or 4 inches of soil should be spread over the banked-up manure outside.

If you have a board fence, the hotbed frame should be placed about 3 feet from it. For covering the frames on cold nights such as experienced here during March and sometimes April, straw mats or those made of burlap are generally used. The burlap may be either single or double or it may be stuffed with straw or other materials.

The size that has been found most satisfactory for hotbed sashes is 3 by 6 feet. When they are larger, they are not easily handled by one man. The sides and upper ends of the sash are made from 3- by 1½-inch strips, grooved to receive the glass, while the lower end is 1 by 5 inches. The centre strips are 1 by 1½ inches.

Single-strength glass (10 inches by 12) is commonly used, as three rows of this size will fill a sash 3 feet wide. While double-strength glass will be less-easily broken, the increased weight and cost are objections to its use.

The sash should receive two coats of paint and may even be given a third coat after the glass has been set in. Whenever the weather is mild enough, the sashes should be opened to allow air into the hot bed. The temperature of the hot bed should be checked at all times. This can be done by placing a thermometer in the bed. A good average temperature for a hot bed when the times comes to plant seeds in it, is 65 degrees. It shouldn't go below 50 degrees.

A good hot bed can become a thing of great interest and a challenge to the amateur gardener.

Admiring geraniums in the City of Calgary greenhouse

HOUSE PLANTS, PLANTERS AND CUT FLOWERS

House plants are those plants which can be grown in the ordinary rooms of dwelling houses. They may be hardy or tender.

In the living rooms of the modern well-built house, in spite of good lighting and in many cases air conditioning, plants still have to contend against difficulties which they do not encounter in a well-regulated greenhouse.

With our central heating many houses are too hot for the successful growing of house plants; others again, are too cold.

Too much heat and dry air are harder for pot plants to endure than insufficient light, but it is also lack of light which makes it so difficult to grow flowering plants in homes. Dust and insects do harm, but these difficulties can be overcome.

For the average home, house plants which are adapted to resist a dry atmosphere, a high temperature, and inadequate light, should be chosen. Alternating high and low temperatures found in some homes are also, of course, most detrimental to the health of house plants.

Speaking of inadequate light, many of the new planters found in the most exclusive homes are not always wisely located in the best interests of the plants. Even though plants which are adapted to shade are chosen for these planters, difficulty is experienced in growing them successfully for any length of time. This is because the planters are placed where they will look most effective rather than where the plants will thrive best.

Foliage plants are easier to grow and care for in the home than are flowering plants. But flowering plants should be introduced from time time, each in its proper season when about to bloom or in bloom, and not considered a part of the permanent arrangement. After flowering they should be removed. Their function is not unlike that of cut flowers, only they last longer.

The best rooms for plants are those which get the most sun, and the best positions are those nearest the windows where there is more light. This does not mean that plants should be placed right up against the glass of a window. Plants can be scorched during the hot weather and frozen during cold weather by being placed directly against window panes.

A large palm, fern, or rubber plant will grow in an entrance hall or poorly-lighted corner, but the best place is that which is well lighted. Plants do well in a kitchen, the moisture from the cooking helping them materially.

Much trouble can be caused by the use of unsuitable potting soil. It should be obtained from an experienced florist. If you make up the compost yourself, use two parts fibrous virgin loam, one part moss, one part sharp sand, and about half a tablespoonful of bone meal to a 6-inch flower pot.

The soil should always be moist when used, not wet, and never dry. It should be made firm, not hard, and a good space left between the surface and the rim.

The best time for potting is just before the plant begins to grow. The next best is just before growth ceases, this gives the plant the opportunity to establish itelf in its new quarters before it stops growing. It is not always easy to do this at home, and large and valuable plants should be sent to a florist.

No set rules can be given for watering, the most important detail of plant growing, except always to use lukewarm water. Water must be given as it is required, a knowledge to be gained by experience only. This may be once a day or once a week, or once in two days; the smaller the pot and the more vigorous the growth, the oftener it will be required.

In hot weather or in dry rooms, more water is needed than in cool rooms and on damp, cloudy days. Water should be given in sufficient quantity for some to pass through the hole in the bottom of the pot. If your flower pot is sitting in some container see that the surplus water is removed after an hour or so.

English ivy and some ferns are not injured by a surplus of water, but some plants are. Water given to the foliage of house plants in the form of a spray is always helpful.

Insects, dust, and fungus disease are troublesome to house plants, due largely to insufficient watering and lack of ventilation. The best remedy is frequently washing with warm water, and a sponge for plants with large leaves.

All plants can be easily cleaned at the kitchen sink or in the bath tub. The forcible application of water will remove most insects, but if scale appears it must be taken off with a stiff brush.

If fungus disease appears, the plants should be isolated, given a chance to recover, or be thrown away. You could spray your plant with Bordeaux mixture, using 8 to 10 tablespoonfuls to a gallon of water.

A list of good foliage plants for the house would include the following: ficus elastica (or rubber plant), ferns in variety, the Norfolk Island pine, palms, dracaenas, aspidistra, English ivy, century plant (agave or aloe), grevillea poinsettia, asparagus plumosa and asparagus sprengeri, and the umbrella plant.

A few flowering plants which could be mentioned are hyacinths, freesias, tulips, narcissi, crocuses, violets, azalia indica and camellia japonica (both of which should be kept in a cool room when not in bloom); calla lilly and begonias (both do well); chrysanthemums; cyclamens, primulas, ovalis, fuchsias, suphorbia, pelorgoniums, geraniums, drooping bellflower, campanula isophylla and azalias. The azalias should be potted in a compost of half peat and half soil, with a mixture of sharp sand.

The hyacinths, freesias, tulips, narcissi and crocuses, if potted in October, stored in a cool dark place until the end of January, and then brought into warm rooms, will flower in early spring. A succession can be maintained by potting at ten-day intervals. After our long, cold winter, they are welcome harbingers of spring.

There are a few plants which will thrive in a dark or dim corner, among which are the aspidistra, certain palms, ferns, and sanseverias, but even these grow far more satisfactorily in a light, airy place.

It is a good plan to move foliage plants in the windows from a darker corner of the room, and the reverse, in rotation thus allowing the various plants to receive the benefits gained by being near the light. Such a change should be made once a week if possible.

Broad-leaved plants, such as the aspidistra and palms, benefit by being sponged once a week with warm water to which has been added a little milk. This treatment removes dust, and helps to keep the plants healthy and the leaves well-colored. During mild weather, and especially if light showers occur, plants should be placed outside for several hours.

When re-potting, plants should be set at such a depth that there is half an inch of soil above the roots and approximately half an inch of pot left for watering. The soil must be pressed firmly all around the old ball of earth clinging to the roots, care being taken that the space between the roots and the sides of the pot is filled with firm soil.

I usually use a piece of lath for this purpose, depending on the size of the pot. It is not necessary to re-pot most house plants yearly, provided they are in a healthy condition. It is wisest to leave them undisturbed except for an annual top-dressing of fresh compost in April. The old surface soil, having been removed, is replaced by about an inch of the newly prepared compost.

Before plants are potted, the flower pot should be scrubbed thoroughly in warm water and soap, and allowed to dry. Sufficient drainage is ensured by means of a few pieces of crockery or pieces of broken flower pots being placed in the bottom of the pot. One large concave piece is used to cover the hole and smaller pieces placed over it. There should also be some larger pieces of turf or peat moss placed over the pieces of crockery, to prevent the finer soil from falling down and choking the drainage.

An occasional application of fertilizer or artificial manure during the spring and summer is of immense benefit to house plants. The concentrated mixtures which are advertised are most convenient to use. One teaspoon of fertilizer to each plant, once every three weeks from May until August may be applied, or if you prefer, the fertilizer can be dissolved in water and used as a liquid manure. It would be wise to use one ounce of fertilizer added to one gallon of water.

If any blemishes appear on the leaves, they should be sponged with a weak solution of permanganate of potash. If the ends of the leaves turn brown, they should be cut off. This is often caused by the plants being placed in such a position in the room that the leaves are in the way of passers-by and consequently become damaged by being rubbed frequently. When leaves of house plants turn yellow and fall, it is an indication that the soil is kept too wet. The drainage should be examined to make certain that it is not clogged.

If the leaves become pale green, the plants are evidently ill-nourished. The soil has probably become too dry at intervals and also lacks the proper nourishment. Sulphate of ammonia, at the rate of half a teaspoon a plant, applied once every two weeks for a month or two, will prove of great benefit.

Sometimes plants are attacked by insects such as mealy bug and scale insects. To combat these, spray with a solution of nicotinic acid with soft soap added. Several good sprayings will afford control of these pests. One teaspoonful to a gallon of water, with enough soap to cause a good lather, will be a satisfactory solution. It is also important to use a sprayer which will function at a good pressure. Several sprayings may be necessary.

The perfection of the flower developing from a hyacinth bulb depends largely upon the strength of the roots and as hyacinths make all their root growths in the fall, the bulbs should be planted early, about the beginning to the middle of October.

For this purpose, large, solid bulbs should be selected and potted singly in 4-inch pots in a rich compost of loam, peat moss, and some sharp sand.

The pots should be filled lightly and the bulbs pressed into the loose soil, until only the apex remains above the surface. The pots are then placed in a dark, cool place in the basement and watered, there to remain for eight to ten weeks until the roots are developed fully and the sprout is about 2 inches above the bulb.

When brought out from the basement, they should be kept in subdued light at a temperature of about 50 degrees, until the shoot has assumed a vigorous green color. The more slowly hyacinths are forced, the finer and more lasting will be the bloom.

Bulbs wanted in flower for Christmas should be potted in September, and for a succession later at intervals as desired. Single hyacinths are handsomer and force better than the double kinds. After plants have finished blooming, gradually withdraw the water until the foliage ripens off. They are then stored in a cool place until the following fall when again they are potted up and the same process is repeated.

Some of the best varieties of hyacinths for potting are: Arentine Arendse (white), Dr. Lieber (lavender blue), Garibaldi (red), Gertrude (rose-pink), Marie (dark violet blue), and Schotel (light blue).

One of the most popular indoor plants is the African violet. In March when the sun is growing warmer, African violets in a window will require more moisture and a moderate increase in balanced plant food. This should be brought about gradually.

African violets, known botanically as saintpaulia, need ample moisture, but like most plants, they should only be watered when the soil feels dry. They should be examined regularly and watered when needed. The best way is to water African violets from the bottom by placing the pots in a container of water.

If you do water them from the top, make sure that the water is tepid, the soil loose enough to absorb the water quickly, and care must be taken not to damage the foliage. Water cooler than the room temperature should never be used, and remember our mountain water is cold even in summer.

It is better to prevent the water from coming in contact with the leaves. If all the water is not absorbed within half an hour discard the surplus. The drainage hole in the bottom of the pot should be checked regularly. It will help if you have pots sitting on some fine gravel to raise them slightly.

Clay pots are best, the kind used by the florists, as they are porous. Freshly potted African violets from the florist will not likely require fertilizer for several weeks and newly-potted plants will not require it until new roots begin to form. Older plants need to be fed every two or three weeks. Liquid fertilizer should be used. To over-fertilize would burn the plants. Then you would get discolored leaves, falling blossoms, and rot in the crowns.

Many ask why their African violets do not bloom although the foliage appears to be healthy. No plant blooms all the time. They must have rest periods and should not be forced with excessive feeding and watering. The feeding should be almost nil during these rest periods.

Another important requirement for bloom is plenty of light. The violets like to be kept about one foot from the windows where light can reach the entire plant. Most African violets bloom more freely when the plant forms open rosettes. Sometimes the leaves grow so thickly that they crowd and shade the centre of the plant, not giving the small flower-buds a chance to develop fully.

To clip off some of the centre leaves with their stems will often help the plants to bloom. They should be cut off half an inch above the crown, using curved scissors. Quite often, the plants will soon afterwards come into bloom.

There are some of the varieties such as the "Blue Chard" to which such dense upright growth is natural. These ought not to be pruned.

If the foliage on African violets look unhealthy, there may be several causes. Fungus infection sometimes attack violets. This may cause the lower leaves to have a dark appearance. Sometimes it takes the form of crown rot— this could be caused by overwatering.

A rough edge on the pot could likewise cause injury to the leaf stems where they hang over the pots, which should be examined at potting time for such defects. These pots can be smoothed with sand paper and waxed to make a protective coating.

Do not be alarmed if a few of the lower leaves turn yellow. They are usually the oldest and this is nature's way of discarding them. They should, of course, be removed to keep plants looking nice.

But flowers or leaf stems should not be removed carelessly. Cut off the leaf stems about half an inch from the crown and the remaining stem will dry up naturally. You could dust the wounds with a mild fungicide. African violets are not very subject to diseases or insect pests, but it is a good idea to isolate a new plant until you are sure that it is healthy.

All diseased or infested plants should be isolated. If African violets become infected with insects, try a water bath before using powerful insecticides. If this does not prove sufficient, a spray preparation can be obtained.

Re-potting should be carried out when the violets grow too large for their pots, for violets grow much prettier and bloom better when only one crown is allowed to a pot.

When re-potting, put a piece of broken pot over the hole for good drainage, and an inch of fine gravel and some charcoal in the bottom of the pot helps to keep the soil sweet. A good compost is one part fibrous loam, one part sharp sand and two parts peat moss or leaf mould.

The most popular method of propagation of violets is by leaf cuttings. Mature leaves are detached with the leaf stalks intact, and placed in a well-drained pan filled with a finely sifted compost of vermiculite and sand in equal proportions.

They are watered and placed in a propagating bench in a warm greenhouse. When roots are formed and the young shoots appear above the soil, the plants are potted in small pots. When well-rooted, put them in 4-inch pots in which they will bloom.

The principal African violet species are: saintpaulia ionantha (purple) and its varieties; albiscens (white) and purpurea (purple).

Planters

Planters both inside and outside the home are increasingly popular, and are a modernized form of window box gardening. The modern planter is usually built in as a planned part of the house design. In this respect it is, of course, a decided improvement. However, some of the old-fashioned window or porch boxes may still be seen.

Let's deal first with the outside planter.

The modern outside planter is usually located at or slightly above ground level, often being merely a raised, masonry-bound bed, along part of the foundation of the house. Naturally, it calls for a somewhat different type of planting from that for potting plants indoors, and it also has the distinct advantage of providing much more root room for the plants to grow in it. Consequently, it is also better suited to accommodate plant materials which will provide more growth during the growing season.

In bedding out planters, annuals can play an important part. For planters, annuals are much less expensive than geraniums, ivy, vicas, marguerites and the other florist plants generally used. Annuals are easily and inexpensively replaced if they are damaged by hail or wind, and a wide range of color and form are offered, with which to create pleasing effects that will show some individuality. Young annuals may be purchased from a florist or raised from seed.

Before selecting varieties of plants for the planter, give careful consideration to the color scheme best suited to your home. A white frame house, for instance, will be enhanced by the bright blues of floss flowers (ageratum) and lobelia; the rich yellows and orange of the dwarf marigold combined perhaps with white alyssum trailing over the edge of the planter to form a foil for the bright colors behind it.

One of the nice things about a white wall background is that you can use any colors you choose in the plant material without fear of having them clash with it.

Brick walls, on the other hand, are particularly trying as a background, and where one is encountered, special care should be taken in the selection of plant material. White, and the many pastel shades that are found in nemesia compacta, may be planted with schizanthus, also petunias.

Another nice color scheme suitable for a dark background is blue and white lobelia with scarlet sage (salvia) or white and purple alyssum with the scarlet sage, and perhaps verbena with its many bright colors. The last two mentioned make a very showy color scheme.

In planters, one is less likely to find an opportunity to use plants of a trailing habit, so we must turn to those of erect and mound-like habit. There are, however, the trailing lobelia, trailing vinca, and trailing nasturtiums.

Many planters will be facing north, and it is important that the right kind of annuals be planted in this aspect — annual balsam, the annual forget-me-not, godetia, monkey flower, pansies, and Virginian stock and English daisy. These are but a few of the annuals that will do well in a northern exposure.

It is important that good drainage is provided in planters. A layer of gravel should be placed in the bottom of the planter. Over the gravel should be placed a layer of sods turned upside-down.

You next prepare your compost, making sure that it is well mixed — use two parts good fibrous loam, one part peat moss, and one part sharp sand. There should be at least a foot of good compost worked in over the sods.

The soil should be kept at least 3 inches below the top of the planter so that you can irrigate plants with the hose, making sure that the water gets down to the roots. When watering, turn on the hose gently, otherwise you could wash the dirt away from the roots, causing no end of trouble.

Here is a list of annual seeds which may be sown in the outside planters when all danger of frost is past.

For a hot, sunny location the California poppy in many shades, 8 to 9 inches tall; mesembryanthemum, 3 to 4 inches tall; gypsophila, 15 to 16 inches tall; jimsonweed (datura), 15 to 18 inches tall; gaillardia, 14 to 16 inches high.

For a foliage plant which may be planted outside in the planter, the castor oil bean is good. It grows quickly and has magnificient and tropical-like foliage of green, reddish, and variegated leaves. This foliage plant grows 2 to 3 feet tall and deserves a place in a planter.

Another seed which may successfully be grown in a planter is godetia, in many shades, growing 8 to 9 inches tall. Clarkia may also be sown outside as well as the Scotch marigold; these two growing about 10 to 12 inches tall.

Be sure and keep seeds moist during the germination period, especially if the planter is facing south, and in a hot, sunny spot.

When seedlings grow to about 2 inches tall, they may be thinned out, giving those that are left a better chance to develop and produce larger and more beautiful flowers.

The soil for planters should be both exceptionally rich and very porous. In order to obtain such richness, plenty of sharp sand and well-rotted manure should be mixed with the compost. This is necessary because the plants will be growing so close together that each one will have little more root room than it would in a small flower pot.

The life of freshly cut flowers may be lengthened by special treatment. Here is a plan which may be tried with some success.

Buckets of clear water are obtained and the flowers are suspended upside down so that they are completely submerged.

Whilst undergoing this treatment, the blooms may be taken out and used for table decoration or other purposes and then put back upside-down in the water again. During the day, the flowers might be used in vases in the house, and at night placed heads downward in the water.

There are several methods whereby flowers may be preserved so that they will last almost indefinitely.

One of the most interesting methods is waxing them. A few lumps of paraffin wax, such as is used in making candles, are needed. These are put in a pan and melted over heat. When the wax is melted, it is important to see that it is free from specks of dirt.

The flowers and foliage to be treated should be in as perfect a state as possible. Much depends on having the petals stiff without any sign of fading.

When the wax is melted, but not when it is actually boiling, the specimens are dipped into the solution. They are held in it for about half a minute, care being taken to move them about all the time to prevent the formation of bubbles. If the stalks are rather weak or fragile, it is a good plan to dip them in the wax as well.

As soon as the blooms are taken out of the wax, they will start to dry. The transparent nature of the wax allows the colors of the petals to be seen plainly, and the blooms may be kept for a long time.

There are many other flowers that may be cut when in full bloom and dried for winter decorating. Some so-called everlasting flowers will last at least two years if properly cared for. These include the sea holly, known as erynigium giganteum, a perennial growing up to 3 feet high, with steel blue flowers, and which is rather attractive when dried, and the straw flowers, botanically known as helichrysum, which is an annual and makes a lovely flower for winter decoration in the home. Straw flowers grow to the height of 2 to 3 feet and come in shades of pink, cream, yellow, and silvery white colors.

The most striking annuals for winter decoration are the sea lavenders, known as statice suworowi, which bear spikes of rose-colored flowers. Statice bonduellii, which bears flowers of various colors, is another choice everlasting plant for winter decoration. Statice sinuata and its varieties make attractive pot plants for the home or greenhouse. The above kinds of statice may be raised from seeds grown in the home or greenhouse and set out in the garden about the first week in June.

There are hardy perennial kinds of statice suitable for the rock garden and flower borders. The most popular of the hardy kinds is statice latifolia, which grows about 2 feet tall and has wide-spreading branches of small purplish blue flowers in summer.

Statice incana is a beautiful free-flowering kind, about 12 inches tall, bearing numerous small pink flowers in spreading clusters. There is a white variety, too.

Several other kinds are available for the rock garden including statice auriculaefolia, 6 inches tall with blue flowers; statice alpina, purple; and statice minutum, lilac, 9 inches tall.

All are easily grown, and flower profusely during the summer.

The soil and location suitable for these everlasting flowers is a light, well-drained, sunny spot in the rock garden or border. If it is desired to cut these flowers for winter decoration in the home, it must be done when the flowers are in the pink of condition and dried slowly upside down in a cool, dry place.

Ammobium alatum is a half-hardy everlasting flower from Australia which belongs to the daisy family. It must be grown in a heated greenhouse or in a home. It grows about 10 inches tall and in summer bears white and pink flowers suitable to cut for indoor vases.

It is treated as a half-hardy annual or biennial. Seeds are sown in the greenhouse in March, grown at a temperature of 55 to 60 degrees in boxes or pots of sifted sandy soil. The seedlings when 2 inches tall are transplanted into 2-inch pots. When they have outgrown those pots, they are then re-potted into 4-, 5- or 6-inch pots where they will produce lovely everlasting blooms. These must also be cut when in full bloom for winter decoration.

Another flower that can be grown here quite successfully to be used for winter flowers in the home is honesty (or lunaria biennis), the silvery seed pods of which are used also for winter decoration indoors.

Bells of Ireland (molucella laevis) makes an excellent cut flower, and the spikes may also be dried for winter decoration like the straw flower.

This lovely Irish annual grows outdoors in ordinary garden soil and the plants should be set 12 inches apart. It has several branching stems which are closely set with big bell-calyces of pale green. Within each calyx lies a perfectly formed little white flower.

ROCK GARDENS

The rock garden has taken a firm hold on the gardening public in Calgary, no doubt because it has been proven in practice that a well-designed and well-constructed rock garden is the best place to grow the majority of alpine plants. Perhaps this is particularly true of Alberta with its high altitude, for so many of Calgary's alpine plants come from high altitudes such as the Swiss Alps and our Rocky Mountains.

A good rock garden provides a wide variety of soils and aspects, and forms an ideal and more or less natural setting in which to show off the plants. The fascination of rock gardens is great, and its strong appeal is no doubt due to the fact that garden lovers enjoy growing the small but brilliant flowers of the alps and hills in semi-wild conditions.

It is also true that rock gardening may be carried out on a smaller scale than almost any other type of gardening and yet be successful. In quite a small rock garden an enormous variety of small, choice, and lovely flowers can be grown to perfection.

To build a really good rock garden is not an easy matter, yet many amateur gardeners have shown great skill and much good taste in this work. Others, I am afraid, spoil the whole effect by rocks which are too small, too rounded and too smooth, and often badly placed.

The first important thing is to choose the site for the rock garden. It has often been said that this should be as far as possible from the house and all formal surroundings.

Against this, it may be said that it is convenient to have the rock garden near the house so that one may always have it at hand for personal attention and enjoyment. So, make your choice!

A small rock garden can usually be made to look better when rounded by a wall, paths, or a background of greenery. There is no more delightful picture to look on through some of your windows than a finely-constructed and well-laid-out rock garden.

It is of the greatest importance that the rock garden be in an open, airy, and sunny position. Any shade that special alpine plants may require should be provided by the contours of the slopes themselves and by dwarf deciduous and evergreen trees and shrubs. The shade and drip of large trees are extremely undesirable, the roots rapidly find their way into the good soil of the rock garden and impoverish it, taking needed moisture from the plant.

Having selected the site, the next consideration will be the rocks. It is well to remember that a porous rock is better than a hard rock, as it absorbs and retains moisture. The best types of stone for rock gardens are sandstone, tufa rock or petrified moss and limestone. There is a considerable amount of sandstone, limestone and petrified moss rock to be found in our province. Possibly the best for the rock garden is petrified moss rock which is both soft and porous and most suited for growing many rare and difficult alpine plants.

It is possible to cut deep holes in the tufa rock with a chisel, fill the holes with soil and plant saxifrages, houseleeks (sempervivums) or sedums in the holes. Tufa rock is a very light rock and a ton of it would go a long way.

The size of the rocks should have some relation to the size of the rock garden. In every rock garden, a few large rocks are valuable for making at least one extra bold feature. Small round river rocks should never be used.

Soil is an extremely important factor in making the rock garden. An overall good basic compost should first be used, such as two parts loam, one part sharp sand and one part peat moss with bone meal added.

The arrangement of the rocks is intensely interesting work and gives opportunity for endless ingenuity in devising arrangements so as to form attractive homes for the plants.

The builder should first form a rough general idea of the effects he hopes to achieve. He should work slowly, thoughtfully, and deliberately, stopping now and again to study what he has done and to consider what he is going to do next.

It is important to avoid a monotonous arrangement of the rocks. In some places the stones may be concentrated, elsewhere they may be spread out more sparsely, leaving open spaces here and there, and then again they may be brought together in heavier building.

Care should be taken not to use up all the best rocks at the beginning, or the last stages will be weaker than they need be.

It is important to pay most careful attention to bedding rocks into the soil so that the lower edge of each is at least a few inches below the surface. Where its base is properly buried, it assures a solid, permanent air and looks as though it were part of an underground rock bed cropping up through the soil.

These are the small but important details which give the rock garden that natural look which we strive for. Every rock throughout the garden should be bedded in this way.

When a rock is buried — maybe as much as half of it — it should be tilted slightly towards the bank. This causes the water to go back towards the roots of plants when the rockery is watered.

The aim also should be to arrange rocks in such a way that they look as though they were all part of one big rock by placing three or four carefully chosen medium-sized ones close together. With care and imagination this should prove to be a great success. It is a good idea also to start at the lowest point and build up to the desired height and design, seeking to create the hill and dale effect with irregularity, avoiding monotony.

Great care should be taken when building, that the basic soil compost be packed fully and firmly under and behind the rocks. Air spaces should be avoided, as these can cause great harm to plants.

As the rocks are built up, you can fill in with the different soil composts which you will require for the various plants you have chosen — that is to say, if you wish them successfully grown.

Some will require peaty soil, some lime, some gravel and others sandy soils. There should be a depth of 18 inches of soil at the least; if it is deeper so much the better.

The main layout should be such that the paths enable one to get to all parts of the rock garden with reasonable ease. For more inaccessible spots, stepping stones can be used to give easy approach for the care of all one's plants.

The introduction of water into the rock garden, if it can be done, will add greatly to its charm. A trickling stream ending in a small pool where lilies could be grown is most picturesque.

It is assumed that much thought has been given to the building of as natural a home as possible for the plants. It is desirable, therefore, to make the planting worthy of the building.

One should not be in too great a hurry in planting. Allow the rocks and soil to settle. It is probable that here and there a rock will shift, and if this happens it is easier to put right if no planting has been done.

Another important phase of planting is placing of a selection of dwarf trees and shrubs, both deciduous and evergreen. These form a framework, giving character to the whole scene. Evergreens are especially nice in the winter when there are no flowers or foliage.

The most effective evergreens are the dwarf varieties of pine, juniper and spruce. The carpet juniper is a lovely shrub for trailing down over a slope or rocks. It is a native of North America.

There are many dwarf deciduous shrubs suitable for growing in the rock garden. The Japanese maple, with its autumn coloring and slow growth is fitted admirably to the rockery. Cinquefoil (potentialla fruticosa) and its varieties are invaluable with their big strawberry-like blossoms in yellow and white. These shrubs are erect-growing and do not exceed 3 feet in height and can be found on our prairies or along the river banks.

It is important in placing dwarf trees and shrubs in the rock garden, to give them positions where they will show up best. It is essential to keep the taller alpines away from them. They should have nothing but dwarf alpines such as the flowering thyme, mossy saxifrages and the very dwarf campanulas or bell flowers.

The following plants should be placed in the shade or part shade. First, the delightfully old-fashioned forget-me-nots in shades of blue, pink and white. Then there are the primulas in rich colors of mauve, pink, yellow, and orange. Another favorite is the multi-colored elephant ear (auricula).

If one wants a bit more blue in the garden, there are the gentians in every conceivable shade of blue, ranging from pale Cambridge blue to the darkest.

There are also quite a number of ferns native to Alberta which form a perfect setting for around a pool. Dwarf trollius do well in a shady place also.

For the open sunny spot in the rockery, here are a few of the better-known plants: the houseleek (sempervivum) with its succulent leaves, which during a dry spell can supply the roots with accumulated moisture for the leaves. The cactus, despite its foreboding appearance, has some of the most fragile blossoms in delicate tones of pink, yellow, and deep crimson.

The fragrant pinks are old-time favorites which in twilight perfume the whole garden.

The alpine or rock pinks (dianthus) like a sunny position, well drained, in gritty or sandy soil. They are exceedingly hardy, and among the most popular here. Among the varieties, all grown in the Reader Rock Garden, are: dianthus caesicus, rose-colored; dianthus arenacius, white flowers marked with purple; dianthus deltoides, the maiden pink; and dianthus alpinus, a fine rock pink.

The dwarf alpine phlox, which when in bloom looks lovely with its profusion of many-colored varieties.

The striking flower of Adonis which has rich buttercup yellow blooms will certainly help toward making a rockery even more lovely.

The dainty blue grape hyacinth looks especially beautiful when planted in masses.

The evening primrose, as its name suggests, opens in the evening to show large bell-like flowers, tinted white and yellow.

The garden gloxinia is a hardy and attractive plant which grows to a height of about 6 inches.

I think the aquilegia jucunda is the queen of columbines. It is almost breathtaking in its loveliness and is in a class by itself. These plants may be obtained at a seedhouse or they may be sown in a greenhouse and later set out in the rock garden.

Saxifrages are a large group of mostly hardy perennials belonging to the family saxifragaceae. Only a few are annuals or biennials. The name is an old Latin name and is derived from saxum (a rock) and fraga (to break). Saxifrages are sometimes called breakstones or rockfoil, and are principally native of north and south temperate and Arctic regions, with a few found in Asia and being rare in South America.

This group of plants is extremely varied, and their principal home is the rock garden. Here the saxifrages are one of the most varied, beautiful, and valuable of all alpine families. They are notable for their lovely flowers and fine foliage. They have a remarkably long-flowering season. A large number of varieties of the saxifrage family have been grown in the Reader Rock Garden.

Among the saxifrage species are: cybalaria—small annual plants with glossy leaves and yellow flowers. Saxifraga sibthorpii is typical and the best known of this group.

Dactylocides — an important group embracing many beautiful species, hybrids, and seedlings known under the popular name of mossy saxifrages. The green rosettes of moss-like foliage form handsome cushions, and the white, pink, and red are carried in numerous erect spikes. Saxifraga hypnoides, the dovedale moss, and saxifraga bathoniensis are typical plants of this species.

Diptera — an unimportant group of which the best-known member is saxifraga sarmintosa or mother of thousands, sometimes called Aaron's beard.

Euaeizoonia — the silver saxifrages such as saxifraga aizoon, saxifraga cotyledon and numerous others. These constitute the most important of the encrusted group which comprise a wide range of easily-grown plants, beautiful both in leaf and in flower. They are mostly rock plants with rosettes of leaves encrusted at the edges with silvery white powder, and graceful sprays of white, pink, or pale yellow flowers.

Kabschia — another important group containing some of the most beautiful of all saxifrages. These plants form compact cushions of small rosettes of narrow undivided leaves, often pointed. They bloom in early spring and the flowers are borne on short erect stems. They are plants for the scree and gritty loam in the rock garden. Saxifraga burseriana, saxifraga apiculata and saxifraga myra are typical of this group.

Engleria — are plants forming rosettes of undivided silvery leaves with many flowered spikes of small flowers with pink or yellowish petals. Saxifraga griesbachii and saxifraga media are typical. A good many hybrids have been raised between the kabschia and the engleria.

Porphyoion — low-growing and creeping kinds of plants of the high alps. The large, almost stemless, flowers in early spring are heather purple or rose purple. Our native saxifraga oppositifolio is typical of this group.

Robertiana — have rosettes of leathery leaves and feathery sprays of small pink or white flowers. Our well-known London pride (saxifraga umbrosa) is typical.

The silver saxifrages are best grown in raised positions in the rock garden. From such raised rocky positions, too, the sprays of white, pink, or yellow flowers can arch outwards in a natural and graceful manner exactly as they do on their own alpine rock and cliffs.

The mossy saxifrages should be grown in cool, half-shady places and given ample room to spread as they are rapid growers. After flowering, it is a good plan to top-dress heavily the clumps with a fine mixture of sifted peat moss and sharp sand.

This mixture may be placed over the plants in a perfectly dry state, and then with the fingers, the compost should be worked down between the rosettes until the plants can absorb no more. When this top compost is dry and fine, it will work down between the leaves quite easily.

A good overhead watering with a fine watering can will complete the work and settle the mixture.

Mossy saxifrages become patchy and go brown with age, and this top dressing serves to keep the plants in a healthy state for a long while.

Eventually, however, it will be found necessary to renew the plants. They should be dug up, pulled to pieces, and the area renewed with new compost. The divided clumps may be replanted a few inches apart. This re-planting is best done in the spring.

It should be remembered that the red-flowered mossy saxifrages fade quickly in the full, hot sun.

Nearly all the kabschia saxifrages are best grown in a soil composed of loam, sand, and peat moss to which has been added a liberal supply of stone chips or gravel. The position should be open and is best if it slopes west or northwest rather than directly south. Sharp drainage is essential and many buried stones are a help, for the roots of these saxifrages love to go down among porous rocks and gravel.

As these plants grow large, they should be top-dressed, also with the compost mentioned in the preceding paragraph. This should be worked well down among the rosettes and stems. This compost is best applied when dry, and should be watered after you get it well worked in and around the plants. This work is best done in autumn.

Seventy different kinds of saxifrages have at one time been grown here in Calgary and they were a delight to the eye. We recommend the saxifrage family as they do very well here.

The grape hyacinth is another dainty and sweet little flower which is suitable for a sunny spot in a rock garden. This bulbous plant multiplies rapidly.

The blue mertinsia virginiana, which is a native of our own woodland, is splendid for planting under the shade of tall trees.

The aubrietia hendersonii, which comes in shades of mauve, pink, and white, also forms a beautiful carpet of dainty blooms. It thrives best in a sunny spot in the rockery.

Other flowers which bloom well in rock gardens here are doronicum caucasicum or the Caucasian daisy; dodecatheon alpinum or shooting star; cyprepedium passerinum or lady's slipper (one of the choicest of plants); arabis alpina; anemone pulsatilla and its varieties; silene acaulis; draba rigida; ribes articus; adonis vernalis; the geum variety Mrs. Bradshaw; actaea alba and actaea rubra.

Sedium or stonecrop also is a plant most suitable for the rock garden. Sedums are a very large group of hardy and tender succulent plants, both annual and perennial. Only one of the annuals found in this family, sedium coeruleum, is of any value in a garden.

The name sedum is from sedo (to sit) from the manner in which the plants fix themselves to rocks and walls. It is an unfortunate thing that the sedums are in a hopeless confused state with regard to naming. In almost any collection of sedums, one is likely to find specimens wrongly named.

This is, no doubt, partly due to the remarkable freedom with which sedums propagate themselves. The smallest scrap will root itself where it falls and so start a new plant. Even single leaves of certain kinds are capable of taking root where they fall and become plants. Thus it must often happen that scraps of leaves of sedums get blown from place to place so that fresh beds spring up around wrong labels.

There are about 500 distinct species of sedum known to botanists, but relatively few of these are, or have been, in cultivation. Then again, of the number actually in cultivation, many are only of interest to botanists and have no horticultural importance.

Therefore, for practical garden purposes, the 500 or so known sedums may be reduced to a much smaller number among which are plants of first-class importance.

The sedums are to be found widely distributed in the Northern Hemisphere especially in temperate countries, but only a few will grow here.

However, the hardy rock garden sedums are best suited when given light, poor well-drained soil and a sunny position. Clumps may be taken up, divided and re-planted almost any time during the growing season.

Many have extremely beautiful and interesting leaves and some varieties take on brilliant coloring in the fall. A novel feature may be created by selecting a good-sized pocket or earth terrace and devoting it to a clump of mixed sedums.

In doing this, it is important to see the pocket of earth you have chosen is well-drained and the location should be hot and sunny. The soil may be mounded up into a sort of low cushion, and planted closely all over with as many different sedums of the smaller kinds as are available.

They should be mixed, for the more varied they are, the better. They will soon join up into one large patch of variegated color, a blending of reds, greens, and purples, quite fascinating and beautiful to see.

Any of the following rock sedums may be used on such a mixed patch: album, acre, dasyphyllum, lydium, hispanicum, oreganum, reflexum, ruprestree, spathuliofilium.

Apart from such specialized use as that described, sedums are invaluable for growing in all sorts of out-of-the-way sunny corners and crevices in the rock garden. Sedum spathulifolium and its lovely purple species purpureum are most decorative when planted in mass to join up and form lovely patches of fine gray, green, or gray purple foliage.

If you have an unsightly wall or bank which you wish to hide, this is an ideal way in which to cover it over. Seldom are sedums so appropriately placed as on a wall and in rock gardens. Many of them will flower in the narrowest crevices between the rocks.

Not in vain has the sedum been called stonecrop. All the smaller sedums make charming plants for the rockery and in rock paths. For this purpose sedum acre in its various forms, album, hispanicum, and lydium are fine. They are easy to establish and are also attractive for planting in an informal way along the sides of garden paths.

They will flourish planted in gravel or stone chips in the scree, and give an excellent affect if tucked in at the bases of the rock to spread outwards.

Sedum sieboldii, a Japanese variety, is not grown half as much as its beauty deserves. It is hardy and could be used with exceedingly good effect in the rock garden or as a neat flower border edging. It is one of the prettiest of all sedums.

Sedum acre is a British native plant, common in many places, especially near the sea. It is the yellow stonecrop and is well worth growing, as it is one of the showiest of the whole family.

Sedium album is one of the commonest. It, too, is a native of the British Isles, but has been naturalized in many places. It is of semi-creeping habit, forming large mats. The flowers are white, fading to pink sometimes.

Sedum aizoon is an old-garden plant with distinct perennial carrot-like roots, erect stems a foot tall. The flower head, 2 or 3 inches across, is yellow or orange. It is a hardy herbaceous perennial and is a native of Siberia, Mongolia, China, and Japan.

Sedum altissimum is a handsome plant with narrow, flattened, pointed leaves and erect stems with heads of greenish-white flowers. The plant varies from 6 to 12 inches in height.

Sedum anacampseros is a distinct type with trailing stems covered with thick rounded leaves and roundish heads of dull-purplish flowers.

Sedum kamchaticum is a first-rate garden plant with erect or ascending stems, 3 to 4 inches tall, broad dark leaves and heads of orange.

o   o   o   o

A new idea in the field of horticulture has taken hold in the British Isles. This is miniature rock gardens, using old stone kitchen sinks and horse troughs as containers. This type of gardening has much to recommend it.

The "sink gardens" as they are called, are to be seen on every hand in the British Isles wherever there is a love for rock plants and their cultivation.

Alberta is ideally situated for this type of gardening and I would like to recommend it as it is intensely interesting. We may not have the old horse troughs and sinks that were once so plentiful in England and Scotland, but they can be cut out from our sandstone or made from cement blocks.

The first and most important operation in making and planting a sink garden is to arrange for efficient drainage. Old kitchen sinks and horse troughs usually had a drain hole which, of course, could be used for drainage purposes, but first it would be wise to place the sink on a pedestal where it is to remain permanently, and then, before filling with soil compost, test the drainage by pouring in a bucket of water. If it all runs away, well and good.

Very likely, however, it will be found that some of the water drains to the end farthest from the drainage hole and a certain amount will perhaps settle in the worn hollows, especially if you have those old-fashioned sandstone troughs or sinks.

Such faulty drainage would be extremely bad when the sink was planted. But it is easily remedied by tilting the sink so all the water runs out at the hole. Usually a little tilting and packing between the bottom of the sink and the top of the pedestal will put matters right.

It may be necessary to drill a second drainage hole in the opposite end of the sink, and in any case, a second drainage hole is a safeguard and a wise precaution in a fairly large sink.

Faulty drainage may soon lead to disaster among the plants. Moss and fungi will soon appear on a badly-drained sink garden, the first danger signal that something is wrong. Later plants will turn sickly and die.

It is important, when placing the sink in its permanent position, to make sure that it is standing on firm, solid ground, otherwise its own weight may cause the pedestal to sink and so upset the otherwise carefully planned drainage arrangement. A slight sinking of the pedestal, one way or the other, will be exaggerated in the sink itself with bad results.

Having arranged the perfect drainage outlets in the sink, the outlet holes should be covered with suitable drainage crocks, and a shallow layer of broken crocks laid over the whole of the floor of the sink or trough.

Over these, should go a layer of fibrous turf. This layer of roughage may be 2 inches thick. Next, the main compost of soil is put in.

A good compost is made by using equal parts of loam, well-decayed manure, sifted fine, and sharp sand, and it would be greatly improved if grit is added.

An excellent form of grit is made by smashing up broken flower pots and crushed gravel about the size of green peas. The grit is added to the compost in about the same proportions as the other ingredients. It is better to err on the side of too much sand and grit than too much loam. The compost should feel sharp and springy and crumbly in the hand.

The sink should be filled to within about an inch of the brim and the soil made firm and level without ramming.

The next operation is formation of the small porous rocks in the sink garden. This of course, lends itself to endless ingenuity in arranging the rocks to produce a pleasing natural effect and at the same time a formation which will grow the plants well and provide a varied assortment of planting spaces to suit their varied requirements. Simplicity should be the keynote.

A good idea is to arrange the miniature rocks in such a way that in the end they will look like one large rock of picturesque and rather rugged outline, which has been split into three and rent by frost and left with a series of deep cracks and fissures in which plants have found a congenial home.

It is convenient to have at hand a selection of smaller rocks of widely varying colors.

For a sink garden 3 to 4 feet long by 2 feet wide, the rocks may vary in size from those as big as one's two fists to others about one and a half times as big as a man's head.

Start by placing the three largest rocks close together on the soil and towards the end of the sink. These three will naturally form the highest point in the rock work. Fit them together rather closely and arrange and rearrange them until you are satisfied that they are in the position in which they most closely resemble one rock which has been split into three.

From the main foundation, build on the rest, aiming still at the idea of outcrop. With rocks of varying size it is possible to make a general upper profile of the rock work descend from the topmost, and then ascend to a second minor headland.

The spaces between the rocks should vary in width from quite narrow cracks to crevices 2 to 3 inches wide. The rocks must all stand firm and solid, each on its own bed. They may come up quite close to the sides of the sink in some place, elsewhere they will likely be 4 or 6 inches away.

The arranging of the rocks is most interesting. It should not be hurried but done deliberately and thoughtfully, arranging and rearranging until it seems impossible to achieve a more natural effect with better planting spaces and crevices.

Now that the rocks are well placed and firmed in with the compost, planting may begin. The first consideration will be a dwarf tree or two, for a few of these miniatures add greatly to the picturesque effect.

Several of the dwarf forms of spruce are good, 3 or 4 inches high. Of these picea nana compacta and picea maxwellii are excellent. Then there is a tiny yew tree known as taxus baccata pygmaea which only adds perhaps half an inch to its growth in a year.

A selection of these and other dwarf trees and shrubs having been planted, attention should be turned to planting the true alpine and rock plants. Naturally, one will use rock-dwelling sorts, too, among the crevices on the rocky hill, while for the "flat lowlands" that surround the hill, low-growing kinds and miniature plants will be chosen. Too great care can scarcely be taken in arranging the plants correctly in the sink garden.

Saxifrages in variety are charming for this type of work, or the lovely rock garden pinks, such as alpinus and neglectus. The cheddar pinks, dianthus caesius, form a curtain of blue-gray foliage with rich rose-colored flowers.

Drabas in variety are excellent for this work with their green cushion producing, in spring, golden flower heads on thread-like stems an inch or two tall.

Erinus alpinus and its variety in lilac and carmine and the quaint house-leeks in variety, especially the miniature and cobwebs, are recommended. Silene acaulis also is a good cushion plant for the sink garden, especially for hanging down over the side of the trough. The flowering thyme in mauve, white and deep rose is splendid for trailing over the tiny rocks, and it also has a lovely smell both in foliage and flower. There are many other alpines.

o   o   o   o

The scree garden is one form of gardening that few people know little about and where the most delightful of dwarf alpine plants may be grown. This type of gardening will grow only certain kinds of plants and the area must be prepared for them in as natural a setting as possible.

The late W. R. Reader, with the help of George Climo and myself did construct such a scree in the Reader Rock Garden where many choice plants from the rocky Mountains and the Swiss Alps grew in splendor.

A natural scree in the Rocky Mountains is a mass of crushed and broken rocks carried down by the glacier and deposited at its base. There is usually a flow of water percolating through a scree, supplied by the melting ice of the glacier above.

Certain types of alpine plants are found inhabiting active screes, and these plants are especially adapted for life among the loose, stony material of which screes are formed, but when transplanted to the close-binding loam soils of the ordinary rock garden, many of them are incapable of existing under such entirely different conditions.

In making a scree it may cover many yards of ground or it may be no larger than a yard square. The gardener wishing to experiment by converting part of the rock garden into a scree should select, if possible, a fairly steep area on the rockery with a sunny exposure. We will suppose that the selected site slopes gently south or southwest, it is roughly eight feet in length from top to bottom and four feet wide. It is surrounded and contained by well-laid rocks.

The soil must be removed to a depth of 18 inches. Rough drainage should be put in the bottom—broken rocks, bricks, and clinkers to a depth of nine inches.

Next, the scree mixture must be prepared. This should consist of crushed rocks and loam in proportion of three parts stone, one part loam, and one part sharp sand. The form of crushed rock usually most readily obtainable is limestone, granite chips, or sandstone.

A porous rock is preferable, and although limestone is excellent for the majority of plants, its use will preclude the cultivation of a few lime-haters. The granite chips will suit the acid-loving plants.

The soil mixture to be added to the broken stones may consist of peat moss or leaf mould, loam, and sharp sand. This mixture is best made in proportion of two-thirds peat moss, and the other third loam and sand, half and half.

These proportions need not be followed too rigidly.

The important thing is to keep the scree mixture very poor in soil. If too much loam is used, the compost will consolidate and lose its special virtue of openness and looseness.

As to the size of the stone chips to be used, they should not be too small and fine, not less than half an inch square chips or rocks. Crushed rocks, similar to those used on city streets, will do very well to mix with the other compost.

Having obtained or prepared the scree mixture, all that remains to be done is to fill up the rest of the excavated site with it. The scree is then ready for planting.

Apart from the free, loose, root run it affords to the special plants which enjoy and even require such conditions, the scree has the great virtue of absorbing water quickly, and retaining it for a long time. A can of water soaks in just as fast as it is poured on, and it soaks rapidly down through the stones as it could never soak into ordinary loam and having soaked in, it is retained by the scree for longer than it would be by ordinary soil.

It is this rapid absorbtion and long retention of water which makes artificial underground irrigation of the scree unnecessary.

The list of plants that may be planted into the scree are considerable, and all have been grown in Calgary in years gone by, and many may still be seen in the Reader Rock Garden.

Among the choice plants to be grown in the scree is androsace arachnoidea and its variety Superba.

Other recommended scree plants are listed at the end of this chapter.

Also there are at least 70 different kinds of saxifrages which may be grown on the scree very successfully.

110

Rock Garden Plants

The following are recommended for growing here:

Name	Plant Height (in inches)	Color
Auriculas (all varieties)	6	Varied
Aquilegia jacunda	10	Blue and White
Aubietia henersonii	3 to 4	Mauve
Arabis alpina	2 to 3	White
Anenome pulsatilla	9	Mauve
Actaea rubra	12	Red Berries
Actaea alba	12	White Berries
Cactus (native)	9	Red and Yellow
Caucasian daisy	12	Yellow
Campanula (bellflower):		
Campanula glomerata acaulis	9	Blue
Campanula alpina	3	White and Blue
Campanula barbata	12	Pale Blue
Campanula caespitosa	3	Blue
Campanula excisa	3 to 4	Violet
Dwarf alpine phlox	2	Mauve, Red, White, Lilac
Draba rigida	3	Yellow
Evening primrose	3	Pink and Yellow
Forget-me-not (biennial)	3 to 4	Blue, Pink, White
Flower of Adonis	9	Yellow
Gentians (in variety)	6 to 9	Blue
Garden Gloxinia	6 to 9	Mauve
Grape hyacinth	3	Blue
Geum (avens) Mrs. Bradshaw	9	Orange
Houseleeks (in variety)	½ to 3	Pink and Yellow
Mertensia virginiana	10	Blue
Primulas (in variety)	6 to 12	Varied
Pinks	½ to 9	Varied
Ribes articus	2	Pink
Saxifrages (in variety)	3 to 12	Varied
Sedums (in variety)	6 to 12	Varied
Shooting Star (dodecatheon alpinum)	9	Mauve and white
Silene acaulis	3	Rose
Trollius acaulis	7 to 8	Yellow
Veronica (or speedwell):		
Veronica apennina	Creeping	Blue
Veronica bona rota	4	Blue
Veronica caespitosa	Dwarf	Pink
Viola tricolor	4	Tricolor
Viola lutea	4	Yellow
Viola arkwrightii ruby	4	Ruby

The following are recommended for planting on Scree:

Name	Plant Height (in inches)	Color
Androsace carnea hallerii	2	Pink
Androsace chamaejasme	2	White
Androsace laetea	2	White
Androsace villosa	4 to 6	Rose and White
Anenome balldensis	3 to 4	White
Anenome vernalis	9	Yellow
Arenaria (sandwort)	Creeping	Pink, Red, White
Armeria caespitosa	Low tufted	Pink
Campanula allionii	9	Deep Blue
Campanula excisa	4 to 5	Blue
Campanula rainerii	9	Blue
Campanula joycii	3	Blue
Chrysanthemum alpina	3 to 4	Red
Dianthus (pink) alpinus	3 to 4	Red
Dianthus boydii	3 to 4	Red
Dianthus neglectus	3	Pale Pink
Dianthus subacaulis	2	Pale Pink
Erodium corsieum	2 to 3	Reddish
Douglasia vitaliana	2 to 3	Yellow
Draba alpina	2 to 3	White
Draba aigoides	2 to 3	Yellow
Draba pyrenaica	2 to 3	Rosy Lilac
Gentiana imbricata	9	Blue
Gentiana acaulis	3 to 4	Blue
Gentiana Farrerii	2 to 3	Green and Blue
Gentiana verna	2	Blue
Geranium Farrerii	4 to 5	Red
Geum reptans	9	Dull Red
Inula acaulis	2 to 3	Yellow
Iris lacutris	3 to 4	Pale Blue
Leontopodium alpinum	3 to 4	Yellow
Linaria (toad flax) alpina	3 to 4	Blue
Pentstemon rupicola	10 to 11	White and Blue
Primula farinosa	3	Pale Pink
Primula scotica	1½	Deep Red
Saxifrages (all mossy and other varieties)	3 to 12	White, Red, Yellow
Sedum aizoon	2 to 3	Yellow
Sedum acre	2 to 3	Yellow
Sedum album	3 to 4	White
Sedum ewersii	2 to 3	Pink
Sedum svebddin	9	Pink

LILY POOLS

Nothing adds greater charm to any garden than a pool in which lovely water lilies are grown. Water lilies, botanically known as nymphaea, are perennial herbs with horizontal or erect rootstocks, or tuberous, rooting in mud covered by three to six inches of water. Water lilies are among the most diversified and universally admired plants in cultivation. Unfortunately, we see all too few of them here.

When building an artificial pond, the most satisfactory method is to build solid walls of masonry with a concrete bottom which has an outlet and overflow. In a city like ours, where there is so much construction, the building of such a pool would not add greatly to the cost of a home.

In all cases, make the pool as large as existing means allow.

In more favorable climates where the lilies may be left outside all winter, a layer of soil 9 to 12 inches deep is sometimes placed in the bottom of the pool. Here, where these plants must be lifted and brought in after the first frost, it is better to grow them in wire baskets which are easily lifted out of the pool in the fall.

These baskets should be filled with the following compost—firstly, line the baskets with peat moss or spagnum moss. Into this place a compost made up of two parts well-decayed manure, two parts rich, fibrous loam, and one part sharp sand to which has been added a quantity of bone flour, about a good handful to each basket.

The baskets should at least be 18 inches long, 15 inches wide, and 12 to 15 inches deep. The rhizomes should be planted in the centre of the baskets, having the crowns level with the soil.

They may be placed in the pool after the first of June.

Water lilies should be started indoors about the beginning of April or a little later. When placing the baskets in the pool, they must not be placed too deeply, just an inch below the level of the surface.

If the pool is too deep, place bricks, or flat rocks, underneath the baskets to raise them to the desired height.

When building a pool, it is important that it be placed in the sunniest location of the garden. For best results, lilies must have sunshine all day long.

The water lilies Nymphaeas Odorata and Rosea are recommended. The first-named variety is white and the latter pink. All nymphaea succeed best when grown as near as possible under their existing natural conditions. This means they must have rich soil in abundance, water, and clear uninterrupted sunlight.

Where natural ponds exist, these conditions are found, but often there is a deficiency of light caused by shade trees.

Let the trees remain, but select an open spot for the nymphaea.

Do not place the plants in a newly-constructed pool immediately after it is finished, as the caustic property of the cement will injure the plants.

Let the water stand a few days, or if the pool is small, the water may be changed before using.

Nymphaea have insect pests like other cultivated plants and aphids prove to be troublesome at times. The best remedy for these pests is their natural enemy the lady bug. A colony of these insects could make short work of the aphids.

Nymphaea are also subject to fungus disease—a leaf spot which is easily discerned after a spell of warm, humid weather. After such a spell followed by bright sunshine, the leaves are scorched and crumpled and as a result the plants are sadly crippled by being denuded of their foliage; new leaves become weak and smaller, and also the flowers, if there are any.

This disease should be checked at once or the plants will be severely set back, if not ruined. The remedy is Bordeaux mixture or any of the various mixtures containing sulphate of copper as a base. A fine spray should be used and the mixture diluted to half the strength recommended for most plants. It is better to spray twice with a weak solution rather than once with too strong a solution and damage the foliage.

After the first frost in the fall, water lilies have to be taken up and stored in their baskets in a frost-proof basement. Make sure they do not dry up during the winter by well-soaking the basket, about once a month.

A plant suitable for planting around the edges of the pool is the Siberian iris, a graceful plant with grass-like foliage and slender flower stems two to three feet in height.

The flowers are much smaller than those of the bearded flag iris, but they are produced in greater profusion. They have slender rhizomes and are suitable for the water-side or they may be planted in the herbaceous border in a sunny position, ordinary garden soil, and abundance of moisture.

Another plant suitable for surrounding the edges of the pool is the Japanese iris (laevigata). It is a distinct type with large flat, clematis-like flowers. The plants grow two to three feet tall.

Others which may be used for the immediate vicinity of the pool are the yellow marsh marigold and the perennial spireas in various colors.

The golden marsh marigold (or caltha palustris), which comes in single and double varieties, is colorful and suitable for planting around the edge of a pool. It likes sun, peat moss and lots of moisture.

The fragrant and lovely lily of the valley never loses its appeal. It grows in white and very pale pink, and should be planted in a peaty soil and a shady location. This plant is also early in flowering in May.

The loosestrife (or lythrum) will likewise add beauty to the vicinity of the pool.

How to build a lily pool? I would suggest that after you have chosen a sunny, sheltered spot you should roughly mark out the pool, remove the soil to a depth of 2½ feet, the sides having a slight inward slope.

Cover the bottom with a layer of stones, ramming them into the soil to prevent cracks by subsequent sinkage of the ground. Put a layer of concrete, 6 inches deep, over the bottom of the pool, working the cement well with a shovel before smoothing with a trowel . . . Concrete for the bottom should be made from one part cement, two parts sand, and five parts fine gravel.

After three days this cement will be hard enough to stand on so that you can cement the sides. The concrete used for the sides should consist of one part cement and four parts coarse sand and five parts gravel.

Before the cement mixture is used, holes must be made in the soil at the bottom and sides with a dibber, or the concrete will not adhere.

It is better to line the sides of the pool in two operations. First apply a 3-inch layer all around. Two days later put on another layer. The first ought to be left roughly finished and the second well smoothed.

Make sure there is a good joining at the points where the sides meet the bottom. An additional filling of concrete at these connecting points will make sure no leaks occur.

To clean the pool, drain off part of the water and fill with fresh. All the water in the pool should never be drained at the same time, as the sudden change in temperature may check the growth of plants.

Of course, if you can have a continual inflow of fresh water into the pool, this is best, unless this water is too cold. A temperature ranging from 70 to 80 degrees is recommended.

The cost of a pool naturally depends on the size and the quality of materials used.

MULCHING

When winter is just around the corner, many think in terms of mulching.

Mulching has four general objects:

1—To conserve moisture in the soil by preventing or hindering evaporation;

2—To keep the surface of the soil loose and friable;

3—To add plant food to the soil;

4—To protect gardens from the effects of our alternately thawing and freezing caused by Chinook winds (this fourth reason is added especially for our peculiar winter conditions).

We have no more welcome visitor during our long, cold winters than the Chinook, but it can cause untold damage and loss to our gardens.

When the garden is carefully mulched, some of the moisture ascends through the mulch and escapes into the atmosphere, but it has been found by long experience and by experiment that mulching does greatly lessen evaporation.

All perennial plants and most shrubs and trees are benefited by a mulch in the fall, no matter how hardy they may be. Nature's mulch is the debris of fallen leaves, grass and other litter.

The autumn leaves that blow into the borders and clumps of shrubbery afford the very best winter covering, but, mistakenly, it is a common practice scrupulously to collect and burn the leaves in the fall, and then, if the plants are mulched at all, to apply a strawy litter. I would suggest that you leave on the garden the natural cover which falls; and that if necessary you add to this a mulch of strawy litter.

Too often, a passion for cleanliness and tidiness sacrifices the welfare of the garden.

A perennial border or bed will be benefitted by a loose, open mulch 6 to 8 inches deep. If the covering is of such character as to become very hard and dense and to hold too much water, it may be injurious.

Leaf mold, peat moss, autumn leaves mixed with strawy litter which will prevent them from packing too hard, fine straw and evergreen boughs are some of the materials which may be used as a mulch to good advantage. Put the mulch over the perennials in the fall after the early frosts have penetrated about 6 inches into the ground. The time for this will usually be in October.

If the mulch has thoroughly decayed by spring, it may be left on the ground, and will make a fine, loamy covering which will be much like the vegetable mold found in the woods.

If bulbs have been planted in the fall, cover them with a mulch of strawy litter to a depth of 4 or 5 inches.

It is of the utmost importance that perennials with persistent foliage be carefully covered with mulch for the winter. Some of these are pinks, foxgloves, saxifrages, sweet rocket, sweet williams, Canterbury bells, verbascums, hollyhocks, campanulas, and brown-eyed susans.

All newly-seeded lawns in particular should be mulched in the fall following their seeding, with well-rotted manure, peat moss, or virgin soil. This mulch should be applied to a depth of a half inch to an inch over the whole lawn.

Trees and shrubs which have been planted in the current year's spring should have a mulch of strawy litter or peat moss placed around the base of the tree or bush. This affords great protection to newly-planted stock which is not yet strongly rooted.

Mulching is most important for berry bushes. Late September is the time to prepare raspberry canes for mulching. Such preparations consist in cutting out all the old canes of last year's growth to ground level.

Also cut out all the weak canes of the current year's growth, leaving from five to seven strong canes in each clump. The latter should then be bent down gradually toward the ground.

By gradually, I mean that the bending over of these canes should only be completed over a period of eight to ten days. They should be bent in a graceful arch with no buckling or breaking of the canes.

After the canes are bent, a stake is driven into the ground to which they are fastened.

You should find it quite easy, towards the end of September, to bend the canes safely, as there is then still lots of sap left in the young canes.

After the first hard frost has penetrated about 6 inches down into the ground, place a cushion of mulch underneath the canes. This cushion acts as a protection and support under canes in case of heavy snowfalls.

Then complete the winter care of raspberry canes by placing a strawy litter over them to a depth of 6 inches. Sometimes, during an open winter, the covering of the canes becomes dislodged, and care should then be taken to see that they are never allowed to remain uncovered.

116

Strawberries require a light mulch of 2 to 3 inches of strawy litter, making sure that the crowns are always covered.

To prepare roses for winter mulching, they must be cut half-way back. Place the mulch over them after the first hard frost, covering the entire rose bush.

For this purpose use one part soil, two parts peat moss, mixed together. After placing this compost over the rose bushes, water it down with a fine spray, compacting but not disarranging the mulch. Be careful throughout the winter to see that the mulch completely covers the rose bushes at all times.

The importance of mulching, particularly in this climate, cannot be over-emphasized. If this were more consistently practised, fewer plants would be lost, and more vigorous plants would emerge in the spring.

It pays to mulch the garden.

FERTILIZERS

Another gardening fact well established by experiment and practice is that fruits, flowers, trees, shrubs and vegetables are benefitted by the intelligent applications of fertilizers and manures.

In the majority of cases, such application is followed by profit.

In the first place, crops should be classified for purposes of fertilization according to their periods of growth. The first class includes the perennial fruits and flowers; the second, the annual flowers and vegetables.

Those in the first class differ in that a longer season of preparation is required, during which the growth is vegetative rather than productive, though upon this vegetative growth depends the quality and value of the fruit or flower obtained.

The growth of both tree and fruit is dependent, too, not only upon the food acquired during its year of growth, but also upon that previously acquired and stored in buds and branches.

For the tree and shrub fruits, it may be regarded as a safe assumption that the fertility elements, phosphoric acid, potash and lime, contribute materially to the proper growth and hardening of the wood, as well as the maturing of the fruit.

The necessity for added nitrogen is, on the whole, much less. It should be applied as the need for its appears in the lack of vigor of the tree or shrub.

By experimental research, it was discovered that, although plants require many chemical substances to build up tissue, only four chemicals were likely to become temporarily exhausted from soils.

These are nitrogen, phosphoric acid, potash and lime. The first three in particular are always required where intensive crops are grown, and hence when fertilizers are added, they should consist of any one or two, or maybe of all three of these chemicals in some form or other.

Nitrogenous manures promote luxuriant leaf growth and rapid development.

Phosphoric (phosphatic) manures promote fruitfulness and early ripening, as well as production of flowers and seeds.

Potash manures are essential for good quality, as they have a tonic effect and promote good health.

Many fertilizers contain more than these three prime ingredients.

In spreading fertilizer from a spreader or by hand, a good guide and one that I have always followed with considerable success, is to use one large handful to the square yard, evenly distributed, and well watered in immediately after spreading.

The nitrogen supply is of paramount importance to all crops; indeed, if a plant is starved of nitrogen it refuses to grow, and a key to successful fertilizing is to be found in a sufficiency of nitrogen.

Nitrogen, is almost entirely taken up by the plant in the form of a solution of nitrates, and all manures which can supply nitrogen are said to be nitrogenous.

Ammonia and other chemicals which contain nitrogen are acted on by nitrifying organisms or bacteria in the soil. They undergo conversion into nitrates, and so they become readily assimiliated by plants. The rate of conversion, or nitrification as it is called, varies with the form in which the nitrogen compound exists.

Nitrogen manures or fertilizers have a striking effect in increasing the growth of all crops. Under normal circumstances, an application is followed in a few days by visible results, the plants become a deeper green, they increase in size, and look healthier and stronger.

Ultimately, a greater crop should be obtained, and often the plants come quicker to the stage when they are ready for harvesting.

The chief nitrogenous fertilizers or manures in use are nitrate of soda, nitrate of ammonia, nitrate of potash, nitrate of lime, and sulphate of ammonia. Many others have nitrogen in them. All the natural manures are more or less nitrogenous.

Nitrate of ammonia is a chemical more expensive than the majority of nitrogenous fertilizers, and on that account is generally used sparingly and only for choice plants. The amount of nitrogen in it is very high—about 35 per cent.

This fertilizer is usually sold in crystalline form. Half an ounce may be applied to each square yard of ground and raked in, or since it dissolves very readily it can be used in liquid form, using half an ounce to a gallon of water.

Both in solid and liquid forms, nitrate of ammonia is a powerful fertilizer, promoting rapid growth of leaf and stem.

But if used in excess, it will promote coarse, luxuriant herbage in plants and will harm production of flowers and fruit. An application of this fertilizer once a month is a recommended maximum usage. Applied to young plants, in liquid form, it encourages rapid growth.

Another excellent fertilizer for choice plants is made by mixing one part nitrate of ammonia and two parts phosphate of potash. This mixture should be sprinkled lightly around the plants, or it may be dissolved in water at the rate of half an ounce to a gallon for watering the soil.

Nitrate of soda is one of the oldest nitrogenous fertilizers. Like others, it promotes growth of leaf and stem. It also makes plants grow quickly. But it requires the addition of phosphates and potash to make it a complete fertilizer.

It may be applied to plants to force them to grow quickly, or to crops when they are nearing maturity. The speedy action is of great advantage where crops are attacked, or may be attacked, by pests such as leather jackets, wire worm and leaf eaters, since it enables the plants to keep growing until the danger period is passed.

On the other hand, an excess of nitrogenous fertilizers induces soft, sappy growth, and thus render plant more likely to fall victims to disease.

Nitrate of soda is used at the rate of an ounce to a square yard of ground, in spring and during the summer. Again, the recommended number of applications is once a month. One ounce in a gallon of water makes a highly stimulating fertilizer for all plants in growth.

In the natural process of decay, when plants die and form humus in the soil, the nitrogen which they contain is rendered available for future plants by the assistance of soil bacteria. This process also is called nitrification.

Since the amount of nitrogen in manurial form in most soils is too little to yield the heavy crops desired in cultivation, gardeners add to the store available by applying as a fertilizer such nitrogenous manures as the nitrates, sulphate of ammonia, and so on.

The legume family which includes peas, beans, and the various kinds of clovers, have molecules on their roots that are the nomes of nitrifying bacteria. These are engaged in preparing nitrates in a suitable form for plants, and it is not considered necessary or advisable to give such plants much artificial nitrogen.

As cultivation becomes more intensive in this country than it is at present, the exhaustion of soils will become a matter for greater study, and keeping the nitrogen content at the necessary proportion will assume greater importance.

Nitrobacterine or similar preparations will then become of the highest value.

The fertilizers which supply phosphorus to plants include super-phosphates, bone manures of various kinds, mineral and rock phosphates, and various others.

In general, the higher the percentage of phosphoric acid the more valuable the fertilizer.

The mineral and rock phosphates are natural rocks ground to a fine powder.

The phosphoric manures effect earlier and quicker development, counteract rank growth, hasten ripening and increase the food value and quality of crops. They, too, should not be used oftener than once a month.

Phosphoric manures should be applied to the soil in powder form and raked in lightly, using two or three ounces to a square yard. These potent manures are good for all plant life, fruits, vegetables, or flowers.

Potassic manures or fertilizers such as sulphate of potash, wood ash and phosphate of potash, which promote plant vigor and also counteract rankness, should similarly be used sparingly. It is recommended that two or three ounces of such fertilizers be used to the square yard, about every two weeks during the growing season.

The main function of lime, which is not really a fertilizer, is to lighten and sweeten soils. Generally, local soils are not deficient in lime, though of course there are exceptions.

If you think soil is deficient in lime, the best way is to have that soil analyzed.

Some plants such as clematis, wallflowers, rose bushes, yucca (or adam's needle), evening primroses, phlox drummondii, pinks, shirley poppies, crocuses and sweet williams, to name a few flowers, and such shrubs as mock oranges, lilacs, spindle trees, cotoneasters, crab-apples and flowering plums all love lime.

Small fruits and berries correspond more nearly to the vegetable crops in their fertilizer requirements. The more quickly available chemicals, particularly nitrogenous and phosphatic fertilizers, are usually applied to these.

In the case of strawberries, it is desirable that the soil in which the plants are placed should be supplied with phosphoric acid, and a fertilizer containing this chemical should be applied to the soil at this time of planting.

Nitrogen also should be present in readily available forms, and should be supplied in sufficient quantities at the time of setting the plants, to enable them to mature and thus to withstand the rigors of winter.

These requirements will be met by the use of dried blood, or its equivalent of nitrates of soda or ammonia. This treatment is advised particularly for soils not previously well enriched with organic nitrogenous matter.

Raspberry and blackberry bushes also require a soil well enriched with the mineral element to ensure an abundant and strong growth of wood.

In the growing of flowers and herbaceous plants, phosphoric acid is particularly needed. It has been demonstrated that bone meal is one of the most practical sources of this chemical, since it furnishes both nitrogen and phosphoric acid, in slowly assimilable forms.

TRANSPLANTING

Transplanting is a general term used to designate the removal of living plants, whereby they may become established in new quarters.

Transplanting may be performed when the plant is in a dormant condition as in fall or early spring, or when it is actively growing.

Small herbaceous plants are usually the only ones that are transplanted when in a growing condition, but this can only be done when the plants are living under special garden conditions where they may have the best of attention as to watering and shading.

Considered from a standpoint of the plants, transplanting is always a drastic operation, for it destroys a considerable part of the rooting system, loosens the plant attachment to the soil, and arrests, for the time being, a large part of its progressive vital activities.

In order to overcome these dangers, the earth into which the plant is set, should be well prepared and moist, so that the plant may quickly re-establish itself. Part of the top is usually removed in order to lessen transpiration, and with succulent and growing plants some shade should be provided for a time.

The deeper and finer the soil, and the greater the quantity of moisture it holds, the more successful the transplanting operation will be, other things being equal. The operation is also more successful in humid regions, i.e., the Pacific Coast, than in dry areas such as we have in Alberta.

The successful transplanting of any plant depends in part on the condition of the plant itself. The younger the plant, as a rule, the better it withstands the operation.

Herbaceous or growing plants which are relatively short and stocky and compact in growth, transplant better than those that are long, leggy, and weak. The stocky plants are able to withstand inclement weather when they are transferred from a protected place to the open air, and they probably also have more recuperative powers to make new roots and to attach themselves again to the soil.

The success of transplanting also depends, to some extent, on the weather at the time that removal is performed. If cool, cloudy, and damp weather follows the transplanting, the plants are much more likely to live.

Trees and shrubs usually establish themselves more quickly in freshly-turned soil, if it contains a relatively large amount of moisture.

In order to bring the oil into contact with the roots, it should be firmed closely about the trees and shrub roots. This firming of the soil tends to bring the subterranean moisture upwards where it may supply the roots.

In order to prevent the escape of moisture from the surface of the soil, it is customary to cover the ground from 1 to 3 inches in depth with a mulch of moss or rotted manure. When practicable, the water may be saved by keeping the surface well tilled, thus providing a mulch of earth.

All types of plants may be transplanted, but some of them can be removed only with great difficulty. In these cases, the special skill which is born of experience with these particular plants must be invoked for success.

Especially in the case of transplanting trees, the difficulties are of various kinds. In some cases, the difficulty may be a tap root system such as the crab-apple and some of the evergreen trees.

In these instances the tree may be prepared a year or so in advance by severing the tap root some distance (maybe 2 to 3 feet) below the level of the ground by means of a spade or other sharp instrument that is thrust underneath the crown.

Sometimes the difficult problem confronting transplanting is probably due to the excessive rate of transpiration from the foliage. In these instances cutting back the top rather severely. Providing shade may also contribute to success.

In other cases, the difficulty is the inability of the tree to make new feeding roots quickly, as in some of the hardwood trees. In the case of large trees and shrubs success may be obtained by transplanting in late fall when the ground is frozen to a depth of two feet, but it is safer in spring.

It is usually better to give the transplanting of large, choice trees and shrubs into the hands of an expert than to attempt to perform it with unskilled help and inefficient appliances.

Only a small portion of the efforts in transplanting very large trees are really successful. The trees may live for several years and yet never fully recover, nor make satisfactory subjects.

The surest and best results are usually obtained only when the trees are nursery-grown and have been transplanted two or three times within a few years of their final transplanting.

But there are some species that remove from their wild state with relative ease when they are of a larger size. The spruce is one of these.

Shrubs which also come under this category include the potentilla, high-bush cranberry, and the native dwarf birches.

To the landscape gardener, a thorough knowledge of trees is absolutely essential. He should know their rate and mode of growth, their peculiarities in regard to soil situation and climate. Many citizens are taken in every year with bargain sales of trees and shrubs, many of which will not thrive, grow and winter here.

As the trees are, after all, the most permanent part of the landscape after the surface of the ground, they ought to be planted with careful deliberation as to the intended artistic effect and their fitness to the soil and climatic conditions.

Mistakes in planting trees and shrubs are, afterwards, not easily corrected and rarely without injury to the original design.

FERNS AND CACTI

FERNS

Ferns are perhaps one of the most popular of house plants. Although ferns may be classified as commonplace, they never lose their popularity and appeal. Proudly they reign in the homes, churches, offices, hotels and green-houses of our land. Wherever a green and graceful background is desired, ferns fill the need.

To grow ferns in the home successfully, a temperature of not less than 55 degrees should be maintained at all times, with a rise of temperature in the daytime of 10 to 15 degrees.

To keep ferns in a healthy and growing condition, to prevent and kill insect pests and diseases, a proper condition of atmosphere always should be maintained.

Extremes in heat, moisture, or dryness should never be allowed.

If the atmosphere is found to be too dry, it will be of great benefit then to syringe the ferns once a day. An excessively dry atmosphere induces the development of the troublesome pest, thrips, and red spider.

In spite of the fact the fern is a moisture-loving plant, an excessive use of water causes parts of the fronds of a great many plants to turn black and to rot off, besides inducing the development of almost incurable fungoid diseases.

In the selection of ferns, the careful buyer should always be on the watch for types which are most perfect in shape, for character of individual fronds, for coloring, for healthy producing spores, and for freedom from the attacks of insects and fungous diseases.

In a large number of ferns, a great difference between the plants of the same species will be apparent to the careful observer. Some plants of the same species may have beautifully developed fronds, but are carried on long, weak stems, and look unattractive.

Others may be of compact, sturdy habit of growth, but with poorly-shaped individual fronds. In some, the coloring will be found greatly superior to others. By closely studying all these points, the buyer may obtain the most perfect types of fern.

When ferns become pot-bound, or the pot appears to be too small for the ferns, they should be shifted into larger pots. The correct compost for most ferns (indoors and outdoors) is two parts loam, two parts peat moss or leaf soil, one part sharp sand, one tablespoonful of charcoal.

Care must be exercised to provide good drainage for ferns. This may be insured by placing pieces of crocks in the bottom of the pot, over which you should then place a layer of peat moss. Do not place ferns in direct sunshine; they like light, but strong sunlight causes fronds to turn yellow.

The adiantum farleyense or maidenhair fern is one of the most beautiful, and one of the hardest to care for successfully in the home. It deservingly ranks as a great favorite among fern lovers.

To attain perfection in growth, the maidenhair fern must be kept in a light, airy room in which every condition of moisture and atmosphere can be kept under absolute control. If they are kept under these perfect conditions, the greatly admired and beautifully pinkish tints may be obtained, and fronds will be hardy and of good substance. For this particular fern a temperature of 70 degrees is required at all times.

There is a lovely and hardy maidenhair fern adiantum pedatium which grows wild in British Columbia and will grow outside here in a shady location. We have it growing here in Calgary in the Reader Rock Garden. In appearance it looks much like the indoor adiantum farleyense, only of coarser foliage.

Another attractive fern is known as polypodium vulgare. It grows wild in the Peace River country and other parts of Alberta. It gives a surprisingly tropical look to a garden, and is particularly attractive when cultivated along a water course or pool.

There is also another hardy little fern which is a native of the Rocky Mountains and grows well here. It is botanically known as polystichum lonchitis, and is commonly known as the holly fern. This, too, is found growing in the Reader Rock Garden. These hardy ferns for out-of-doors are worthy of study and admiration; they seem to require so little care and yet give such general satisfaction, and are so greatly admired.

Some dreary outdoor places shut off from the sunlight may be beautified by a clump of ferns which fill the place as no other plant can do. The dreary spot may become an enchanted corner of your garden with the addition of these graceful and verdant plants.

It is much better to move ferns in the garden in spring or autumn when not in growth. If it is necessary to plant them in summer when they are in full growth, cut off all new fronds. This will retard evaporation to keep the plants from wilting. Get the roots into the soil with as little exposure to air as possible, and (with a few exceptions) new fronds will spring up, giving nearly a good results as if planted in early spring.

Failures from planting when in full growth are probably due to not cutting back.

A shady and moist location and peat moss are musts for ferns.

A recommended greenhouse fern is the osmunda, which grows to a height of 6 feet. The spores are produced on special structures on the ends of the fronds.

The allosorus belongs to a group of dwarf, hardy ferns with finely divided fronds, all of which must be grown indoors. The parsley fern (allosorus crispus) is one of this group.

The pteris (pteriscretica) is another greenhouse fern. It has ribbon-like fronds, and is closely related to common bracken.

One of the best known here is asparagus fern, the popular name for several kinds of ornamental asparagus grown in greenhouses.

Another popular and well-liked greenhouse fern, and one of the easiest to grow indoors, is the Boston fern.

Several kinds of aphis attack ferns which are also subject to white fly, thrips, red spider and scale insects.

Fumigation with hydrocyanic acid gas (which is POISONOUS) is the most effective way of getting rid of these pests.

Other ways of treating these diseases include using a spray with nicotine and soap or other efficient contact insecticides.

CACTI

The cactus is a peculiar family of plants which many people find intriguing. The many unusual forms found under this name constitute the family cactacea. They are especially characteristic of the warm and dry regions of North America, and are found in even greater numbers in Mexico.

It is believed that the drought-resisting habit of this family seems to be the result of perennial drought conditions to which they have become remarkably adapted.

The twofold problem presented by such conditions is the storage of water and the regulation of its loss. As a result of water storage, the plant bodies are characteristically succulent; loss of water by transpiration is reduced to a minimum by the heavy outside coating and other features of the plant.

Most cacti do not bear foliage leaves, the stems are flat, columnar or globular, and the flowers unusually conspicuous and in many cases, remarkably large and brilliantly colored.

Others again, are diminutive. The sepals and petals are numerous, arranged in an overlapping series; the stamens are indefinite in number and insterted at teh base of the corolla. They contain numerous seeds which ripen into a smooth, bristly, or spiny fleshy fruit, often edible.

To enable one to be fairly successful in the cultivation of cacti, always endeavor to obtain plants in the spring, whether for indoors or outdoors, and always be sure that the plant is in perfect condition before potting.

Plants collected from their native habitat are usually received without roots, as the roots are often damaged in transit. They have to be set in sand to form new roots before being placed in the regular compost.

This compost is composed of one part fibrous loam, one part old lime rubble or crushed brick, and one part sand; with some dried cow manure.

Before being potted, it is a good idea to carefully examine the plant for any sign of disease or decay. If any decay is found, the bad parts should be cut out until healthy tisue is reached. After this operation, the plants should be placed in full exposure to the sun and wind until the treated parts have become covered with a dry and perfect callous.

If you are given very large and old plants, or the bottom has become dry and woody, or the roots injured, then the woody part should be cut off to living tissue and planted only after the wounds are dry.

Treated thus, the plant will produce an abundant supply of new roots in a very short time. Never take the hard trunk of a plant for propagating purposes, but choose the active growing parts in which the cells are full of life.

In potting cacti it is generally supposed that a pot as large as the body of the plant is sufficient. But I prefer to select pots of a rather larger size. During the growing season even cacti must be supplied with water, and when pots are too small this cannot be done effectively.

In the process of potting, fill one-third of the pot with pieces of broken pots, covering the crockery with peat moss or fibrous sod to ensure good drainage, and then the finer soil in which to place your plants or cuttings. Take care to plant a very little way below the surface. Be sure the soil is fairly pourous and will hold water for some time.

If the weather is very warm and bright, a very light syringing of the foliage with tepid water may be given once each day.

It is a mistake to pot a cactus very often unless it has become infested with some pest. Should this occur, the plants must be turned out of the pots, roots thoroughly washed with tepid water, and planted in new pots and new soil. If imperfect drainage is found in any of the pots, this should immediately receive attention.

In the summer, some people turn their plants out of the pots into the open garden. They may do well during the season, but there is always a danger of bruising or injuring in taking them up from the open ground and re-potting. Therefore this practice is unwise.

It will be found a much safer practice to plunge the plants in their pots in the soil. Any warm, well-drained bed, border, or rockery where they may receive sunlight and lots of air may be selected for this.

Cacti may be propagated from seed, or by division of large clumps, or cuttings, or offsets. Propagation, however, is most interesting, instructive, and more permanently successful when done from seed. Plants grown from seed will furnish the grower in two or three years with a fine stock of these most interesting plants.

Raising seedlings is much more effective than importing the plants from their native habitats if one desires to obtain a fine collection of cacti. There would be many more amateur collectors of cacti if persons would start by raising these plants from seed.

A sandy soil should be chosen for the seed bed, and lightly shaded after the plants show the first true leaf. When large enough they should be potted into small pots of porous soil, not too rich and made light by the addition of sand. The cacti plants, especially some kinds, grow rapidly and must be moved into larger pots as their size requires.

Care should be taken to harden off the plants gradually in the house so that they may not be chilled when planted out of doors.

Many cacti are found growing in different parts of Alberta. Many people enjoy them as house plants because they require so little care, and have surprisingly beautiful blooms. What is more beautiful than the Christmas cactus, with its rich, deep pink, drooping blossoms at that season of the year for which it is called?

TREES, SHRUBS AND HEDGES

With our wide-open spaces and vast expanses of prairie, how much we need to cultivate the many lovely shrubs and trees which can be grown so successfully in our region!

How true the words of the poet who said "I think that I shall never see a poem lovely as a tree!"

No home is complete without the introduction of trees and shrubs into lawns and borders, and nothing adds more to the beauty of a home, whether it be in the city or in the country.

But in the beginning, a word of warning to all . . . do not buy trees or shrubs without finding out definitely if they will thrive in our severe and variable climate.

There are many lovely and attractive shrubs and trees which will do well here in Alberta, and those are the kinds to choose. At the end of this section there is a list of all trees and shrubs suitable for our climate, listed in categories, and also graded according to the heights to which they normally grow. Fruit trees are described in the chapter after this.

The last week in April and the first two weeks in May is the best time to plant shrubs and trees. In a late spring, planting can be continued approximately until May 24. In the spring, fresh roots develop quickly, but in the fall the roots are likely to be so inactive in the cold ground that the supply of plant food to the plant may be curtailed, resulting in injury to the shrub or tree.

Choice evergreen trees and evergreen shrubs are more difficult to transplant successfully than deciduous or leaf-losing kinds. Unless precautions are taken, they are liable to perish, particularly if the specimens are large. It is wise to choose small evergreen trees and shrubs, 2 to 3 feet tall, for they may become established more readily than larger ones, unless these have been specially prepared for removal during the previous year.

One of the commonest failures in transplanting shrubs and trees is allowing the roots to become dry while they are out of the ground. If this happens, it is probable that many of the needles or leaves will shrivel and die. It is most important that the roots be kept thoroughly moist, and the soil should be soaked with water as soon as planting is finished.

Care should be taken when planting ornamental trees to avoid a spotty appearance or one lacking in individuality. See that trees do not obstruct the view or cause damage. By this I mean keep them far enough away from the buildings to prevent the roots getting into pipes or cement work, or from blocking out window views, etc. All trees should be planted 6 or 8 inches deeper than they were in the nursery. They should be staked and tied for the first season.

For years farmers in all parts of Alberta have been planting poplars for windbreaks. In irrigated areas or places having a heavy rainfall this is fine, as the poplar is a moisture-loving tree. In dry areas such as our prairies the poplar, although fast growing, soon deteriorates. If planting poplars, the Russian and Northwest are preferable to the other varieties, as they do not produce cotton.

It is my personal opinion that hardwoods such as ash and elm, although slow-growing, make a hardier, drought-resisting and more durable windbreak.

The spruce and birch need more moisture but also make fine windbreaks.

Choke-cherry, caragana and lilac villosa are excellent for hedging boundary lines.

When planting a windbreak see that the trees are well spaced. A distance of 15 to 18 feet should be left between trees. This will give the tree a better chance to grow and develop. Trees, especially in a dry area, will do much better if kept well cultivated. This, of course, applies to trees and shrubs anywhere.

But before discussing some of the more popular trees, here is a brief description of the way to plant trees:

Dig a hole 2 feet deep and 2½ feet wide. Place 6 inches of fibrous loam in the bottom of the hole. Place the tree carefully, spreading the roots, after having cut off broken roots.

When the tree is planted and the hole filled in and firmed down, a depression of 6 inches should be left surrounding the young tree to retain water, which will then make its way to the roots. When such a depression is not left, much of the water given at watering time merely runs off and is lost.

It is also important to place a stake, 2 x 2 inches and about 6 feet high, beside the tree, and fasten the tree securely to it. This gives the new tree the necessary support until its rooting system becomes established.

Let's briefly look at some of the trees which will grow in Calgary.

ASH

The ash is a useful hardwood tree, fairly easy to grow and a good ornament. Its main fault here is that it is slow to leaf in the spring and is one of the first trees to shed its leaves in the fall, and its summer consequently is very brief.

The common ash (fraxinus excelsiori) is possibly the best ash for our climate, and especially for this city. It is a shade-loving tree, the hardiest of all the ash species, and the most popular in Calgary. Normally it grows here to a maximum height of about 30 feet, maybe to 40 feet under exceptional growing conditions.

The tallest ash of the three species I recommend for growing here is the North American white ash (fraxinus americana) and will go up to 80 feet. Advantages are that it grows and then gives lots of shade, generally growing straight. But it will require lots of room.

The third kind for us is the green ash (fraxinus pennsylvanica). This also is a very nice ornamental shade tree, generally a little shorter than the white ash, at between 50 and 60 feet at maturity.

Ashes do well generally in ordinary soil in shade or sun, though they do like moisture.

BIRCH

A top favorite with our citizens is the birch (betula), especially the cut leaf weeping birch, known botanically as betula laciniata alba or betula pendula gracilis.

The birch tree are a family of hardy, leaf-losing trees and shrubs. Various kinds are found wild in Europe, Asia, and North America and are conspicuous by their graceful habit and white, or otherwise attractive, colored bark which peels off in papery flakes. The flowers are small catkins produced during May and are not showy.

As many of the birches grow naturally in cold regions, some being found farther north than any other broad-leaved trees, they are hardy and withstand a considerable amount of exposure. However, a few do sometimes suffer from injury to the young shoots by cold winds or frost in the spring, owing to premature growth or planting.

They succeed in a great variety of soils. Some are especially suited to sandy and peaty soils. The birches do not transplant well as large trees, and should not be transplanted when they are old or over a height of 15 feet.

Two of the most popular birches are pendula youngii and laciniata alba, both of which are weeping birches. The weeping branches of the smaller pendula youngii hang to one side. There are specimens of this birch to be seen in the Reader Rock Garden. During our long, cold winter, the birch are lovely without their leaves. The beautiful, delicate branches and white, clean-looking bark are attractive in themselves.

One of the common silver birches which does well here is the papyrifera or paper birch. It grows to a height of 30 to 40 feet when fully developed. It is conspicuous on account of its white, flaking bark.

In direct contrast is the river birch, (etula nigra) or black birch, which is found growing wild on the river banks and hillsides here. It, too, makes a lovely specimen for your lawn. The bark of the black birch is rough, flakey, and dark reddish brown in color.

For those who may be landscaping new grounds, and find these lovely trees already there, do not dig them up and throw them away. On the outskirts of the city where many new homes are under construction, the black birches are to be found growing, particularly along the banks of our rivers.

The yellow birch, betula lutea, has yellowish bark and it not as hardy as those already mentioned.

There are also some lovely shrubs found in the birch family, some of which are native of this country. These are to be very highly recommended for their extremely dainty leaves and branches. Two of these are betula pumila and betula nana. The pumila grows to a height of 4 to 5 feet. The nana is of low-spreading habit and rarely grows taller than 3 feet. These two shrubs will grow well in a moist, shady place or will likewise thrive in a sunny place.

The oak tree has been called the king of the forest, and the birch tree has sometimes been referred to as the lady of the woods. How very fitting is such a title.

ELM

One of the relatively newer trees for this part of the world, and one which is still being experimented with, is the stately elm. We still don't know too much about how the various kinds of elm will do in Calgary, but so far I think it safe to recommend only three elms for here, and they are the American elm (the best bet), the Chinese elm and the European.

The American elm is the biggest and hardiest and when it takes and matures is a tree of which anyone may be proud.

The smaller European elm can also be grown, and there are many Chinese elms here. This latter is the smallest of the elms, growing to a maximum of about 25 feet here, and it also may be trimmed into a hedge .

These three elms will do well, if properly cared for, in nearly any type of garden soil.

LARCH

There are two species of larch trees, the European and Siberian, which grow well here. They are of a stately, erect habit.

The European larch (larix decidua), is a deciduous tree growing to a height of 50 to 60 feet. It is of very slow growth and most graceful. Even though it is of slow growth, it should, nevertheless be planted where it will not come in contact with wires or a building.

Larix siberica is a native of Siberia and naturally hardy for our climate. This Siberian larch also is to be recommended for this province, and I might mention that the siberica also will grow to a considerable height.

The larches turn a lovely golden color in the fall.

MAPLE

The maples are another beautiful tree, especially in the fall when their leaves turn to bright shades of red which add their own rich splash of coloring to the landscape.

But many of them are difficult to grow.

The Manitoba maple is most attractive and hardy, but it is not recommended for growing in this area because unfortunately it is most susceptible to aphids on account of its sugar content.

This tree, also known as the green-leaved box elder or by its botanical name acer negundo, will grow to a height of 30 to 40 feet, and makes a fine wind break when it is grown successfully.

The Rocky Mountain maple (acer glabrum) will grow well here, as a shrub. It is distinguished by its smooth, bright dark green leaves which are paler on the underside. It can be grown as a tree—up to 25 feet—but is more popular and useful here as a shrub. In this role, it is usually trimmed to a maximum height of 10 to 12 feet.

The amur maple (acer ginnala or acer talaricum), is one of the species which doesn't winter well here, and to grow at all it must be placed in a very sheltered location.

The amur, like the Rocky Mountain maple, grows up to about 25 feet as a tree, but it also is better trimmed to a bush, where its handsome foliage is an added attraction.

MOUNTAIN ASH

I am quite sure that there are many Calgarians who, in the words of the old Scottish song, would say of the rowan tree, "O Rowan Tree, O Rowan Tree—Thou e'er be dear to me!"

129

This old and well-loved tree is botanically known as sorbus and is commonly called the mountain ash rowan tree. It is a native of Europe, and is also native to North America, growing wild as near as Field, B.C.

In its natural habitat, the mountain ash grows in the shade of other and larger trees, and can be grown successfully here if the location in which it is placed is carefully chosen. It must be planted in a shady spot, preferably on the north side of a building, because if placed in a sunny location, it is subject to "sun scald" in the late spring.

For those gardeners who may already have chosen the wrong location for their mountain ash, I would recommend that they wrap burlap around the trunk of the tree. This should be done (maybe in October) after the first hard frost in the fall, and should be left on until the sap begins to flow in the late spring, maybe in April.

The two varieties of mountain ash which will do well here are the sorbus americana and sorbus aucuparia. The latter is the European species, and about the only difference between the two is that the americana has larger leaves and bigger berries than the other and is also a little hardier.

They grow to a height of 25 to 30 feet, and are covered with creamy white blossoms about the month of June.

During a favorable year, when the blooms escape frost, this lovely tree is later clustered with rich orange-colored berries. These berries, which are called rowans, remain on the tree until the cedar waxwings bear down on them during the winter.

POPLAR

The populus or poplar is a tree well-known to Albertans. There are about 10 varieties or more grown in our city and province. They are deciduous, soft-wooded trees, and of medium height. It is perhaps not so well-known that they belong to the willow family. This is why they give so much trouble in blocking our sewers. They are moisture-loving, and send their roots deeply into the earth in search of that moisture.

Poplars are among the easiest of all trees to grow. They grow readily from cuttings of ripened wood from the current year's growth. They thrive in almost any soil, although the cottonwood is most at home in lowlands and along streams or river banks. For shelter belts they are most useful, because of their rapid growth and great hardiness.

Here on the prairies the populus certinensis, commonly known as the Russian poplar, is the most stately and among the hardiest.

People generally plant too many poplars, especially around public places. It is better to use them for temporary shelter-belt effects, allowing better but slower-growing trees that are planted with them to take their place gradually, a few poplars of the best varieties being allowed to remain.

As a rule, poplar are less adapted to isolated planting as specimen trees than to use as parts of general groups.

Poplars are really gay trees, especially the ones similar to the aspens which have a trembling foliage. Their trunks and leaves are bright and attractive.

The common aspen is really a poplar, and because of its trembling foliage is botanically known as the populus tremulioides. Its light-dancing foliage and silver grey trunk and limbs are always cheering, and its autumn color is one of the purest golden yellow of our landscape. To have a common aspen tree standing in front of a group of evergreens is effective.

Of all the poplars, the Northwest is probably the best as a single specimen. It is a noble tree, spreading its grey branches far and wide.

But I am afraid that in spite of their beauty and gay appearance, there are some poplars growing in Calgary which are not so popular. This is on account of the cotton shed by these cottonwoods, and in which the seed is contained. This elusive bit of fluff looks quite pretty and attractive hanging on the tree, but when it is blown earthwards into the nostrils and homes of our citizens, it becomes a real nuisance.

Some of the silver or white-leaved poplars produce the most striking contrasts of foliage, especially if set near darker trees such as evergreens. Bolles poplar, or populus bolleana, is one of the best of these. Its habit is something like that of the Lombardy (which we cannot grow satisfactorily in Calgary). The upper surface of the leaves of the populus bolleana is a dark dull green, while the under surface is almost snowy white. They are of slower growth than many poplars and make a most attractive and shady tree for home grounds.

Among the varieties which shed cotton, so that readers may be forewarned are the balm of Gilead (populus balsamifera and populus wobbstii). These are the chief offenders around Calgary. The Russian, Northwest and birch poplars are among the few which do not bear cotton.

Another thing which makes poplars unpopular is their tendency to work into sewer pipes. The small thread-like roots enter the pipes and then grow and expand rapidly, blocking and sometimes bursting the pipes.

Poplars can be beautifully shaped if they are pruned symmetrically and carefully.

Despite the faults of some of them, they are still to be highly recommended for parks, large areas and locations removed from sewers and overhead wiring.

WILLOW

Here in Alberta, many kinds of willows may be grown successfully and are rather beautiful both in foliage and their deciduous form during the winter. Take, for instance, the golden willow (salix vitellina), with its lovely bark, the osier willow (salix viminalis), with its light green wood. These are most attractive during the winter.

Also most lovely is the pussy willow, known as salix discolor, with its gray-green foliage during the growing season, its catkins in early spring, and its green and red wood during the winter.

The willow is considerably used as a nurse tree for slower-growing trees that require part shade while young.

The red, green, yellow branches are bright and cheering in winter and especially when the snow is on the ground. The weeping forms are popular where they do grow. Unfortunately, the weeping willow known as salix babylonica will not grow satisfactorily here in Alberta.

The willow family has been used effectively to hold stream banks against erosion. The root system is extensive and when well established, withstands the effect of heavy rapid streams as well as wave action. All species of willows are readily propagated by cuttings.

Salix pentandra, known as the laurel leaf willow, is a shrub or small tree which grows to a height of 8 to 20 feet with shining dark green leaves above and paler beneath. The laurel leaf willow will make a fast-growing hedge or a specimen tree on the lawn, and is most attractive all year'round.

The pussy willow is a shrub or short-trunked tree 10 to 20 feet tall. The buds are large and nearly black, the leaves smooth and bright green above and whitish beneath. It produces its lovely catkins before any leaves appear in the spring.

Salix viminalis, or osier willow, a shrub or small tree, grows 10 to 20 feet high, with slender and upright branches. This shrub is used for making basket material for production of which the plants are cut near the ground each year. This graceful shrub grows here in Alberta, and grows best when headed hard back at pruning time in the spring (about March).

The golden willow becomes a large and venerable tree, and the rather short trunk is often 2 feet or more in diameter. It is often headed back, producing rich, golden branches, most colorful during the winter.

Salix humilus or the prairie willow, a shrub 3 to 8 feet high, varies much in stature and size and shape. It will grow in the driest location and makes a nice hedge.

Salix caprea or goat willow is a small tree, 15 to 20 feet high, with upright branches and fairly large leaves 2 to 5 inches long and 1 to 3 inches wide. It makes an attractive specimen in the garden.

Salix sericea or silky willow is a dwarf shrub, usually 4 to 8 feet tall, diffusely spreading from the base of the branches, often reddish leaves, silky beneath; hence the name silky willow. It is densely flowered, followed by the leaves, the stamens often orange red and very showy in the spring of the year.

Salix arctica or arctic willow, among the few woody plants extending into the extreme arctic regions, is among the most diminutive of woody willow plants. Some of these species grow only 6 inches tall with very tiny and rather leathery leaves. At one time, salix arctica grew in the Reader Rock Garden and it certainly did make an attractive shrub for this type of gardening.

With the exception of the weeping willow, most of the willows are hardy here in Alberta, and are to be recommended for fast growing as well as for hedge-making and as specimens on the lawn or in the border.

The only thing you will have to lookout for is to plant willows too near water pipes or sewer pipes or where they may get entangled in electric light wires.

The willow is a clean tree and shrub, and not subject to many diseases. However, sometimes they do get infested with greenfly.

Willows will grow in any type of soil provided that they get sufficient moisture during the growing season.

Evergreens

PINE

The evergreen firs which can be grown here, and do well, are a relatively small group of pines and spruce.

In the pine family there are four species which I can recommend: the Austrian, Scotch, mugho and jack pines.

The pinus sylvestris, the well-known Scotch fir, grows successfully here, reaching great heights (for local trees) of 70 feet. It has grey-green, pointed leaves which have flat upper surfaces.

All the pines seem to thrive in almost any type of soil, including gravelly soil.

The mugho (botanically known as the pinus mughus mugho) is a compact, dwarflike species, grows slowly and reaches a height of about 8 to 10 feet.

132

It has long and rich dark green needles; and would be effective on each side of a garden path, or on a terraced lawn.

The Austrian pine is a comparative newcomer to Western Canada. It grows up to 25 feet, and has long green needles.

The jack pine also grows well in gravelly soil. It is of erect habit with very long needles; and also makes a fine specimen for a lawn.

SPRUCE

A striking and noble tree—called by some the queen of the evergreens—is the blue spruce. It is hardy wherever it is tested. Strong, sturdy and upright in growth, its form alone would make it an impressive tree on any grounds, and it seems to thrive in all varieties of soil.

Its lovely colors vary from a silvery blue in some specimens to a darker blue or almost purple in others.

It grows usually to a height of between 50 and 60 feet, but under exceptionally favorable circumstances it may go up to 70 feet, and it is well to remember this when planting a new tree.

It must be kept away from walls and shrub borders, or from any place where it would obstruct the view.

There are really two types of blue spruce—one is called the blue spruce (sometimes the Colorado spruce) and this is the picea pungens. The second is the Koster blue spruce (botanically, picea pungens kosteriana).

The first type, the blue spruce, is grown from seed; and the second type, Koster spruce, is a grafted variety in which the needles are bluer.

Actually, the Koster blue spruce is my favorite spruce.

The Canadian spruce (picea canadenis) is one of our own evergreens, and can be highly recommended for a windbreak.

The black spruce has very dark green leaves, but this tree, though it can be grown here, attains better growth in the East rather than the West.

The white spruce, a native of North America, grows very straight and lives to a great age.

The Black Hills spruce, best known surrounding the Idaho mountains it is named for, also grows here, and is notable for being able to withstand extreme drought conditions.

Spruces are some of the finest trees for windbreaks. Although they are of slow growth, they are worth waiting for.

Shrubs

Shrubs and plants have two values: (1) a real value as individual or isolated specimens, (2) a value as part of the structure or design of an ornamental place. As individual specimens, they are grown for the beauty of the species itself; as part of the landscape they are often grown in masses constituting a shrubbery.

Many shrubs may also be used as hedges, and their use as such is further described in the section which follows on hedges.

It is often advisable to plant shrubs as single specimens in order to produce the characteristic beauty of the species. But plants scattered indiscriminately over a lawn, destroy all appearance of unity and purpose in the place. The place has no meaning or individuality, the plants are in the way and they spoil the lawn.

However, an ordered mass of planting emphasizes particular parts of the area. It can give the place a feeling of strength and character. The shrubbery border usually should have an irregular outline and generally contain several different species. In this way, variety and interest are increased. The shrubbery border should be placed on the boundaries.

It is a fundamental concept of landscape gardening that the centre of the place shall be kept open. The boundaries are the lines between properties, foundations of buildings, borders between walks and drives.

Individual specimens may be used freely, but only rarely should they be wholly isolated or scattered. They should be planted somewhere near the borders so that they may not interfere with the continuity of the place, and also have a background to set them off.

The background may be a building, bank, fence or a mass of foliage. In most places, the border planting should be the rule and the isolated specimens the exception. It is not to be understood, however, that boundaries are always to be planted or that foundations are always to be covered.

The line between trees and shrubs is not definite. A shrub generally has a number of stems springing from the ground, and a tree usually has a single trunk, but this is not uniformly true in either case.

The chief value of shrubbery comes from its use in an artistic way, although some shrubs have edible fruit.

Included among some of the best early shrubs are the daphne, spirea, the wild gooseberry, the forsythia (or golden bells), choke-cherry and saskatoon, which produce leaves early in May, to be followed by a profusion of blossoms later that month.

Many shrubs, like some of the viburnums and dogwoods, grow to a height of 8 to 10 feet, while others like the daphne (cneorum) grow to a height of only a few inches, and are more suitable for rock gardening.

Daphne tangutica and daphne mezereum grow to a height of from 2 to 4 feet and they are most fragrant.

Many deciduous shrubs are well worth planting even if it be only for the ornamental fruits they bear, like the honeysuckle, cotoneaster, and cherries. Some of these fruits are so richly colored and so abundant that they can be seen for a long distance. They remain on the shrubs well into the winter until the waxwings and other hungry birds gradually eat the berries.

Throughout the season, the foliage of a goodly collection of shrubbery will present the greatest variety of color, including the many different shades of green as well as yellow, red, gold, white, silver, gray and purple.

Even in winter, shrubbery is wonderfully attractive in appearance— from the gracefulness of its stem and branches to the color of its bark. With the right selection it will serve almost as well as evergreens to shut out from view any unsightly objects.

The great variety in foliage, flower, fruit and habit of growth makes shrubbery adapted to extended use in the development of landscapes. Shrubbery is especially appropriate on steep slopes and in the immediate vicinity of buildings where foliage and graceful lines are needed to connect the wall of a structure with the ground.

Shrubbery could be called a charitable thing in that it often covers a multitude of sins. It might replace the grass with advantage upon all surfaces too steep to walk upon with comfort.

In planting borders or groups of shrubs, the ground to be occupied should be deeply spaded over, and manure dug into the soil. The bushes should then be planted far enough apart to allow for full development of the shrubs. Many people plant their trees and shrubs too closely. If placed closer they would have a crowded appearance, but if placed too far apart the effect is also bad.

Generally, the effect should be that of a continuous mass of varying foliage.

In the placement of shrubs one should avoid too uniform a slope. Usually the taller shrubs are placed at the back with the odd one brought forward, then the intermediate with the lower species along the front of the border.

The arrangement should be varied so as to avoid monotony. Straight rows should be avoided wherever possible. The ideal condition of a group of shrubbery is to have all the individual plants healthy so that the foliage will appear fresh and of good color. The value of shrubbery is perhaps not fully appreciated. It could, if more wisely used, transform our city.

In planning a shrub border, it is well to keep in mind the size of your shrub and its coloring. For example, the yellow dogwood, the many varieties of red dogwood, the golden willow and the green laurel-leaved willow are beautiful both summer and winter.

The lovely foliage and berries of the dogwood and the glossy leaves of the laurel present a pleasing picture in summer, while the vivid coloring in their wood is effective throughout the winter. These shrubs all do well in a shaded location. The laurel willows grow fairly tall and should be placed towards the back of the border. The dogwoods are not as tall and do nicely in a central location.

Another shade lover is the Ural false-spirea (spirea sorbifolia). This shrub produces a white flower but is noted mainly for its beautiful foliage. It grows about 3 feet high and should be placed to the front of the border. It should be kept in bounds, as it has a strong tendency to sucker.

The red and black berried cotoneaster can be grown well in either shade or sunny locations. The berries remain on these shrubs all winter, making them attractive then as well as in summer.

There are many shrubs that do well in a sunny border. I would like to mention a few of these. The red-berried elder (sambucus) with its palmate leaves is a rapid-growing shrub which will hide any unsightly corner in the garden. When fully developed, it is about 7 or 8 feet in height.

The sweet-smelling mock orange, the tamarix, the flowering almond, and several varieties of spirea will provide a pleasing foreground for a border. These shrubs will thrive in light, rich soil.

The bush honeysuckle (lonicera tartarica), of which there is a white variety, is one of the best types of honeysuckle to plant in a shrub border. Along with the Nanking cherry it will fill the central or back portion of the border.

Euonymus alatus or burning bush is another shrub which may be recommended. It is not commonly grown here, but should be well known to nurserymen. The common name burning bush is derived from the color of the leaves in fall, and particularly because of the bright brick-like red of its berries.

The height to which this shrub grows is 4 to 5 feet, and the blossoms are a pale yellow and not showy.

Owing to the square shape of the branches, this bush is sometimes known as spindle bush.

There is a dwarf rock garden variety of the euonymus known as nana which is really a creeper, and is particularly suited for the rock garden because of this trailing habit.

CARAGANA

Many people believe the caragana bushes are all commonplace because of the common variety caragana arborescens, so widely used for hedges and other purposes. But this shrub, like most of the ordinary, well-known plants, has its fancy varieties too. I will name, and can recommend highly, some of these.

There is the caragana frutescens and the lovely little pygmy caragana. Also highly recommended are the caragana chamlagii and the fern leaf caragana, lorbergii.

The lorbergii is the loveliest of the caragana family, tropical in appearance and deserves a prominent place on your lawn or border. Its branches are so fine, and the foliage so lacy, that the branches fall gracefully down in a semi-weeping habit, although it is not a "weeping" caragana. It grows to a height of 8 to 10 feet.

The chamlagii has rich, dark green leaves, and the blossoms are two-toned, bronze and yellow. This colorful shrub grows to a height of 4 to 6 feet.

The frutescens has pale green leaves and produces an abundance of rich yellow blossoms. Contrary to the habit of the lorbergii, the frutescens grows erect and compactly and to a height of about 4 feet. It is striking when used in a border, especially when in bloom.

The pygmy as the name denotes is a dwarf and has fine wood, tiny leaves, and like the chamlagii has two-toned blossoms. It grows to a height of about 3 to 4 feet, and should be placed towards the front of a shrub border.

This pretty little caragana makes a perfect hedge which can also be kept to a height of 1 foot or 3 feet. For a hedge, pygmy should be planted about 1 foot apart.

There are more or less 20 species of caraganas. The shrub is a native of Russia and China. Its Mongolian name is leguminosoe, meaning pea tree, a name derived from its pea-like pods and blossoms.

COTONEASTER

In the cotoneaster group there are only a few which are suitable for our climate, namely cotoneaster acutifolia, cotoneaster integerrima, multiflora and horizontalis.

The acutifolia is splendid for hedging or for planting in the shrub border and its foliage turns many lovely shades of red, yellow and bronze in the fall. This, along with its black berries, makes it a most desirable shrub or hedge.

The integerrima is also showy in the fall, with red berries which remain on the bush well on into winter.

The acutifolia and integerrima both grow to a height of 3 feet.

Horizontalis is a low shrub, gaining its name from the fact that its branches grow almost horizontally. It is most suitable for planting in a rock garden.

The name cotoneaster comes from the Greek kotoneon, quince and aster.

No shrubs are more easily cultivated than the cotoneasters. They thrive in almost any kind of soil including poor, dry ground, although this, of course,

136

should be dug deeply and manured previous to planting. However, they do dislike a too shady or too moist a location.

Cotoneaster vary from a few inches to several feet in height and their uses in the garden are many and varied.

BUCKTHORN

The hippophae, known as the sea buckthorn, is a colorful shrub which does well here. It is most decorative during the autumn and winter, because of its bright orange berries, thick clusters of which remain on the bush long into the winter.

The sea buckthorn requires a light, sandy, and rich soil, and can be placed on steep banks. When buying the shrub, it is advisable to have three or four of them, as both the male and female species must be present for pollinating purposes, and must be grouped together. They grow to a height of 5 or 6 feet, and the best species to buy is hippophae rhamnoides.

DOGWOOD

Another very popular shrub which does well in shady places is the dogwood, also known as cornus. It is a hardy, ornamental shrub with handsome foliage. It is brightly colored at all times, but assumes a more brilliant color in the fall and winter. Seen against a background of snow, it presents a warm and pleasing picture.

Among the better species are cornus serecea, which grows from 3 to 4 feet tall, cornus baileyii and cornus stonifera, all red-wooded with white berries.

A yellow-wooded dogwood is cornus flaviramea, which grows to 5 or 6 feet.

ELDER

The golden elder is another shrub which I recommend. It grows from 3 to 4 feet high, and the beauty of this shrub lies in its yellow foliage.

The sambucus aurea must be planted in a hot, sunny location. If it is planted in a spot which is too shady, the leaves will turn green instead of the rich golden yellow which gives this lovely shrub its name.

The elder must be treated in autumn like a perennial. By this I mean that you must cut back the wood to within 2 inches of the ground, to ensure a new, strong, vigorous growth next spring.

HAWTHORN

The hawthorn grows in almost any soil and position, but are best in rich loamy, somewhat moist soil, and also in heavy clay. The flowering hawthorn belongs to the family crataegus and is the true English may day tree. The tree which is commonly called the may day tree in Alberta is the improved chokecherry. It has been called the may day tree here because it customarily blooms around May 24.

North America has furnished our gardens with a wealth of beautiful hawthorn shrubs which are particularly attractive in spring with beautiful blossoms, and in autumn with highly-colored fruits and autumn-tinted leaves. About 90 species are found in Europe, Asia Minor, China, Japan and Himalayas and some 800 in America, though evidence points to a considerable number of the latter being natural hybrids.

The name crataegus is from kratos (strength) in allusion to the strength and hardness of the wood. The hawthorn belongs to the rose family rosacea.

The hawthorn which is best for our climate is the Alberta native crataegus crusgalli, the cockspur thorn with large thorns and brilliant red foliage in the fall. If allowed to grow in tree form, it will bear rich scarlet fruits which would remain on the shrub throughout the winter, and will attain a height of 10 to 15 feet.

The crusgalli derives its common name from the position of the thorn which grows in the form of spurs on a rooster's legs. It produces an abundance of small scalloped leaves and large white blossoms followed by red berries which remain on the shrub throughout the winter.

HONEYSUCKLE

A hardy shrub is the Tartarian honeysuckle, known also as lonicera tartarica. There are pink, white, and red varieties of this shrub which, after the flowers fade, bear crops of red and yellow berries. These remain on the bush all through the fall and part of the winter.

Honeysuckle will grow in any well-tilled soil, and can be planted in either the sun or shade, and grow to approximately 8 or 10 feet high.

LILAC

Lilacs never seem to lose their popularity and appeal, and here are a few of the choice varieties of French grafted lilac:

Edith Cavell (double white), General Pershing (double deep purple), Charles Joly (double dark purple red), Marechal Foch (carmine rose), Charles X (deep red), Madame Lemoine (double creamy white), Marie Finon (single white), Marechal Lannes (violet), President Lincoln (blue), Lucie Ballet (pink), Ludwig Spaeth (purple).

These lilacs all grow to about 6 to 8 feet in height and require a sunny spot in the garden.

For those of you who feel that you cannot afford the expensive and choice varieties just named, two of the common and less costly kinds are lilac vulgaris in white and purple single, and the villosa in pale mauve, a single. It should be remembered, however, that the vulgaris bushes are a bit of a nuisance because they produce lots of suckers.

The villosa, although not so rich in color, is particularly sweet smelling.

Lilacs should be placed well back in the border. When planting roots, pace them 6 to 8 feet apart. At the time of planting, this may appear too far apart. When, however, the shrubs are fully developed, they will just be touching.

Correct spacing of shrubs is important, as it will produce finer specimens. Trees and shrubs, being live things, do not thrive in overcrowded conditions any more than human beings do.

The fragrance of most of the varieties is sweet, although some species have little perfume at all. Lilacs are showy in bloom, especially when massed in groups. Do not mix too many kinds which differ in habit and blooming season, as this spoils the effect.

Lilacs grow in any good garden soil, although they do better if a handful of lime is cultivated into the soil around each bush.

DAPHNE

The rose daphne (daphne cneorum) is a dwarf shrub suitable for the front or a narrow shrub or perennial border or even more suited to a rock garden. It grows 6 to 8 inches only and has tiny, narrow leaves and sweet-smelling flowers, and may be obtained with pink or white blossoms.

Another among the several types in the daphne family, is daphne tangutica. This Chinese daphne grows to about a foot tall, bears white blossoms and red berries. It, too, is suitable for the border or rock garden.

English daphne (mezereum) is a native of England where it is to be found in its wild state. It was introduced in Calgary years ago by the late parks superintendent, W. R. Reader. This plant is the taller variety, growing up to a height of three feet and bearing little rosettes of mauve-pinkish flowers which appear before the leaves and along the branches. Daphne mezereum blooms early in the season and is to be highly recommended, as are all the daphne family.

MOCK ORANGE

Another lovely shrub is our own native mock orange, which has been found growing wild around the Waterton Lakes district in southern Alberta. This shrub enhances the appearance of any garden, because of its large white flowers and striking yellow stamens. It has also a perfume faintly suggestive of that of the orange blossom.

Out of the 30 or more varieties of philadelphus or mock orange which are grown in different countries of the world, only one variety will grow successfully here. It is philadelphus lewisii watertonii, the later name indicating the fact that it was discovered growing wild at Waterton Lakes. This, of course, ensures us that it is a hardy variety.

This native Albertan grows 2½ feet to 3 feet tall, and it will do well in either a sunny spot or in part shade.

PRICKLY SPINE

The prickly spine, or acanthopanax senticosus, derives its name from the fact that it bears thorns similar to a rose bush. The beauty of this shrub lies in its palmate-shaped, large and almost tropical leaves. The flower is rather insignificant. The shrub grows to about 4 feet.

PRUNUS (Plum, Cherry and Almond)

The double-flowering plum, botanically called prunus triloba, is another shrub that shows to best advantage when planted as a lawn shrub. It is interesting to note that the large double pink flowers appear before the leaves. When fully developed, it is only about 6 feet high, so you can afford to have two or three of these around your home. It's my favorite among the flowering fruit trees.

The prunus pennsylvanica, known commonly as the pin cherry or wild bird cherry tree, grows to a height of 20 to 25 feet. It is also most decorative for a lawn or border. It is usually covered with clusters of little white flowers, followed by masses of tiny red cherries in the autumn.

Prunus padus, or the improved choke-cherry, is another lovely tree belonging to this family. It also grows to a height of 20 to 25 feet, and when developed, provides fine shade on a lawn. It can also be kept down to shrub size if you wish to plant it in a shrub border. To grow it as a shrub you must allow several branches to come up from the base.

The prunus padus is, also, sometimes in the West, called the may day tree, because it blooms approximately at that time of year. The tree originally known as the may day tree is the English hawthorn, botanically known as crataegus.

Three other shrubs which belong to this large and exciting family group of prunus are: prunus tomentosa, prunus besseyii and prunus amygdalus nana.

The tomentosa grows to a height of 5 to 6 feet, and is of an erect habit. It blossoms with pink, single flowers in the spring, and in the fall produces quite large, red berries. These are sweet and edible. This shrub should be planted in a sunny spot in the border. The common name of the tomentosa is Nanking cherry, and as the name Nanking implies it is a native of China.

Prunus besseyii, or the western sand cherry, is a dwarf shrub growing to a height of only 3 feet, and having a spreading habit. The blossoms on the besseyii are white, and it yields an abundant crop of edible dark-colored cherries when the season is favorable. This exquisite little shrub is suitable for the front of a shrub border, and it, too, should be planted in a sunny location.

The amygdalus nana, which is commonly known as the Russian almond, is also of a dwarf nature. It grows to a height of only 2 feet, and bears single, pink flowers, which come out before the leaves. This early-spring shrub is an offender in that it producers suckers, but if these are kept under control, it is still a worthwhile shrub, requiring a sunny location in the front of a border.

SIBERIAN SALT BUSH

The halimodendron or salt bush is a native of Siberia, and is a very hardy, deciduous shrub.

It grows to a height of from 6 to 8 feet, and with its silvery leaves and delicate mauve blossoms it presents a charming picture indeed against a green lawn.

It is not as well-known as some other shrubs, perhaps, and when purchasing ask for halimodendron argenteum.

SPIREA

This is one of the loveliest little shrubs I know. The word spirea is a Greek one, the name of a plant used for making wreaths.

It is an ornamental, deciduous shrub with rather small leaves, and small white, pink or almost crimson flowers. It grows to 2 or 3 feet in height and is outstanding arranged in groups of four or five. It is well adapted for borders of a shrubbery or as single specimens on the lawn or in the rockery.

Some of the best varieties are Van Houtii and Arguta, both of which are pure white, Spiraea Trichocarpa, also white but which grows a bit taller than the others, and Anthony Waterer, which is somewhat smaller than any of these three (about 2 feet) and is a deep red.

Some spirea will bloom in June, others in July, and some until well on in August.

To keep spirea in good condition, the branches that produced the blossoms should be removed immediately after flowering so young wood can take their place in preparation for the following year.

TAMARISK

The tamarisk, commonly known as tamarix, grows to a height of 6 to 8 feet, and should be planted in a hot, sunny spot, where the soil is light and sandy. If your soil is too heavy, introduce quantities of sand around the base.

This shrub produces lovely purplish, pink flowers, with light feathery foliage. It has a charmingly graceful appearance, and should help to enhance any garden.

There are two varieties which I will recommend to you, namely pentandra and purpurea, both of which have been grown successfully here for many years.

Hedges

A well-grown hedge is a great asset to a garden and, providing a suitable kind of shrub has been chosen, it is preferable to a board or wire fence, and definitely more decorative.

Unfortunately the common caragana arborescens (the variety most commonly grown here) although a lovely shrub in itself, can be produced so quickly and cheaply that it is planted too often and becomes monotonous. It is also planted to the exclusion of more interesting and decorative caraganas, such as pygmy caragana. The pygmy caragana normally grows to a height of 3 to 4 feet and forms a more attractive hedge. For a hedge, caragana pygmy should be planted about a foot apart. It can be clipped to a smaller hedge height of from 1 to 3 feet.

Hedges provide protection, shelter, and also a boundary.

One of the most protective (and attractive) hedges which we can plant is the hawthorn, because of its long and sharp thorns. It is said that dogs or cats will not go through a hawthorn hedge. This is believable when you test the sharpness of the long thorns.

However, the shrub I personally prefer for hedging is the cotoneaster acutifolia, or the black-berried Peking cotoneaster.

This in my opinion is the most colorful hedge for Calgary. It is one of the easiest to grow, makes an effective hedge, and in fall its reds, golds and greens and its black berries contribute eye-catching splashes of color which make our gardens a delight.

Dig a trench early in April about 18 inches deep and about 18 inches wide, put in manure, and plant your Peking cotoneaster roots about 15 to 18 inches apart. Water immediately after planting, and let the water soak the soil firmly around the roots. It is a good idea, too, to mulch the soil.

Also after planting it is advisable to cut down the plants to a uniform height of from 6 to 12 inches above the ground.

Clip the cotoneasters back in the early summer (toward the end of June) to give them a chance to branch out and grow stems and foliage close to the ground.

The acutifolia grows to a height of almost 3 feet.

The slow-growing spruces always make a handsome hedge. They are, of course, evergreens of considerable importance from a decorative and intrinsic point of view. They are widely distributed in temperate countries in the Northern Hemisphere, being found as far north as any trees and in alpine altitudes.

They can be kept down to 2 or 3 feet for hedge work or allowed to grow to 8 or 10 feet for the same purpose.

Prunus virginiana, a choke-cherry, makes a fine hedge and is certainly something different. It may be found growing wild along the banks of the Bow, the Elbow and in the foothills. This choke-cherry bears a lovely white blossom.

Another hedge which is not as much seen is the Japanese lilac (syringa villosa). This shrub makes a thick and fast-growing hedge. The word syringa is sometimes used as a common name for the mock orange (or philadelphus), but its correct use is as the botanical name for lilac.

You can allow the lilac villosa to grow to a height of 3 feet or 15 feet in your hedge. When allowed to grow naturally, these shrubs may reach a height of 20 feet or more. They can be grown successfully from seeds which have been allowed to ripen fully. Sow the seeds in the garden in the fall, just before freeze-up, about the end of September, at a depth of 2 to 3 inches.

The lonicera tartarica honeysuckle also makes an attractive hedge. It may be raised from seeds or propagated by cuttings, and bears pink and white flowers.

Ural false-spirea (spiraea sorbifolia) is likewise a shrub which makes a pretty hedge. It grows to a height of 2½ to 3 feet and will do well in a shady location as well as in the sun.

When planting any hedge make a trench from 12 to 18 inches deep and up to 2 feet wide, depending on the species. These measurements should be about the minimum required for any shrub or hedge plant.

Ornamental Berries

Many kinds of trees and shrubs are worth growing for the sake of their brightly colored fruits during the winter, apart from any other ornamental characteristics they may possess. Not all the fruits borne by the following trees and shrubs are true berries, but for the sake of convenient reference, these types are grouped together .

Two kinds of cotoneaster which do well here are known as cotoneaster acutifolia and cotoneaster interregima. The acutifolia turns beautiful in the fall with its varied-colored leaves and large dark berries which remain on the bush all winter. The cotoneaster interregima is usually loaded with bright red berries in the fall and is most attractive against the snow.

The fruits of many of the shrub rose family are particularly showy during the winter.

The rose rugosa, which has large red hips or fruits more than an inch in diameter and glossy red color, can be used for making jelly. Another rose with large fruits is rose altaica which is whitish yellow and single flowered when it is in bloom. It has large chocolate-colored hips and is of an unusual color.

Rose rubrifolia, with its tiny red clusters of bloom and red foliage during the growing season, is another showy members of the rose family. Its clusters of red fruits are about half an inch in diameter.

The hawthorn known as crataegus oxyacantha has dark brownish red berries, while crataegus crusgalli, a native to Alberta, has dark red berries.

The mountain ash is well-known for its large clusters of coral red fruits, but there is a variety of the common mountain ash with yellow fruits. The American mountain ash is also an attractive tree with bright red fruit.

The crabapple trees, especially the ornamental kinds which have red leaves and flowers during the summer and red fruits during the fall and winter, are most attractive. The fruits stay on the tree during most of the winter until the grosbeaks come in flocks and clean up the tree in a few minutes.

Very lovely, too, are the barberry (berberis), but is must be remembered that the common barberry (berberis vulgaris) is illegal in Alberta. Its pollen is a rust-carrier; and dangerous to our grain fields. It is therefore banned in this province.

Among the species which may be grown, however, are three very beautiful berry bushes, the purple leaf barberry (berberis thunbergii), Japanese barberry and poirets barberry (berberis poiretii).

The dwarf shrub Oregon grape (mahonia aquifolia) has deep purple fruits, with foliage resembling the holly, only dull in color.

The burning bush or spindle bush known as euonymus alatus is another attractive shrub by reason of the highly colored fruits which split open and disclose brightly colored seeds within. The outer part of the fruit is in most cases of a reddish brick hue, the seed being orange .

The sea buckthorn, known botanically as hippophae rhamnoides, which bear orange-colored berries, are most attractive all winter long if planted in groups in a hot sunny place in the garden.

The bush honeysuckle (or lonicera tartarica) has handsome fruits, scarlet and translucent berries. One variety of the honeysuckle bears rich yellow berries which stay on the bush pretty well all winter.

The snow berry, symphoricarpus, bears round white fruits.

Virburnus, or highbush cranberry, produce showy berries, all of which have red fruits.

FRUIT TREES AND BUSHES

APPLE TREES

There are very definite limits in Calgary, as well as in most parts of Alberta, to the growing of fruits from trees as well as bushes, but particularly from trees.

Very few apple trees can be grown here, and no edible pear or plum, peach, or apricot trees.

I myself have not experimented in growing apple trees, so I cannot give you too much information about them from my own first-hand knowledge. Generally speaking, I think we shall need a change of climate before we can produce edible apples from any number of varieties.

Among the few apple trees which have been grown successfully are the varieties Heyers No. 9, No. 12 and No. 20.

The variety Transcendent can be grown here, also, and it will yield a good crop of fruit.

Also the varieties Haralson, Battleford and Allgood have been grown successfully in Calgary.

All apple trees need to be planted in April in a sunny, sheltered location. Special care should be taken in planting them. The hole should be 2 feet deep and 3 feet wide. In the bottom, place a flat stone, large enough to cover all of it.

This flat stone stops the tap-root from growing down into the sub-soil, causing the roots to grow horizontally in the good soil.

When the tap-root is allowed to grow too far down in the subsoil, it retains excessive moisture, causing the tree to become woody.

All trees should of course be staked immediately after planting.

For winter care, strawy litter should be piled around the base of the tree.

CRAB-APPLE TREES

There are a great many lovely crab-apple trees growing in this city and province. Their popularity, no doubt, is because of their beauty in the spring when they are laden with white, red and pink blossoms.

Again, in autumn, they are almost as colorful with clusters of richly painted fruits.

And the delightful jelly which may be made from crab-apples is undoubtedly another reason why they are becoming increasingly popular.

There are an increasing number of hardy crab-apple trees suitable for our climate, but a gardener should still carefully check when he buys a new tree to make sure it will withstand our weather.

Some of the best crab-apple trees for this part of the country are the Dolgo, Bechtel's, Osman's, Siberian, Wealthy and the Hopa.

All of these are extremely hardy and are suitable for our Calgary climate.

The crab-apple tree should be given lots of room when planted. In April, dig a hole 2 feet deep and 3 feet wide for the new tree.

Crabs should also be planted in a sunny location, and it is necessary to pick a sheltered spot, especially from winds.

All crab-apple trees should be carefully mulched for winter protection.

Fruit Bushes

GOOSEBERRIES

The gooseberry is a hardy fruit which, grown wild in the British Isles or cultivated in Alberta, has a delicious tart fruit. It also grows wild in some parts of Alberta, but then the fruit generally is so small it is barely worth picking.

But it can be cultivated with moderate success here. There are, however, only about two varieties which succeed in this part of the country.

I recommend Whitesmith and Pixwell. They are easy to grow in almost any type of soil, but they must be in a sheltered location.

STRAWBERRIES

Appetites, both large and small, are whetted when the delectable combination of "strawberries and cream" is mentioned. The strawberry, which is a herbaceous perennial, has been growing wild on the prairie regions of North America probably for centuries. With cultivation, and the accompanying conservation of moisture, the plant has now reached a standard unattainable in its wild or natural state.

The strawberry propagates by means of runners that form chiefly after the blooming season. Plants, started from the runners, either transplanted or allowed to remain where they form, will bear fruit the following year.

Usually the plants will continue to produce for four or five years, but the second and third crops are generally the best. It is therefore the custom to dig up strawberry beds after they have produced from three to four crops.

The better the soil and the more intensive the cultivation, the shorter the rotation should be. The strawberry delights in a rich, rather moist soil with good drainage, and a fairly sunny location.

The young plants may be separated from the parent plant, and placed in a new location in the garden in August. But if the weather is hot and dry, I suggest the young plants be left in the old bed until the following spring, when they can be planted (in April) with good results.

Plants that have not borne fruit are the best for transplanting. They are plants of the current year's growth, i.e., plants which start in the spring of 1961, will be suitable for planting in the late summer of 1961, or in the spring of 1962. The young plants have many long fresh light-colored roots. Pots are sometimes plunged under the new runners during June and July, and they become filled with roots by August or September. These pot-grown plants are excellent for August planting in the garden, but this method is seldom employed in extensive commercial practice as it entails too much labor and expense.

For best results plants are generally set in rows 2 feet apart and 15 inches between the plants. All flowers and runners are removed the first season in order to allow the young plant to build themselves up for the production of better fruit in following years.

Strawberries are usually mulched in the fall in order to protect them during the winter and early spring, and to prevent the soil from heaving. In some cases the mulch is allowed to remain on the plants rather late in the spring (maybe until early May) to retard the season of bloom. Sometimes the crop may be retarded a week or ten days by this means.

The mulch is usually more essential in Alberta than in other climatic zones because of the Chinook winds and uncertain snowfalls during the winter and spring.

Experience has taught me that the best mulch is usually made up of some strawy material, and should be placed over the beds to a depth of 2 or 3 inches. The mulch is applied late in the fall (October) after the ground is well frozen, and if the mulching material is abundant, both the plants and the intervening spaces should be covered.

Among the best strawberry plants are Royal Sovereign, Sir Joseph Patton and the Ever-Bearing Varieties.

When the mulch is removed from the plants generally as soon as the plants show signs of growth, it must be done carefully, and a little at a time. If all the mulch is removed at one time, your plants may be sun scalded, and may possibly die.

The flowers of the strawberry may be either perfect or imperfect, and the nature of the flower is characteristic of the variety. Some varieties have flowers that are perfect, i.e. having both stamens and pistils, and are consequently self-fertilized. Other varieties bear flowers which are pistilate, producing no pollen, and therefore require pollination from a pollen-bearing variety.

Exposure of the roots of strawberry plants for any length of time during hot sunny weather — even 15 minutes — will damage the young plants so much that one should hardly risk setting them out. Be careful also not to have the crowns covered with earth, as this will damage them. All this can be prevented by gardeners with a little experience, but it must be remembered that correct planting will make the difference between success or part failure.

RASPBERRIES

Most of the fruit of the raspberry, whose botanical name is rubus idaeus, ripens here during August and September; though you may even get some in July if the weather in early summer is unusually hot. The raspberry bears a satisfactory crop when planted in any good garden soil which is well cultivated, provided adequate protection is afforded during the winter.

Among the best raspberry canes to buy are Indian Chief, Lloyd George and Reliance.

Raspberries thrive best in light, rich soil or even in a very light sandy soil. They will grow briskly and produce abundantly if the bed is given a mulch of manure each spring to prevent the surface roots from drying out during drought. Although sufficient moisture at the roots during the summer is essential, a water-logged condition often proves disastrous, and if planted in soil which is largely clay, a great many canes may die outright.

When planted in rows, the canes should be set at 18 inches to 2 feet apart, and there should be a space of 4 feet between the rows. The space between the rows could be cropped with small vegetables, such as radish, spinach or lettuce.

Before planting a row of canes, a strong post should be driven into the ground at each end of the row, to which wires can be attached, and if the row is long, smaller, intermediate posts must be placed at intervals of 12 to 15 feet.

The best time to plant raspberry canes in this climate is during the spring, about the middle of April. Fall planting rarely brings good results. The material selected for planting should consist of sturdy young canes of the current year's growth. Great care should be taken to obtain healthy canes from robust, fruitful stock of a good variety.

A common mistake of amateur gardeners is to plant the canes much too deeply. Upon examining the roots of raspberry canes, it will be seen that there are several white, spear-shaped buds on the topmost fibrous roots. These are the buds which produce the young canes during the first spring and summer.

When the roots are buried too deeply, these buds are smothered and die, so that no new growths are produced during the first season. When planting, the uppermost roots should not be more than 2 inches or at the most 3 inches below the surface of the ground.

CURRANTS

Black currant bushes, known as ribes nigrum, are more widely planted in Alberta gardens than the red or white currants — the berries being greatly in demand for jams, jellies, and preserves. These bushes are found growing wild in the woods of Europe and North America.

Successful cultivation is possible in most gardens, and, although there is misunderstanding among amateurs as to the correct method of treatment, the general management is quite simple.

Experience and experiment have taught that excellent crops can be grown even in light, sandy soil, and that well-drained, loamy soil is preferable to the heavy ground sometimes recommended.

Whatever the garden soil, it must be deeply dug and well-manured before planting. Any hard subsoil likely to cramp root development must be broken and a liberal dressing of farmyard manure, or peat moss worked into the soil.

Black currant bushes blossom early in the spring. Therefore, a cold wind-swept location is not conducive to good cropping. Protection from a windbreak, so the pollinating bees and insects may work in comfort and effect good settings of fruit, is desirable.

In this part of the country, planting should be done about the middle of April if the conditions are suitable. One- or two-year-old bushes are the most satisfactory for planting; if well grown, they should yield a crop of fruit in their second summer.

Care must be taken to avoid burying the fibrous roots too deeply; a covering of 3 to 4 inches of soil over the top layer of roots is ample. After the soil has been firmly pressed over the roots, a thick mulch of well-rotted manure should be placed around each bush and allowed to decay.

Black currant bushes are easily propagated by cuttings. The easiest and best method is to strike hard-wooded cuttings in the greenhouse in the early spring (March) before leaf growth starts up. But cuttings from outdoor canes should be taken just before the leaves come out (maybe in early May). All the cuttings should be 9 to 10 inches long and cut from healthy, fruitful bushes. No buds are removed from the shoots, which are planted firmly about 9 inches apart, in sandy soil, and with the top 3 or 4 buds left above the ground.

By the following spring, the cuttings will have rooted strongly and made good growth, and will be ready for transplanting in April to their permanent quarters.

Another method is to take soft-wooded cuttings in June. The advantages of this method is that the soft shoot tips which provide the cuttings are then free from what is known as big bud mites and so a healthy stock of mite-free bushes can be raised.

To prepare the soft-wooded cuttings, the top 3 or 4 inches of young side shoots are taken and inserted in sandy soil in a coldframe, or planted in pots kept in a cool greenhouse. The cuttings are inserted with the base an inch or two deep.

These cuttings are made the same way as geranium cuttings — by removing the two lower sets of leaves, and then cutting square across below the bottom joints, leaving two sets of leaves on the cuttings. For the first few weeks the cuttings are kept shaded and in a moist, close atmosphere with a temperature of 55 to 60 degrees, then gradually hardened off preparatory to being planted in the open garden in early autumn (late August), and before cold weather sets in.

There are several excellent varieties of black currant bushes of which I believe Boskoop Giant is the best. This is the earliest to ripen; it makes a strong spreading bush and bears long bunches of large, sweet berries.

Another good variety is Seabrook Black. It is a strong grower and a heavy cropper.

Goliath, a mid-season variety which I recommend, is of upright, compact growth and bears short bunches of very sweet, large berries.

Red Currants are another popular species.

I would recommend Red Lake, Laxtions No. 1 and Perfection.

The best white currant bush, in my opinion, is the variety known as White Grape.

The cultivation of red and white currant bushes is similar to that of black currants, but the big different in the culture of the bushes is in the pruning. This is dealt with in the section on pruning.

147

Maximum Heights and Pruning Times

FOR TREES, SHRUBS AND HEDGES

Here is a list of trees, shrubs, bushes and hedges which are recommended for growing in Calgary district, according to the maximum heights to which they normally grow, and with the best times for pruning (some plants may be in both the tree or shrub sections):

TREES

(Including deciduous, evergreen and fruit)

Common Name	Botanical Name	Maximum Height (in feet)	When To Prune
APPLE:	Malus	18 to 20	Early April
Allgood		18 to 20	Early April
Battleford		18 to 20	Early April
Haralson		18 to 20	Early April
Heyers No. 9		18 to 20	Early April
Heyers No. 12		18 to 20	Early April
Heyers No. 20		18 to 20	Early April
Transcendent		18 to 20	Early April
ASH:	Fraxinus	30 to 80	March
Common Ash	Fraxinus Excelsiori	30 to 40	March
Green Ash	Fraxinus Pennsylvanica	50 to 60	March
White Ash	Fraxinus Americana	70 to 80	March
ASPEN:			
Common Aspen	Populus Tremuloides	30 to 40	October
BIRCH:	Betula	10 to 40	June
Black (or River) Birch	Betula Nigra	25 to 30	June
Cut Leaf Weeping Birch	Betula Pendula Gracilis (or B. Laciniata Alba)	30 to 40	June
Paper (or Silver or White) Birch	Betula Papyrifera	30 to 40	June
Yellow Birch	Betula Lutea	30 to 40	June
Young's Weeping Birch	Betula Pendula Youngii	10 to 12	June
CHERRY:	Prunus	20 to 25	March
Improved Choke-Cherry	Prunus Padus	20 to 25	March
Pin (or Wild Bird) Cherry	Prunus Pennsylvanica	20 to 25	March

Common Name	Botanical Name	Maximum Height (in feet)	When To Prune
CRAB-APPLE:	Malus	14 to 30	Early April
Alma Crab	Malus	14 to 15	Early April
Betchall's Crab	Malus	15 to 20	Early April
Dolgo Crab	Malus	15 to 20	Early April
Ele's Purple Crab	Malus	15 to 20	Early April
Hopa Crab	Malus Hopa	15	Early April
Osman Crab	Malus Osman	20	Early April
Siberian Crab	Malus Baccata	25 to 30	Early April
ELM:	Ulmus	20 to 70	February and March
American Elm	Ulmus Americana	60 to 70	February and March
Chinese Elm	Ulmus Parvifolia	20 to 25	February and March
European Elm	Ulmus Campestris	40 to 50	February and March
FIRS: (See Pines and Spruce)	Abies	—	
LARCH:	Larix	50 to 60	Never Prune
European Larch	Larix Decidua	50 to 60	Never Prune
Siberian Larch	Larix Siberica	50 to 60	Never Prune
*MAY DAY (Also known as the improved choke-cherry)	Prunus Padus	20 to 25	March

* The Hawthorn is, especially in England, traditionally known as the May Day tree, but here in the West the improved chokecherry, or prunus padus, is often referred to as the May Day tree, though incorrectly, according to traditionalists.

Common Name	Botanical Name	Maximum Height (in feet)	When To Prune
MAPLE:	Acer		
Manitoba Maple (or Green Leaved Box Elder)	Acer Negundo	30 to 40	October or November
MOUNTAIN ASH:	Sorbus	20 to 30	March
American Mountain Ash	Sorbus Americana	20 to 30	March
European Mountain Ash (or Rowan)	Sorbus Aucuparia	20 to 30	March

Common Name	Botanical Name	Maximum Height (in feet)	When To Prune
POPLAR:	Populus	30 to 80	
(some Cottonwoods)			January
°Alberta Cottonwood	Populus Deltoides	60 to 80	to March
°Balm of Gilead (or Balsam Poplar)	Populus Balsamifera	30 to 40	January to March
Birch Poplar	Populus Betuifolia	50 to 60	January to March
Bolles Poplar	Populus Bolleana	50 to 60	January to March
Common Aspen	Populus Tremuloides	30 to 40	October
Northwest Poplar	Populus Acuminata	50 to 60	January to March
Russian Poplar	Populus Certinensis	60 to 70	January to March
	°Populus Wobbstii	60 to 70	January to March

° *These "Cottonwoods" shed cotton fluff in June.*

PINE:	Pinus	8 to 70	April (trim only)
Austrian Pine	Pinus Ostiacus	20 to 25	April (trim only)
Jack Pine	Pinus Banksiana (Lamb.)	30 to 40	April (trim only)
Lodgepole Pine	Pinus Contorta	30 to 40	April (trim only)
Mugho Pine	Pinus Mughus Mugho	8 to 10	April (trim only)
Scotch Pine	Pinus Sylvestris	60 to 70	April (trim only)
White Pine	Pinus Strobus	60 to 70	April (trim only)
SPRUCE:	Picea	30 to 70	April
Blue (or Colorado) Spruce	Picea Pungens	50 to 60	April
Black Hills Spruce	Picea Glauba (?)	30 to 40	April
Black Spruce	Picea Nigra	30 to 40	April
Canadian Spruce	Picea Canadensis	60 to 70	April
Koster Blue Spruce	Picea Pungens Kosteriana	50 to 60	April
Norway Spruce	Picea (Excelsa) Abies	50 to 60	April
White Spruce	Picea Alba	60 to 70	April

Common Name	Botanical Name	Maximum Height (in feet)	When To Prune
WILLOW:	Salix	12 to 30	
Goat Willow	Salix Caprea	15 to 20	October or later
Golden Willow	Salix Vitellina	15 to 20	October or later
Laurel Leaf Willow	Salix Pentandra	20	October or later
Osier Willow	Salix Viminalis	15 to 20	Feb. or Mar. also October
Pussy Willow	Salix Discolor	20 to 30	October and later
Sharp Leaf Willow	Salix Acuitfolia	12	February or March

SHRUBS, BUSHES AND HEDGES

Common Name	Botanical Name	Maximum Height (in feet)	When To Prune
ALMOND:	Prunus		
Russian (or Flowering) Almond	Prunus Amygdalus Nana	2	After Flowering
BIRCH:	Betula	3 to 6	June
	Betula Nana	3	June
	Betula Pumili	4 to 6	June
BERRIES:			March and early April
Gooseberry	Grossularia (or Ribes)	4 to 5	March and early April
Raspberry	Rubus Idaeus	6 to 8	September
Strawberry	Gragaria	Creeping	Never Prune
BLACKTHORN:	Rhamnus Cathartica	4 to 5	March
BUCKTHORN:	Hippophae		March and October
Sea Buckthorn	Hippophae Rhamnoides	5 to 6	March and October
BUFFALO BERRY:	Shepherdia Argentea	10 to 11	March
BURNING BUSH (or Spindle Bush):	Euonymus Alatus	4 to 5	March
Dwarf Burning Bush	Euonymus Nana	Creeping	March
CARAGANA:	Caragana	1 to 20	Jan. to March
Common Caragana	Caragana Arborescens	20 to 25	Jan. to March
Common Caragana	Caragana Chamlagii	6	Jan. to March
Common Caragana	Caragana Ftruescens	6	Jan. to March
Fern Leaf Caragana	Caragana Lorbergii	8 to 10	Jan. to March
Pygmy Caragana	Caragana Pygmaea	4	Jan. to March
Russian (or Little Leaf) Caragana	Caragana Frutex	7	Jan. to March
Weeping Caragana	Caragana Arborescens Pendula	6 to 7	Jan. to March

151

Common Name	Botanical Name	Maximum Height (in feet)	When To Prune
COTONEASTER:	Cotoneaster	Creeping to 6	Feb. & March
European Cotoneaster	Cotoneaster Integerrima	3	Feb. & March
Many-Flowered Cotoneaster	Cotoneaster Multiflora	5 to 6	Feb. & March
Peking Cotoneaster	Cotoneaster Acutifolia	3	Feb. & March
Rock Cotoneaster	Cotoneaster Horizontalis	Creeping	Feb. & March
CHERRY:	Prunus	3 to 12	
Common Choke-Cherry	Prunus Virginia	4 to 6	July
Nanking Cherry	Prunus Tomentosa	5 to 6	March
Pin (or Wild Bird) Cherry	Prunus Pennsylvanica	10 to 12	March
Prinsepia Cherry	Prunus Sinensis	6 to 8	March
Western Sand Cherry	Prunus Besseyii	3	March
CINQUEFOIL:	Potentilla Fruticosa	3 to 4	March
CURRANTS:	Ribes	4 to 6	March
Black Currant	Ribes Nigrum	6 to 6	March, early April
Flowering Currant	Ribes Aureum	5 to 6	March, early April
Red Currant	Ribes Sativum	4 to 5	March, early April
White Currant	Ribes Alba	4 to 5	March, early April
DAPHNE:	Daphne	½ to 3	After Flowering
Chinese Daphne	Daphne Tangutica	1	After Flowering
English Daphne	Daphne Mezereum	2 to 3	After Flowering
Gerald's Daphne	Daphne Geraldii	2 to 3	After Flowering
Rose Daphne	Daphne Cneorum	6 to 8 inches	After Flowering
DOGWOOD:	Cornus	3 to 6	March
Bailey's Dogwood	Cornus Baileyii	5 to 6	March
Golden Twig Dogwood	Cornus Flaviramea	5 to 6	March
Purple Twig Dogwood	Cornus Kesselringii	4 to 5	March
Red Osier Dogwood	Cornus Stolonifera	5 to 6	March
Siberian Dogwood	Cornus Sericea	4 to 5	March
Variegated Dogwood	Cornus Alba	3 to 4	March

Common Name	Botanical Name	Maximum Height (in feet)	When To Prune
ELDER (or Elderberry):	Sambucus	3 to 10	
American Elder	Sambucus Canadensis	8	February and March
Common Elder	Sambucus Nigra	4	October
Golden Elder	Sambucus Aurea	3 to 4	October
	Sambucus Racemosa	8 to 10	February and March
FORSYTHIA (or GoldenBells):	Forsythia	5	March
HAWTHORN (or English May Day Tree):	Crataegus	5 to 25	March
Chinese Hawthorn	Crataegus Pannatifia	12	March
Cockspur Hawthorn	Crataegus Crusgalli	10 to 15	March
	Crataegus Oxyacantha	5 to 25	March
HIGHBUSH CRANBERRY (Viburnum):	Viburnum	5 to 25	After Flowering
Common Highbush Cranberry	Viburnum Trilobum	5 to 25	After Flowering
Snowball Highbush Cranberry	Viburnum Opulus Sterilus	5 to 25	After Flowering
HONEYSUCKLE:	Lonicera	Creeping to 10	March
Amur Honeysuckle	Lonicera Maackii	8 to 9	March
Scarlet Trumpet Honeysuckle	Lonicera Hybrid	Creeping	March
Tartarian (or Bush) Honeysuckle	Lonicera Tartarica	8 to 10	March
LILAC:	Syringa	6 to 15	Immediately After Flowering
Common Lilac	Syringa Vulgaris	6 to 7	Immediately After Flowering
Japanese Lilac	Syringa Villosa (or Japonica)	3 to 15	Immediately After Flowering
Manchurian Lilac	Syringa Amurensis	6 to 7	Immediately After Flowering

(French-grafted lilac varieties include: Edith Cavell, Gen. Pershing, Charles Joly, Marechal Foch, Charles X, Mme. Lemoine, Marie Finon, Marechal Lannes, Lucie Ballet, President Lincoln, Ludwig Spaeth.)

Common Name	Botanical Name	Maximum Height (in feet)	When To Prune
MAPLE:	Acer	10 to 15	October
Amur Maple	Acer Ginnala (or Talarica)	10 to 15	October
Rocky Mountain Maple	Acer Glabrum	10 to 12	October
MOCK ORANGE:	Philadelphus		
Waterton Mock Orange	Philadelphus Lewisii Watertonii	2½ to 3	After Flowering
NINEBARK:	Physocarpus	3 to 6	March
Common Ninebark	Physocarpus Opulifolius	5 to 6	March
Golden Ninebark	Physocarpus Opulifolius Luteus	3 to 4	March
OREGON GRAPE	Mahonia Aquifolia	1	March
PLUM:	Prunus		
Double-Flowering Plum	Prunus Triloba	6	After Flowering
PRICKLY SPINE	Acanthopanax Senticosus	4	March
SHRUB ROSES:	Rosa	4 to 10	April
—	Rosa Alpina	5 to 6	April
—	Rosa Altaica	8 to 10	April
—	Rosa Grootendorst	5 to 6	April
—	Rosa Harrisonii	5 to 6	April
—	Rosa Rubrifolia	5 to 6	April
—	Rosa Rugosa	4 to 5	April
SIBERIAN SALT BUSH	Halimodendron Argenteum	6 to 8	March and After Flowering
SNOW BERRY	Symphoricarpus	2 to 3	March
SPIREA:	Spiraea	1 to 4	After Flowering
Anthony Waterer Spirea	Spiraea Bumalda	1 to 2	After Flowering
Bridal Wreath Spirea	Spiraea Arguta	3 to 4	After Flowering
Korean Spirea	Spiraea Trichocarpa	3 to 4	After Flowering
Oriental Spirea	Spiraea Media Sericea	2	After Flowering
Ural False Spirea	Spiraea Sorbifolia	2 to 3	After Flowering
Van Houti Spirea	Spiraea Van Houtii	2 to 3	After Flowering

154

Common Name	Botanical Name	Maximum Height (in feet)	When To Prune
TAMARISK (or Tamarix)	Tamarix	6 to 8	April
—	Tamerix Pentandra	6 to 8	April
—	Tamerix Purpurea	6 to 7	April
WILLOW:	Salix	½ to 8	
Arctic Willow	Salix Arctica	6 to 12 inches	October
Laurel Leaf Willow	Salix Pentandra	8	October
Osier Willow	Salix Viminalis	10	March
Prairie Willow	Salix Humilus	3 to 8	October
Pussy Willow	Salix Discolor	10	October
Silky Willow	Salix Sericea	4 to 8	October

A display of hedges in the City of Calgary nursery

PRUNING

In the field of horticulture, the pruning of trees and bushes is of great importance. It should not be done by inexperienced amateurs, but if you are inexperienced and have to do the job, then I'll try and tell you what you should do.

Pruning may be grouped around three principles:

(1) Pruning proper, or the removal of parts of a tree or shrub for the purpose of bettering the remaining part or its product.

(2) Training, or the disposition of the placing of the individual branches.

(3) Trimming or shaping a tree, shrub, or hedge into some definite or artificial form.

The principles that underlie pruning proper, may be associated with two ideals: The lessening of the struggle for existence, and the cutting away of certain parts for the purpose of producing some definite effect in the formation of fruit, buds, or leaf buds; or in modifying the habit of the tree or shrub in question.

There are more branches in the top of any tree or shrub than can persist. Therefore, there is struggle for existence, and those which have the advantage of position persist.

Nature prunes. Dying and dead branches in any neglected tree top are illustrations of this fact. When the struggle for existence is greatly lessened, the remaining branches receive a greater proportion of the plant's energy, and they make stronger growth or are more productive in flowers or fruits.

In itself, pruning is not a devitalizing process — it is essentially a thinning process. It becomes devitalizing when it is carried to excess or when the wounds dot not heal and disease sets in.

Properly done, it is an invigorating process, since it allows more nourishment to be distributed to the remaining parts of the tree or shrub.

The larger the wound the greater is the liability to infection. This is as true of trees as it is of the human family. It is, therefore, important in pruning that the wounds be as small as possible.

This means that the best pruning is that which is practised annually so that none of the branches to be removed attain larger size. This is particularly true in the case of trees.

When trees and shrubs are transplanted, the roots are pruned in the process of removal, and the tops must be reduced in proportion.

For some time after the tree or shrub is transplanted, it has no vital connection with the soil, and if all the top is allowed to remain, there is much evaporation from it and a loss of energies of the tree or shrub.

How much of the top should be removed depends on how much of the roots were removed in digging. It is a general practice to cut back the top at least one-half when transplanting.

In the case of young seedling trees, it is wise to cut away all side branches for the first year or two, leaving just the centre leader.

The pruning of ornamental trees and shrubs for the production of flowers is controlled largely by the flower-bearing habit of the shrub or tree in question. Most early-blooming trees and shrubs develop their flowering buds the year before. Heavy pruning, therefore, particularly heading back when the tree or shrub is dormant, cuts off the flower buds and the amount of bloom is lessened.

In the case of lilacs, many of them are robbed yearly of their finest blooms in this manner. Some even clip lilac bushes into rounder shapes in spring, cutting off most of the flowering buds. Lilacs should be pruned just after the flowers have died in early summer.

Other shrubs which should be pruned immediately after flowering are the prunus triloba or the double-flowering plum; the viburnum or highbush cranberry; the spireas in variety; the halimodendron or salt bush; all shrub roses and the flowering almond.

When these are pruned immediately after flowering, the new growth will then develop flower buds for the following year.

It may be advisable, however, to prune such shrubs in winter for the purpose of thinning them, thereby allowing the flower buds which remain to produce larger blooms. But in most ornamental shrubs, it is the number of flowers rather than the size of each which is desired, so don't thin too much.

There is relatively little training for artificial shapes of trees and shrubs done in this country, as it is in the older lands.

Fruit trees, such as crab-apple, can be trained against a wall or building of any kind. They are particularly attractive when trained in this manner. They have to be started when young right out of the nursery.

When large wounds are made in pruning a tree, it is well to dress the wound with "pine tar," grafting wax, or ordinary paint. This dressing does not hasten the healing of the wound, but it does keep the wood from decay. The dressing prevents bacteria and fungi from obtaining a foothold, and thereby prevents the rot.

Wounds that are exposed for some years nearly always become unsound at the centre because of the intrusion of organism, and even if the wound should subsequently heal over, the infection may still extend down the heart of the tree. The dressing should be applied heavily and renewed occasionally.

The rapidity with which wounds heal depends largely on the position on the tree. Wounds along the main branches, which are leading avenues for distribution of food, heal more speedily than those on the weaker side-branches. The closer the wound sits to the main branches or the trunk, the more quickly it will heal.

The general rule which applies in all pruning is: All dead, diseased, weak or badly-placed branches should be removed. In the elimination of these, try to keep trees and bushes symmetrical.

In order to prune successfully you must, of course, have the correct tools to work with. These include a pair of secateurs, a pruning saw, a pair of loppers, and a long-handled pruner.

TREES

Ash trees need no pruning apart from removing all dead and diseased branches. If the tree, however, becomes too crowded, remove those branches which are best taken out.

Prune ashes in March.

Special care is needed in pruning birches. Old trees do not respond well to pruning. Therefore, enough pruning to encourage birch trees to grow into shapely specimens should be carried out while they are young.

June is the best month for the pruning of the young birch trees, when they are in full leaf. This latter statement may sound strange to the amateur, but the dead wood in a leafless birch is hard to discern, whereas a leafless dead branch is obvious when the rest of the tree is in leaf.

Do not prune birches before June. If the branches are cut off before the leaves develop, a good deal of bleeding takes place. If, however, pruning is carried out in summer, the sap does not exude from the wounds, and before the fall of the leaves the surface of the wound becomes hard enough to prevent the flow of sap.

Here again, pruning consists mainly of removing dead, diseased and badly-placed branches. If the birch is too spindly, cut back the top a foot or more, depending on how spindly the tree is. Also, cut back all lateral shoots a few inches, thus causing the birch to thicken out.

Always try to shape the tree symmetrically.

Prune maples in October or November. Pruning is necessary only for thinning out crowded branches, shortening long branches which tend to spoil the shape of the maple, or for the removal of dead or diseased branches.

But prune mountain ash in March, for the same reasons you prune maples.

Prune poplars in winter or early spring. In pruning poplars it is wise to remove as many branches as you think desirable before the trunks exceed 8 inches in diameter.

Pruning willows is important in keeping the wood colorful during the winter. About the first week of April those willows which produce beautiful wood must be cut back hard. Other willows may be pruned either in spring or fall.

What I mean by cutting hard back is to cut back the wood of the previous year's growth to within a few inches of the main branches.

In this way, new and strong shoots will be produced from below where the cut was made, giving you rich colors in green, yellow, gold or reddish-green wood.

This applies to the golden willow (salix vitellina), the laurel leaf willow (salix pentandra), and the osier willow (salix viminalis).

Other varieties of willows, as trees or shrubs, should be pruned in the fall to remove dead and diseased wood and to keep the plant well shaped.

EVERGREENS

Pruning of ornamental fir trees requires great care, and the same is true of any ornamental tree.

There is a tendency for firs (pines or spruce) to produce large branches low down on the stem. If these are not removed, they will take the food which should have gone to build up the trunk.

So those persons who like a bushy fir with branches down to the ground will have to be especially careful in supplying enough food for their kind of trees.

The others who like their pine with a longer amount of branch-free trunk should cut off the lower ones to suit their preference, and the pruning should be done in March or April.

If you don't want a clear trunk, then don't prune.

FRUIT TREES AND BUSHES

When you start to prune established fruit trees, see that you prune them in such a manner that the branches are well spaced. This allows sun and air to circulate freely throughout the trees. After trees are uniformly shaped, you then cut back the wood or shoots which formed last year's growth to within 2 or 3 inches of the main branches. This forms the fruiting spurs for two years hence.

For those who wish to let their apple trees grow taller, allow the terminal growths to remain 9 to 12 inches in length. When pruning terminal growths, always cut on a slope and make sure the top bud is on the outside to ensure outward growths of branches.

If the bud was left on the inside of the branch, it would cause an inward growth and crowding of the trees would result. All badly-placed, diseased, or dead branches must, of course, be removed, cutting them off close to the trunk or main branches as the case may be.

The last year's growth or young wood of the apple tree may be recognized by the following description. It is very dark in color and has small buds, which are leaf buds growing very close to the young shoots.

When pruning the apple trees is completed, you should paint over all the larger cuts with pine tar or paints.

Next let's discuss pruning crab-apple trees.

When it comes to the pruning of the red, pink and white-flowered crabs, all you do, early in April, is remove the dead, weak and badly-placed branches. Contrary to the habit of the apple trees, this young wood or growth on the crab-apple tree produces blooms and fruits, and must not be cut back.

The white-flowering crab, however, is spurred back in the same manner as the ordinary apple tree.

To get good black currants, regular pruning in the spring is a must.

After a black currant bush is four years old or more, you will find the wood of each year's growth varies considerably in color. Black currant bushes should not be pruned until after the fourth year, and at the fourth year, the old wood should be removed in March or early April down to the base, as this will rejuvenate the bush. You will readily recognize the old wood which is much darker in color. It is important that these old branches be cut off at ground level.

The second and third year wood produces the fruit on the black currant bushes. After the first pruning, the process of eliminating the old wood must be carried out annually.

After the removal of the old branches, young shoots will grow up in their place. The best and healthiest of these young shoots must be left, and the weak and spindly ones cut out at ground level.

Next, consider the red and white currant bushes. The wood which must be removed on the pruning of these species is very light in color. This is because it is the young growths or last year's wood which must be spurred back on both

159

the red and white currant bushes. The young shoots are cut back in March or early April to within 2 or 3 inches of the main branches. It is on these young spurs, formed all along the main branches, that the fruit grows.

To encourage the formation of strong spurs and to produce maximum fruiting, annual pruning is essential. Cut back all lateral and side shoots which have grown out along the branches to within two or three buds, or to within about half-an-inch, of the base.

The young leader shoot at the end of each branch should not be cut hard back, but should be shortened by about half its length if the growth is only moderately strong, or by one-third if the growth is more vigorous. Try to prune so that the centre of the bush is open and free from crossing and tangled growths.

Pruning after planting is most vital in the cultivating of raspberries. If left unshortened, the young canes would possibly bear a few berries during the first summer, but that would be at the expense of the new growth from the base, and it would seriously weaken the plants.

In an established row of summer producing canes, pruning should be done as soon as all the fruit is gathered.

The month of September, after all the fruit has been picked, is definitely the correct time to cut out old canes. There is an old saying, "Better late than never," and this most certainly applies to raspberry canes.

You may recognize the old canes by their grayish-white color; in contrast to the young canes (which will produce fruits this year) which are of a rich brown color or tone.

Gooseberry pruning must be carried out in March or early in April within a few weeks of planting, or just before the buds begin to show in early spring.

In the main, pruning consists of shortening all crowded, ill-placed laterals or side shoots, especially those crowding the centre of the gooseberry bush, to within two or three buds of their base. Leave the well-placed, sturdy young shoots practically full length wherever there is ample room.

The heading shoot, extending each main branch, should be shortened by about one-and-a-half or a third, according to its vigor.

In the cultivation of strawberries, it is necessary only to remove the young runners for propagation. This should be done in June or July.

SHRUBS, BUSHES AND HEDGES

The same principles apply to pruning shrubs, bushes or hedges.

Caragana bushes, or hedges, require only the basic pruning-out of dead, diseased, badly-placed or overcrowding branches.

Do this work from January to the end of March. Then, of course, if you want a well-kept caragana hedge, you'll be kept busy trimming from May to August.

Cotoneaster needs practically no pruning except when used as a hedge, then during February and March.

Burning bush (euonymus alatus) needs little pruning. Every second or third year, during February and March, you may want to remove a few old branches to encourage new growth.

Sea buckthorn shrubs may be pruned also during February and March, or in October, every three or four years to remove old wood.

The various cherry shrubs, plum-cherry or flowering plum, wild bird cherry, and choke-cherry, need pruning every year as they have a tendency to overcrowd.

The double-flowering plum (prunus triloba), should be pruned as soon as the flowers fade by removing all weak and badly-placed branches. Watch for suckers around the roots. The reason these appear is that the flowering plum is grafted on to the wild plum, and the latter has a tendency to rob the shrub of its vitality, and may eventually kill it. Remove the suckers.

Keep all these shrubs open to sunlight by removing surplus branches, and, of course, take out the dead and diseased parts.

About every three years, in the spring, cut out the old wood in dogwood to encourage young and more colorful new wood.

Each fall cut back golden elder to within 2 inches of the ground.

The cockspur hawthorn requires only the dead, diseased, or surplus branches removed, usually in March.

Honeysuckle needs little pruning the first few years. After this, however, an occasional thinning out of old wood in March may be beneficial, and if it grows too tall or spindly, then cut it back.

After lilac has bloomed, the faded flowers should be removed and the pruning should be done as far as necessary. As explained earlier in the introduction to pruning, the pruning of lilacs must be done just after the flowers have died off in early summer.

Pruning lilacs during the fall or very early spring when they are dormant will remove the coming year's flowers. Lilacs produce their flowering buds the year before. Pruning during the winter or spring, unless great care is taken, will therefore destroy a large part of the flowering buds for the next season.

When lilacs are too tall, cut back a few branches here and there in each bush, yearly. To do this, cut back in March to a healthy, dormant bud on the main branches. In the course of two or three years, your lilacs then will be the desired height, and you will not have deprived yourself of blooms each year. If the whole bush is cut back in one season, you'll have no blossoms for a year.

The common lilac, syringa vulgaris, produces a great many suckers. These must be dug out each year.

Mock orange must be pruned as soon as the flowers fade in August. All old wood must be cut out to the point where young shoots are appearing near the base.

If there appear to be too many new shoots, cut a few of the old shoots to the ground line.

The prickly spine, a most compact shrub, needs practically no pruning, but when it is necessary, prune in March.

The daphnes need no pruning, but the old flowers should be cut off immediately they die.

But the tamarisk should be pruned each year, cutting back half the current year's growth. This is best done in March or April.

Another shrub which needs pruning only every third year is the Siberian salt bush. In March, shape the bush and cut back the too-long branches, or any others which spoil the shape. Also cut off the dead flowers each year.

Spirea should be pruned in August immediately after flowering. Cut back the old wood then and remove all spindly growths.

161

LAWNS

It is the desire of every property owner to have a good lawn, because the lawn enhances the whole aspect of the property. The various scattered landscape features are brought together as a common unit by its introduction.

Since the lawn is a permanent thing, and adds so much in beauty to the home, no effort should be spared in its development.

In laying out the lawn, the preparation of the soil is of primary importance. It is important the uppermost soil be saved if it is at all good. In ground operations, the fact must not be lost sight of that the upper 9 or 10 inches of soil is more fertile than beneath, and the deeper one goes, the less fertile the ground becomes. Even though the soil may look good, that which has been deeply buried for a number of years is actually sterile.

But for a new lawn or for improving old lawns the planning of what you want comes first.

First you have to decide where you want the lawn or lawns, then the grades, then what grass seed you prefer, and finally how you're going to do the job, especially whether you're going to tackle this back-breaking job by hand and by yourself, or whether you've lots of good neighbors to lend a hand as well as lending advice, or whether you can afford to call in professional gardeners and machinery.

Planning is one of the most important phases of gardening. I believe strongly in planning on paper the things that will be needed and where they should go. One may spend many an interesting hour during the long winter nights engaged in this profitable and fascinating pastime.

A general plan might be drawn of the entire grounds and separate ones on a larger scale of the different sections.

In planning a general layout for new grounds, especially if of considerable area, one must remember the effect that the proposed planting will have in after years.

The lawn should have an open expanse of green and an open outlook. This can be done by keeping the trees and shrubs at the back and on the sides.

So, now, having decided what you want, let's get down to work, either with machinery or with your own two hands.

Let's first discuss the easier job either of making a new lawn where the ground is reasonably suitably graded and where the soil is rich enough; or where an old lawn is to be re-seeded.

Nowadays, if it isn't a small job, it is customary to use machinery, generally a roto-tiller for digging and a seeder for sowing—though I'm still old-fashioned and think a better job usually is done by hand with a shovel and wheelbarrow.

The digging, by roto-tiller or by hand, should be done in fall whenever possible. If this isn't possible, dig it as early as reasonable in spring, possibly the last two week in April if frost has gone out of the ground and also providing the soil isn't too wet.

It should be dug several weeks in advance of seeding (the first preferred seeding period is June), so the soil will settle firmly.

It is worth while taking pains with preliminary work. As the ground is dug, care must be taken to remove all weeds. However carefully the rest of the work is done, weeds are bound to appear later in the new lawn if this part of the job is skimped.

Then comes levelling. This is done similarly for the simpler lawn-making and as for the more difficult job of making a new lawn on a new site which has to be completely re-graded and where more than likely the builder has left an awful mess.

Where you have to re-grade, the first job is to save any of that fertile topsoil—if any has been left. We are not too well blessed with depth of soil here, so it is of primary importance not to waste any of it.

So if you have any good topsoil left, take off as much as you can down to possibly 10 inches, and put it close at hand (but not where it'll interfere with the job) so that it can be used again when the site is graded and shaped the way you want it.

You'd better use a tractor or back-hoe to remove this topsoil and rough-level the ground beneath.

Satisfied with the grading and levelling, now replace the preserved topsoil. If you didn't have any topsoil, then of course you have to buy loam—at least enough to give you a spread 4 to 6 inches deep.

If you were lucky enough to have had topsoil preserved, but feel this soil isn't sufficiently enriched, place another layer of maybe 3 or 4 inches of good, clean virgin loam over your replaced soil. Or mix the new load of loam with the pile of old surface soil if you've still got it unspread in a corner.

When purchasing loam, make sure it is free from weeds such as quack grass, dandelions and buck brush. Virgin prairie, stacked for two years, is the best buy.

The job of grading and levelling is difficult, so I'd like to come back again to describe that more fully, especially for re-grading a lot for a lawn, though the method is similar for levelling more even ground for a lawn.

After removal of the top soil, the ground must be properly marked out. The way in which this can be done is by spirit level and straightedge board.

When using the spirit level, at least two people are required. A good supply of strong pegs of varying lengths is also necessary, with a spade for digging holes and a hammer or mallet for driving in pegs.

The straightedge may be any length, but 12 to 14 feet is usually long enough. It must be accurately worked and may be made of ash or oak, well seasoned, so that it will not change in shape by exposure to weather.

By placing the straightedge on two given pegs, and placing the spirit level on the straightedge, the position of the air bubble will indicate whether the two pegs are the same height.

After the pegs have been inserted, it is essential they should not be disturbed until the levelling is finished, and it is wise to test the pegs occasionally in case of accident. It is also a good idea to mark the position of each peg by a conspicuous stake, for it is easy to wheel over the peg and upset the general level.

After levelling pegs have been inserted and properly checked, transference of soil from point to point may take place. Care must be taken to use the original surface soil for the top and to make the ground firm where much filling up has been done. The removal of the levelling pegs should be the last job and the levels ought to be all checked before the pegs are removed.

When levelling slopes, get a straight line along the top and bottom of the slope with the necessary levelling pegs driven into the required depth, and if the slope is a deep one, put in one or more rows of intermediate pegs. A general levelling to get rid of small lumps and hollows may be necessary, particularly on new garden soil.

For some who may prefer a gently sloping lawn, make sure that it slopes away from your building. A pitch of 12 inches in 30 feet will give you enough slope for adequate drainage. The grade can be established by using a line and line level.

RAKING AND ROLLING

The next step is raking the soil. It should be raked thoroughly, removing stones, sticks and debris, and at the same time all hollows should be filled in and humps levelled. The ground should then be rolled in both directions from end to end and from side to side, to ensure a firm and even surface. This must be done while the soil is fairly dry, so that it does not stick to the roller.

This operation will reveal any spots that are too high or too low. Next rake the area over again, correcting and eliminating the hollows or hills, and then rake again in both directions as before. You will have attained a fine tilth, and a good seed bed.

Now you're reading for sowing the grass seed, having, of course, already decided what kind of seed or mixture of seeds you prefer.

Nowadays seeding is generally done with a spreader or seeder, though some still may prefer to broadcast the seed by hand.

The amount to sow is generally 6 pounds to 1,000 square feet of area. This works out at about 400 seeds in a 12-inch square.

Again, generally speaking, grass seed should be sown very thickly, so that the seed almost completely covers the surface of your lawn-to-be. It is better to spread too much seed than too little.

To ensure the inexperienced gardener of an even growth, the seed should be carefully apportioned, and sown on a calm day. Even distribution of the seed should be carefully attended to. It is unwise to sow lawn grass in windy weather, as the seed is very light and easily blown about.

Measure the area you plan to seed at that time, put the required amount of seed for that operation in the spreader (or in a carrying receptacle if you're hand-seeding) and then push your seeder in straight, slightly overlapping swathes at an even, slow pace, making sure the seed is evenly and thickly distributed.

If you're seeding by hand, hold the seed container in your left hand (unless you're left handed, in which case you hold it with your right hand); walk in a straight line at a steady, slow pace, scattering seed evenly at each step with the right hand. A small, similar-sized handful of seed should be scattered at each step.

Immediately after, rake the newly-seeded lawn lengthwise and then crosswise. In this way you will be assured of better distribution of the seed and more coverage. It is impossible to cover all the seed, but the more you get just underneath the soil, the better the chances of good germination.

After this, the lawn must be rolled again from side to side, to compact the soil around the seed.

By no means the least important is the watering of the newly-seeded areas. At no time during the germinating period must the lawn be allowed to dry out.

This germinative period is approximately 10 days, but during cool weather the grass takes longer to germinate. Care must also be taken that the lawn is never flooded. Always use a fine spray, giving it a gentle but thorough watering.

If it is not watered by hand, never leave the spray too long in one place. Flooding causes a spotty and patchy lawn, the seed having been washed into heaps, leaving some areas without any seed. Flooding also packs the soil, making it difficult for the tender young grass to come through.

Newly-sown grass should not be cut until it is about 3 inches high, though it may be rolled several times before then, when the soil is just moist but not wet.

Whether cut by a hand mower or power mower, when the new lawn is first cut the blades of the mower should be raised fairly high, and must be well sharpened. The grass, being young and tender, is easily uprooted by a blunt mower.

At the second cutting, the blades may be lowered a notch. By the time you mow your grass for the third time, you can lower the blades to the finally desired height.

If you find the lawn is not as healthy as it should be at this period, you might feed it with some artificial manure, spreading it preferably by the spreader (or by hand-shovel), in the quantity of one large handful to the square yard, spreading it evenly, and watering it in well.

There is an old saying that states, "Thirty days from sowing, your grass will need mowing." Let's hope that all your new lawns will require mowing after 30 days.

A monthly application of any good fertilizer will keep a lawn in healthy shape.

It is generally known that the various kinds of bent grasses produce more beautiful and velvety lawns. Unfortunately, these grasses are not hardy enough for our climate.

Four varieties of grasses which are to be recommended for use here are Kentucky Blue, Creeping Red Fescue, Chewing Fescue and Merion Blue.

I recommend a mixture of these as follows: two parts of Kentucky Blue Grass, two parts Creeping Red Fescue, one part Chewing Fescue, and one part of Merion Blue. This mixture can be made up for you at any seed store.

For those who may like a little clover in their lawn, White Dutch Clover is best, and should be added at the rate of one teaspoonful to a pound of the grass seed mixture.

The three most favorable periods for sowing grass seed here are June, July, and the first two weeks in August.

A fungus known as snow mold, brown patch, winter kill or dollar spot (sclerotinia nomococarpa) is fatal to grass. It is caused by unusually heavy snow smothering the grass roots, and becomes visible in spring when the snows melt, disfiguring a lawn with dead, brown patches.

It can be prevented if lawn owners treat their gardens around September with a mixture of bichloride of mercury and clean sand.

However, for those who fail to take precautions against snow mold, here is what I advise you to do in spring when and if the mold appears:

First, brush the moldy spots with a rake and a brush to remove as much of the growth as possible. Then the lawns should be spread with the mercury bichloride mixture.

I recommend that the preparation be mixed outside in a wheelbarrow, with two ounces of mercury bichloride (I suggest you ask for Layton 2-1) to a bucketful of clean, sharp sand, minus any gravel. The sand should be well mixed so that the poisonous chemical cannot be distinguished from the sand. Mix outside, because bichloride of mercury is a virulent poison as well as a general disinfectant, and you must use it with the utmost care and caution.

Then the mixture should be spread on the lawn, one handful to a square yard of lawn. This will help. But the treatment should be applied in the fall.

Prevention being better than cure, it is wiser to take steps in the fall, before the first snow is likely, to avoid this mold.

The wise gardener will therefore prepare this mixture of bichloride of mercury and sand early in September, and spread it as suggested above. If he does this, he will not have snow mold next spring.

Of course the preparation may be spread by a spreader as well as by hand. With a mechanical spreader you have the advantage of not having to handle the poison, and it may also do a more even job, and an even distribution over all your lawn is necessary, because you just can't guess where the mold may strike during the snow season.

Whether you use it doing the spring or fall, I would suggest two applications with an interval of two weeks between; here again this suggestion is more applicable to the preferred fall prevention than the spring cure.

The proportions when the bichloride of mercury is used in a spreader should be one ounce of mercury to an average-sized bucket of sand.

Another preventive is a 2:1 mixture of Calomel and corrosive sublimate, spread in the early fall at the rate of 3 to 4 oz. per 1,000 sq. ft. This material can be mixed with dry sand for easier spreading.

The best preventive for weeds and dandelions is 2,4-D, but this may only be used safely on lawns, driveways and paths.

It cannot be used on vegetables, trees, shrubs or flowers.

It must, therefore, only be used on a calm day. On a windy day the fumes carry, and will destroy nearby flowers and other plants.

In using 2,4-D on weeds in your grass, follow carefully the directions contained on the container of this weed killer.

MUSHROOMS

For centuries, men have used certain fungi for food.

Mushrooms, which are considered quite a delicacy today, are a fungi.

The Greeks and Romans esteemed them highly and gave a great deal of consideration to favorable times and places for gathering them, and to choice methods of preparing them for the table.

It has also been known for centuries that some fungi, however, contain virulent poisons. Still, through ignorance of those points which distinguish the poisonous from the edible, frequent cases of poisoning occur. These mistakes have caused many persons to have a dread for all fungi.

To many people the only fungi known are toadstools and mushrooms. They give the name mushroom to the species known to them as edible, and regard all other fungi as toadstools, things dangerous and poisonous. This distinction has no scientific basis, and in fact most of the species called toadstools are edible.

There are about 35,000 species of fungi known to botanists. I'm going to confine myself to writing only about the mushrooms, which after all are classified among the higher forms of fungi.

But perhaps I had better deal first with a question which many persons ask — how to tell an edible mushroom from poisonous ones?

I regret to state there is no simple, short answer. Some of the most poisonous mushrooms closely resemble the edible ones.

The difference between non-poisonous and poisonous species cannot be ascertained always by coloring or shape or any other lazy method.

It seems the only way to tell the difference is by experience. But I would advise you not to try to obtain that experience by tasting — you might guess wrong and never live to gain the knowledge from experience.

Some persons seem to have a gift of knowing which can be eaten, and which can't. Sometimes this information is passed along from parent to children, sometimes from a person who has made a long and careful study of fungi.

Maybe the best advice I can give is to tell you always to be very careful; if you're not sure, then don't take a chance — or you may not live to regret it.

Mushrooms grow in warm, moist places, and where cattle and especially horses are pastured you will find them growing outdoors.

Fungi are plants which have no green leaves and which do not grow from true seeds but from dust-like bodies resembling in appearance the yellow pollen of roses or lilies.

For those who might like to experiment with growing mushrooms, I'll tell how to construct a mushroom bed in a properly constructed mushroom house or shed, or even in a basement (though I can't imagine many persons wanting to grow them in their modern basement!).

167

You make sure there is no danger in your mushroom shed of frost, and that the temperature is kept at a steady 70 to 75 degrees Fahrenheit.

Unlike most plants, fungi such as mushrooms like to grow in dark places, so the shed or mushroom house should be kept dark.

For making the mushroom bed you will require a few loads of good fresh horse manure that does not contain too much straw. Allow it to stand for 7 or 8 days until it begins to heat; then turn it.

The manure bed is usually built flat, and should have a minimum depth of at least 18 inches after the manure has settled. The length and width of the bed will depend entirely on how large you wish to make it.

After completing construction of the manure bed, place a thermometer in it to test the temperature of the bed. At first, it may rise to 100 degrees or above. When it recedes to 75 or 70 degrees (generally in about a week), it is ready for the soil which must be placed over the manure.

Place a 6-inch layer of loam over the manure and be sure that it is firm. First the temperature will go up a little. When the temperature has gone down again to 70 or 75 degrees (and this may take another week), the bed is ready to receive the mushroom spawn.

The spawn is a material made in the form of a brick, and impregnated with the white thread-like material of the mushroom mycelium. Break each brick into pieces 2 inches square, and insert these into the soil 9 to 10 inches apart about 4 inches deep.

The bed should be watered with tepid water, using a fine spray. Such a mushroom bed usually produces for about three to four months.

If the spawn is good, the manure bed well prepared, and the heat maintained, mushrooms should appear in about 8 to 10 weeks.

Mushrooms mature quickly, so the bed must be examined frequently. Mushrooms should be gathered when the film which has been joined to the stem has become separated, maybe the day after they first appear.

Gather mushrooms by twisting and pulling — never by cutting. If you cut, and then leave the stem, the remains of the stem will decay and do harm to oncoming mushrooms. To pull them up without twisting would be likely to uproot smaller, adjoining mushrooms.

When a bed ceases to give a profitable crop, it should be replaced by another. The spent manure is invaluable for horticultural purposes, and for enriching garden soils. All weed seeds are usually killed by the terrific heat of the bed, another reason the manure from the mushroom bed is still valuable.

Although mushrooms do well in dark places, it is not true to say darkness is essential to their growth. They are often found growing in pastures, and in lawns which have been heavily fertilized by horse manure at some time or other, provided that moisture conditions are right for them.

Mushrooms are propagated by spores, and spawn later.

Spawn is the mycelium. It may be dried and will resume growth when congenial conditions co-exist. It will keep for a number of years in a cool, dry place. Dryness is essential.

This spawn may be obtained from any place where mushrooms grow or may be purchased. It is grown in some prepared material which is dried and may be then transported easily. The making and "bricking" of spawn is a business in itself.

168

Mushrooms may be grown successfully under the greenhouse benches, providing the drip from the roof can be kept off the beds, but the best place is a mushroom house built for the purpose.

Failure in a mushroom crop is hard to explain. The fault may be in the making of the bed, or it could be in the spawn, but this very uncertainty is a challenge to the enterprising.

KITCHEN HERBS

What herbs will grow in our climate?

A herb is plant which dies to the ground each year. It may be an annual as dill or summer savory; a biennial as parsnip and parsley; a perennial as horse-radish, mint or sage.

To the gardener, however, the word herb is ordinarily associated with herbaceous perennials, and he usually has in mind those particular perennial herbs which are grown for ornament, and which remain where they are planted.

To many other persons, however, especially the housewife, the word herb means the kitchen or savory herbs and it suggests such as sage and thyme.

In this chapter I'm going to deal with the savory kitchen herbs which most women are anxious to have included in their gardens. Many wives take a delight and pride in looking after the herbs as their particular eden in the garden.

A reasonably good selection of kitchen herbs includes both annuals and perennials.

Some good kitchen herbs for flavoring which may be grown here include:

Sweet basil, for salads and soups; chives, for salads; dill, for pickles; fennel, to eat raw like celery or to cook; mints, for teas and sauces; rosemary, for seasoning roasts, and chicken; sage, for dressing; savory, for flavoring vegetables, and dressing; sweet marjoram, for pickles; thyme, to season foods and salads; tarragon, to flavor salads:

Some perennial herbs which may be grown for their scent are bee balm, lavender and scented geraniums.

The following kitchen herbs are particularly good for a beginner's garden: mints, sage, tarragon, parsley, chives, basil, dill, rosemary, some of the thymes, and sweet marjoram.

Ordinary, well-drained garden soil, poor rather than rich, and not too acid, suits the majority of kichen herbs. However, mints prefer a fairly rich, moist and acid soil.

With the possible exception again of mints, which require considerable moisture, the majority of herbs do well in sandy loam if some humus is added and moisture is provided in very dry weather. But parsley, like mint, is an exception to the general rule of dry soil conditions; parsley and mints do well in moist places.

A southeast location is ideal for a kichen herb garden, but any site that gets full sunshine during the growing season will do. The soil and cultural practices which include winter protection are equally important.

The general cultural requirements for most herbs also include warmth, sunlight, and the free circulation of air. Space plants adequately according to the kinds. Keep weeds down and surface soil well-cultivated.

This is a generalization. A number of herbs require distinctly different conditions.

The perennial herbs should be planted together; and the annuals should also be planted together.

The majority of true herbs require no fertilization. Feeding them this way induces rank growth but does not favor the production of the essential oils which give them their flavor and fragrance.

The seeds of the perennial sweet basil may be started indoors in April and the seedlings transferred outdoors later, in June. Allow 12 inches apart between plants. Basil yields abundantly. Plants may be lifted in the fall and potted for winter use indoors if desired; or dried.

Chives may be grown from seed sown out of doors when the ground warms up generally late in April. Thin out the small plants to about an inch apart. They are hardy perennials and multiply rapidly, needing little attention.

They should be divided every three or four years. And they like a moderately moist soil.

Dill is a fast growing annual that matures in a little more than two months. Sow in spring (late May), in well-prepared soil outdoors, in rows 2 feet apart. The plants grow about 3 feet tall. Thin out seedlings to 4 or 5 inches at first, later giving a final thinning so that they are 10 to 12 inches apart.

With annual fennel you may sow the seeds outdoors in spring (late May), where the plants are to mature. The seedlings are thinned out to 6 to 8 inches apart, and the plants mature in about 60 days.

Mint, the common garden perennial herb so much in demand in the kitchen, is easily cultivated in rich garden soil of a good depth which does not dry out quickly in hot weather. In a hot, dry spot it will fail, or will make such weak, woody growths as to be useless. A half-shady place will do.

Mints spread so rapidly that they may become a nuisance. The underground stems travel along the bed or border, and the shoots push through the soil some distance away, and so they may spoil or overcrowd other plants.

The best mint is obtained from single, vigorous plants. It is thus advisable to lift the old plants every year or two. In the spring (late May), separate them into rooted pieces and replant. Later the old central parts of the plant, which have become woody, should be discarded.

Mint may also be started from seed in the greenhouse. Sow the seeds in February and they should be ready to set out in the garden by the end of May. Mint is very hardy.

Parsley is another popular biennial herb. It may be started from seed in the greenhouse in February, and set out after May 24. Or you may sow the seed, but after May 24, in the garden outdoors, in rows 2 inches deep and 15 inches apart.

Moss parsley is perhaps the best species.

Parsley usually takes a longer time to germinate than most vegetables and herbs; the seedlings may not appear for almost four weeks.

Rosemary is a tender annual herb, but it may be plunged outdoors in pots in a sunny, sheltered spot in June, and carried over the winter indoors in a cool, light place. It should be potted in well-drained soil to which a sprinkling of lime has been added. It is propagated by cutting.

Sage likes best a light, well-drained and rich soil. Sow the seeds indoors, in February, and when large enough set them out when all danger of frost is past in the spring, generally after May 24. Do not give sage too much water, but cultivate frequently during the growing season. Sage, a perennial, is not too hardy, and should be taken up in the fall and brought indoors if you wish it to continue its growth.

Savory, another perennial, grows best in rather poor but well-limed soil in an exposed, sunny spot. The seeds are very small and are best sown indoors in February in pots or boxes, and barely covered with soil. Water by immersing the pots or boxes in water, as the seeds wash out easily.

Seedlings should be set out when all danger of frost is past. Set them in rows 10 inches between plants and 48 inches between rows.

Tarragon is a hardy perennial. It needs a well-drained, moderately rich soil with considerable lime added. It grows best in slightly shaded areas in the garden, and can be propagated by stem or root cuttings, or by division. It can be planted in the same way as savory.

Perennial thyme may be sown from seed outdoors in the spring in a light, rich, sandy loam. Transplant the seedlings 6 to 8 inches apart. Do not over-water them or apply fertilizer.

When harvesting herbs in the fall, both annual and perennial, care should be taken that they are fully developed or ripened before being cut down.

The time for drying varies according to the kind and the weather at the time. They should be dried as quickly as possible in a warm, airy, well-ventilated place without exposure to the sun.

If you wish to harvest the seeds, they should be picked when fully matured before they fall off the plant . . .

Collect the heads or the seed pods and spread them out on a tray, placing it in a well-ventilated room. Turn them frequently, and at the end of a week or so they will be dry enough to separate the seed from the pod.

Mint may be cut from plants late in the summer, and hung in bunches in a cool, dry place. The leaves should be stripped from the stems and placed in tin containers to keep them dust free. They are then readily available for winter use.

Perhaps the greatest problem with mint is that it spreads so rapidly that it may become a nuisance. It is a good idea to sink an old zinc vessel in the ground, fill it with soil, and then plant the mint inside it. This method will prevent this herb from spreading all over the place.

Some gardeners surround the mint patch with 12-inch boards or planks for the same purpose.

In a similar way, an herb garden might well be planted in the form of a wagon wheel. You might even use an actual wagon wheel (if you're lucky enough to find one) for an herb garden, putting the various different herbs you want each within two spokes of the wheel.

171

Of course, if an actual wheel can't be obtained in this western rangeland, a similar result could be improvised by a structure, from wood, brick, cement, or whatever you like, in the shape of a wheel, with dividing materials radiating out from the centre like the spokes of a real wheel.

Herbs which may be seeded outdoors include: chives, dill, fennel, mint, parsley, rosemary, sage, sweet basil, tarragon and thyme.

Generally speaking, herbs should be sown outdoors after May 24, the date depending of course on whether it's an early or late spring. Also generally, herbs like lots of sunshine.

DISEASES AND PESTS

Diseases and pests have taken their toll of food crops and ornamental plants since the beginning of time, often to the extent of influencing the course of world events.

It is also well-known that weather conditions have a great influence on the activities and general behavior of insects of all kinds. Certain climatic conditions are highly favorable to severe attacks by one pest or another.

The red spider attacks are most severe during hot, dry weather, but little trouble is experienced from them when it's wet and cool.

But aphids of most kinds usually increase rapidly during warm, humid weather.

Wet weather also increases the damage from the second principal disease danger—fungous diseases.

So the only good thing that can be said about this is that seldom do the two classes of disease sore spots hit at the same time in this part of the world.

Fungi need moisture and cannot survive dry conditions except in the resting state. To enable fungi to multiply, the weather must be favorably moist not only for spore formation, but also for spore germination.

That is the reason why we are not so troubled by fungal diseases in Alberta. Our dry atmosphere and comparitively low rainfall are not favorable to their growth. This does not mean, however, that we are entirely free from fungal diseases.

The class fungi includes all those growths popularly known as mushrooms or toadstools, rusts, smuts, molds and mildews.

However, these form but a small part of the total number. All the parts of a fungus plant are seldom seen. That part which is usually exposed to view and which is popularly designated as a fungus is merely the fertile or fruit-bearing part of the fungus plant. A mushroom is the fruit of a fungus.

The vegetable part, that which supplies materials for the growth of the fruit and which in a way, corresponds to the roots and leaves of higher plants, is hidden away in the ground in organic matter or within the tissues of other living plants upon which the fungus feeds.

In spring, Calgarians may find their lawns disfigured with patches of a fungus botanically known as sclerotinia nomococarpa, commonly called snow mold or brown patch. The cure: bichloride of mercury, which is a general disinfectant and a virulent poison. The way to prevent or cure snow mold is more fully described in the chapter on lawns.

Mildews form a clearly-defined group, the different species of which attack all types of plants. The true mildews are fungi which grow over the surface of plants, not inside the tissues. Fortunately, satisfactory control methods are available in sprays.

Nearly any fungicide will kill mildews, but they are particularly easily killed by sulphur. First spray with water the leaves of plants attacked by mildew and then apply sulphur dust, the dust adhering to the wet leaves.

Potato ring rot, potato scab, potato leaf curl and potato stem rot or black leg are only a few of the many diseases which attack potatoes.

Quite a number of potato diseases may be prevented by frequent spraying of Bordeaux mixture, if this is carried out at the proper time. The correct time of application is just before blight appears and afterwards at intervals of three weeks. Experience is the safest guide to tell you when to spray, but as a very rough guide to the amateur, I would suggest spraying when the potato plant is about a foot high.

If gardeners formed the habit of spraying gardens to keep them clean, many of the pests and diseases would not appear, and if they did, they would be under better control. Again, as a very general guide, I suggest spraying annuals once a month, starting late in May.

The Colorado beetle, or potato bug is one of the worst pests. As the name indicates, it was originally a native of the Rocky Mountain area in the Colorado region and then fed on weeds belonging to the wild potato family. When that part of the West was developed, and real potatoes were planted, the Colorado beetle improved its diet and turned its hungry attention to this crop. It has been a pest of the first order ever since.

This bug can be exterminated by spraying potatoes with paris green, using three to five tablespoonsful to a gallon of water.

The beetles emerge from the soil and lay clusters of small, yellowish eggs on the under side of the potato leaves.

Soon, the eggs hatch into grubs which feed on the leaves for about three weeks, at the end of which time they are fully grown.

So when spraying the potato leaves be sure to spray under the leaves as well as the upper side of the leaves.

Green-fly or aphis is another pest which attacks all sorts of trees, shrubs, and plants, also generally on the under side of a leaf. To be rid of this pest, spray with Black Leaf 40, using two teaspoonfuls to one gallon of water, melting one inch square of soap and mixing with the water.

Spray plants every eight or ten days until rid of the aphis. Remember to spray the under side of the leaf, particularly.

Malothine may also be used for spraying aphis and other bugs, using as directed on the instructions.

Bordeaux mixture is an effective fungicide for controlling any diseases affecting perennials. Use eight tablespoonfuls of mixture to a gallon of water.

This fungicide is particularly effective against stem rot or black leg on peonies, if the disease hasn't progressed too far.

Asters are subject to a disease known as aster wilt, particularly during a wet, cold spring and summer. With this disease, a malformation of the buds and blooms takes place, marring the beauty of the plants and causing many of them to die early.

You can't do anything for the asters already infested.

When the disease has been present, it is unwise to plant more asters in the same soil the following year. The disease is known to stay in the soil and again attack asters the next year.

The soil should be sterilized with formaldehyde.

Asters require a fairly dry location in the garden. There are, however, several varieties of asters on the market which are disease-resistant, and you are advised to buy these when you go shopping for asters.

Delphiniums may be attacked by the aster beetle in the early part of the season, cutting out the flowering spike.

Soot and wood ashes poured over the crowns of delphiniums in the early spring will help eliminate this nuisance.

Also, delphiniums may be sprayed with Black Leaf 40, using two teaspoonsful to one gallon of water. Melt a square inch of ordinary soap, and add this to the water. Spray every week until you get rid of the beetles.

This spray also is effective against greenfly, to which delphiniums also are subject.

For the widespread treatment of soils which are disease-infected, an effective disinfectant is potassium permanganate. This will eradicate spores of fungus diseases on plants.

Stir half a teaspoonful of the crystals into a gallon of water. This is enough to make an effective solution which is not, however, harmful to plants. Disinfect the soil before crops are sown by soaking it thoroughly with the solution; then wait ten days before planting any crop.

Potassium permanganate crystals sprinkled around plants will help greatly in keeping away cut worms and other destructive insects.

Another useful chemical for sterilizing soil is formaldehyde. This liquid should be used at the rate of one pint in six gallons of water, and the soil should be soaked with the solution.

The soil should be dug over and loosened first, and care should be taken that it is not made too wet.

The area can be used for planting after ten days, or when there is no odor left.

If the soil is treated in this manner before planting, fungus diseases or insect pests won't gain the upper hand in your garden.

LAYOUT OF GROUNDS

When planning the laying out of the grounds around a home, it is wise first to make a plan on paper.

It is easier to remedy a mistake made with pencil on paper than when the work, often back-breaking, is completed or even partly completed on the grounds.

With a sketch of your grounds, you will know just where you wish every tree and shrub to be placed, as well as your perennial and annual flower beds.

The nature of the terrain must be considered when landscaping grounds. You must provide suitable depth of good soil, and you must avoid, as far as possible, the need for extensive earth-removing to ensure acceptable grades.

Often it is possible to reduce the amount of grading needed and at the same time add to the interest of the garden by making it in one, two or more levels with steps and low retaining walls of stone or bricks. Grassy banks may also be used to set up terraces.

A garden, beds, or borders for the cultivation of perennials should for the most part be located in the open. Some shade is not objectionable over part of the layout provided there is not too much competition from tree or shrub roots.

The area should be related to its surroundings. Some times it may be an informal affair, roughly parallelling the outlines of a shrub border with a curving front edge, the lawn in the foreground, and the border providing a suitable background.

This is perhaps the simplest way of locating a perennial border, but it has some troublesome features. There is the competition with tree and shrub roots to be dealt with, because ultimately the growth of the shrubs will gradually eleminate the back row of perennials.

If this happens, it would necessitate of course re-planting the border, moving it forward, and stealing another 2 or 3 feet from the lawn.

One way of meeting this situation if you have enough space is to maintain a walk between the shrubbery and the perennials to eliminate root competition. By restricting shrubs by annual pruning, it is possible to maintain a border in this way for many years.

A formal clipped hedge makes an excellent background for perennials. Here again there should be a space of at least 2 feet between it and the flowers, not only to avoid root problems but to prevent mutual injury and to permit clipping the hedge without interfering with the flowers.

But often, in the case of smaller properties, a strip 2 or more feet wide right alongside the boundary fence or alongside a wall may be the most satisfactory location for a border.

A fence or a wall may be covered with vines or climbing shrubs to enhance the background.

175

On even larger properties, the flower garden can be screened by shrubs or a formal clipped hedge, with the perennials displayed in the bed and borders, which may be informal or partly formal in character.

If you wish annuals, and any other plants grown as annuals, to do the most they are capable of doing to beautify the garden and grounds, you must also give considerable thought to where and how you are going to use them.

There is a mistaken but all-too-widely held assumption that annuals are merely pinch-hitters to be stuck here or there where other plants have not yet been established, or have failed.

Learn to look upon annuals as one of the most important of several different types of plant material you can use to create a well-rounded and constantly colorful home landscape, and you will find them rewarding indeed.

This involves, on the gardener's part, some definite decisions as to the effects or the results he or she wishes to obtain; and, following that, careful planning as to what and where to use plants.

It is true many gardeners, even experienced ones, do not take the trouble to work out a plan. It is also true, however, that those who do, get the most satisfactory results.

Morever, making a plan for the annuals, like making a plan for the general layout of the garden, saves both time and labor — time, because when it comes to planting, the gardener knows just where each basket of annuals is to be planted and where each packet of seed, or group of plants, is to go, and he has the ground prepared in advance.

It can prevent mistakes such as placing the tall-growing varieties in front of lower-growing ones, thus partly or completely hiding the latter from view, and making it impossible to carry out a desirable color scheme.

Also it can result in spots of flowerless foliage here and there in a mixed border through having annuals with the same blooming season planted next to each other.

Many beginners have a slight dread of the thought of attempting to make a plan. They seem to feel that course in landscape architecture is essential to anything they regard as so complicated. Their fears are groundless.

They may bolster their hesitant spirits by saying: "It's a poor thing, but it is mine own." And the very fact it is their own will add immeasurably to its value. Nobody can make a plan without acquiring a great deal of valuable knowledge about the different plants involved in its component parts.

Now to set about making a general plan for a garden layout.

There are two main steps. First, decide on the different areas to be planted and the general size and shape of each; secondly, work out details for each area.

Following is a suggested procedure:

1—Attach a sheet of cross-ruled paper (which you can obtain from any stationary store), to a piece of cardboard or light plywood. This makes it easy for you to carry and to rough-draw your plan.

2—Indicate on this sheet the boundary lines of your property, using a scale of an eighth of an inch to a foot, or whatever scale is convenient. Now locate on the sheet the house, garage, driveway, paths, trees, rockery or any other feature you have in mind.

3—Now comes the first planning. Indicate in a general way the areas to be assigned to different uses: lawn, play yard, vegetable garden, main shrub and flower beds and borders, shade trees, rock garden, pool and maybe even a sun dial.

4—This preliminary work having been done in rough, you are now ready to draw a detailed, more exact plan for each area where annuals, perennials, borders, shrubs, trees, and any other plants you desire are to be planted.

Then, all that is necessary is to go to it and do the job!

Long flower borders, straight or curved, should be at least 3 feet from back to front, and better still, a foot or two more.

If the front is arranged in a series of sweeping curves, providing a succession of small bays and promontories, the effect will usually be much more pleasing than if it is made a straight line. Not only will the front edge actually be longer, but to the eye it will appear even longer than it is.

If the design is to be formal, similar to Calgary's Memorial Park, then floral beds, rectangular in shape or of some other fixed geometric pattern, will of course be in order.

To get effective masses of color and also to avoid a spotty appearance, several plants of each variety should be planted in a group. In the large gardens these groups may be repeated as often as desired; never less than five, and preferably more, should be planted together.

The few exceptions to this rule are such large or dominating plants as castor bean (ricinus) and the large type of sunflowers.

The larger the bed or border, the larger should be the size of the individual units of color (that is the number of individual plants in each group).

Whether annuals are used by themselves in an all-annual border or as supplementary material in a mixed border, it is all-important to keep in mind the height to which each kind will grow. Unless this is done, the border will be jumbled and ragged in appearance, with a large proportion of the flowers hidden by taller ones in front of them.

It is especially necessary to have a plan before planting trees and shrubs in the spring, because in this way you will be sure of the exact location where you really want to plant them. And also because trees and shrubs cannot be moved around like flowers without the danger of severe setbacks.

Transplanting trees or shrubs in the fall is not good here. Spring definitely is the best time for this operation. Fall planting may be carried out more successfully in moderate climates, but not in Alberta.

Central Park, Calgary

177

VEGETABLES

Introduction

Just because there are so many flower lovers in Calgary we should not forget that there are very many fine vegetable growers here, too.

There is a great deal of satisfaction in growing tasty vegetables. What can compare with well-grown fresh vegetables from your own garden?

But before those good-tasting vegetables appear on your table there is work to be done.

The first thing to be considered is selection of the site; then the preparation of the soil.

Location of the vegetable garden is important. One thing essential is an abundance of sunshine. The shade of tall trees or a hedge that casts a continually shifting shadow upon the vegetable rows will not be too serious, but every square foot of garden should get at least six hours of full sunshine daily.

More sunshine than that is preferable in early spring, for asparagus and for rhubarb which then make their most rapid growth, but will stand considerable shade later in the season.

Lettuce, on the other hand, is rather benefited by slight shade during very hot weather. But even lettuce as a general rule likes a fair amount of sunshine.

Every vegetable garden should have good drainage. A boggy or swampy location, in which water has a tendency to remain and to become sour, is not a good place for a garden.

The garden should also be protected from injury, damage by dogs, cats, or children not trained to have proper respect for the garden or for the plants. The experienced gardener would not think of attempting to plant a garden where injuries from such sources are likely. The amateur may go ahead without thought of such things, and regret it later.

Chicken wire with a 2-inch mesh and 4 to 5 feet high, supported by posts firmly set in the ground at intervals of 8 to 10 feet, will supply adequate protection.

The lower edge of the wire should be buried 2 or 3 inches deep and firmly pegged down.

Such protection will, of course, make an additional item of expense the first year, but it is a worthwhile investment. If kept in repair it will last for many years.

Such a fence will also serve as a permanent support for sweet peas, green peas, tomato plants and can also be used for the growing of vines such as clematis, Virginia creeper and other climbing plants.

To obtain a good vegetable garden you must have well-prepared soil. Many think that there is not much skill required in digging, but to dig a garden correctly is quite an art.

Start at one end of the vegetable garden, and take out one spitful of earth across the area. A spitful is a clump of soil the width and depth of a spade. It should measure 9 to 10 inches square.

This soil should be wheeled in a barrow to the opposite end of the vegetable garden to be used for filling in the last trench. As digging is continued, each spadeful is placed upside down in the empty trench.

The secret of smooth, level digging is to have each spitful exactly the same size.

Many do their digging in the spring, but when done in the fall the soil is more mellow, and easier worked than in the spring. The soil also benefits from exposure to the elements during the winter.

Whether done in the spring or fall, manure should be spread into each trench as you dig, 3 or 4 inches deep.

If dug in the fall, all that is necessary when spring comes is to fork the soil lightly. This forking serves to break up the lumpy soil, which is then raked into a fine tilth, making a smooth and level seed bed.

If you have left digging until spring, rake the ground immediately after it is dug. This is necessary, as soil dries out rapidly from wind and sun in the spring.

Many persons nowadays of course prefer to have their garden dug by roto-tiller — and there are still some who use a hand-plow (if they can find a horse) for large gardens.

The same rules apply for those who have their garden dug by roto-tiller as apply for hand digging. Only its harder on the pocketbook, and easier on the back.

It is better to use the roto-tiller in the fall, having first spread manure or fertilizer over the top and mixing it in the soil when you till it. Then in spring all that is necessary is a light turn-over of the soil — if you want to, this can again be done by roto-tiller.

In planning the planting of a vegetable garden, taller-growing products should be planted on the north or west sides. Planted otherwise, they can prevent smaller vegetables from receiving necessary amounts of sunshine.

Most vegetables should be sown or planted after May 24. However, there are some which should be sown a bit later because of their susceptibility to late frost.

Among these tender vegetables are: sweet corn, dwarf beans, tomatoes, cucumbers, pumpkins, squash and vegetable marrows.

These should not be set out or sown until all danger of frost is past, usually after the first week in June.

The equipment required in the care of a moderate-sized garden need not be too extensive or expensive, but it pays to have well-made tools. The best are the cheapest in the long run. Cheap tools will likely break after a short time and so eventually cost you more than the best.

For the average garden you will need a spade, four-tine fork, an iron rake with wooden handle, a draw hoe, Dutch hoe, edging iron, garden line, garden hose, wheelbarrow, and mower.

A small sprayer will be needed, too, for the control of weeds, pests, and diseases, if you are to keep your garden clean.

When possible, I prefer that all vegetables should be planted or sown with the rows running north and south. The garden line should be used to ensure straight rows. Rows of vegetables look most unattractive, I think, unless they are straight.

Regular cultivation between the rows and hand-weeding in the rows is of supreme importance, if proper growth is to take place.

A great many vegetables can be grown here from seed started outdoors in the garden, but there are some of the more tender types which are better started indoors in the greenhouse where they can have an earlier start free from the dangers of our unpredictable spring with its dangers of frost.

Muskmelon, cucumbers and watermelon are among those best grown from start to finish in the greenhouse.

I shall not write about all the vegetables that may be grown here, only about some of the more popular ones. Also I have not touched on such vegetables as artichokes, broccoli or brussels sprouts because it is most difficult, if not impossible, to grow these in this part of the country.

Most of the everyday vegetables like beets, carrots, lettuce, onions and spinach are generally sown between 12 and 18 inches between rows, but if the vegetable garden is quite small these distances may of course be reduced.

There are many excellent varieties of seeds available in the stores. It is unnecessary for me to mention them all, but I have listed several varieties in most types of vegetables to give you a choice. These varieties I can recommend after many years' experience with them in Calgary, and I know that these, given proper care, are suitable for growing here.

Generally speaking, I also recommend planting the earlier varieties for local gardens, because in most cases the late varieties will not mature in this climate. This especially applies to potatoes.

A final tip on watering: as a rule, don't water late in the cool of the evenings. It is generally better, with some exceptions, to irrigate in the noontime heat. Watering in the evenings may bring on rust and mildew, especially in the case of leafy vegetables.

Following are details about growing some of the vegetables most suitable for our climatic conditions, the vegetables being listed in alphabetical order, with a summarized "planting guide in brief" for each type added for the readers' fast information:

ASPARAGUS

Asparagus is one of the most delicious of early spring vegetables, and its cultivation gives little trouble, providing the soil bed is prepared correctly before the plants are set in.

Rich, light, loamy soil provides perfect conditions for the cultivation of asparagus, but this vegetable can be made to thrive on any good garden soil by thorough and correct cultivation of the site.

This should be prepared in the fall, so that everything may be in readiness for planting in spring.

In making an asparagus bed, the ground should be excavated to a depth of 2 feet. If the soil is clayey, drainage must be provided by laying in a bed of gravel. It is an advantage to have the surface of the asparagus bed raised about 6 inches above ground level.

Partly decayed farmyard manure should be mixed in with the lower layer of soil, and coarse bone meal in the proportion of 3 or 4 ounces a square yard. The upper soil should be mixed with bone flour.

A convenient width for an asparagus bed in a limited space is about 3 feet. The length will of course depend on the area of ground available. A bed of this width will take two rows of plants, set 12 inches apart and a foot in from each edge of the trench.

As an asparagus bed will continue profitable for at least 20 years, and probably much longer, it is worthwhile taking great care in preparing the site so that there will be 2 feet of rich, fertile, well-drained soil.

The best time to plant asparagus is in late April. Roots two years old may be set in. Small ridges of soil should be drawn up where the plants are to be set, so the crowns (that is, the dormant buds) are on top of the ridge, and the roots down the sides.

A soil-covering of 5 or 6 inches is necessary. The roots should be 12 inches apart. If asparagus roots are exposed for a long time and are allowed to become dry, they will start into growth slowly, if, indeed, they start at all.

It is most necessary to keep them moist during the time they are out of the ground. While waiting to be planted they should be covered with wet sacks, and it's a good idea to soak them in water before they are set in the soil.

The routine work in connection with management of an asparagus bed is not heavy, but it must be attended to carefully. A dressing of salt should be given in late April, or early May, using an ounce to the square yard of surface.

If one-year-old roots are planted, asparagus should not be cut until the third year.

If two-year-old roots are put in, the produce should not be cut until the second year.

Three-year-old roots will produce asparagus the year following planting.

Do not cut asparagus tips after the end of June. They are sour then.

During the summer, when the plants are growing freely, the bed, or rows, must be kept moist in hot, dry weather by watering. The shoots ought not to be cut after the third week of June, otherwise the plants will also be prevented from making vigorous growth and building up strong crowns for next year's crop.

After cutting has stopped, an occasional watering with liquid manure will prove helpful in assuring development of strong plants. When the foliage turns yellow in the fall, the stems should be cut to ground level.

Those who wish to raise their own asparagus plants may do so by sowing seeds outside in May. Make a small trench 2 inches deep and scatter the seeds along the trench. Cover them over, and when large enough, the seedlings may be transferred to their permanent position in the garden.

Planting Guide in Brief

Recommended Varieties:
Early—Mary Washington and Paradise.
Mid-season—Giant Dutch and Early Giant.
Late—Connover's Colossal (extra vigorous roots and large-size asparagus shoots).
Main Crop—Giant Dutch.

How and When to Plant:

Plant 3-year roots outside in late April; 5 or 6 inches deep; 12 inches between roots; 12 inches between rows; water well, salt and cultivate.

Crop Available:

In Mid-May from early varieties to about mid-June from later varieties.

BEANS

BROAD BEANS

The broad bean, favored by many, is a hardy annual. Its botanical name is faba vulgaris, and it belongs to the pea family leguminosae.

The plant has erect quadrangular stems and grey-green leaves, and bears clusters of five to eight pea-like flowers which are followed by pods. Each pod contains five to eight edible, flat seeds.

Deeply dug ground, enriched with decayed manure, should be prepared for broad beans a week or two before planting, providing the weather is favorable. One ounce of sulphate of potash should be applied to each square yard of ground. On light soils, two ounces of bone meal a square yard is recommended.

Broad beans may be planted outside early in May, or earlier, weather permitting. They should be planted in rows 6 to 8 inches apart, and 2 to 2½ feet feet between rows. The bean seeds should be planted 4 to 6 inches deep, depending on the nature of the soil, deeper in light soil and 4 inches in heavy soil.

The growing tips of all broad bean plants are pinched out as soon as the lower trusses of flowers have set pods, generally when the plants are about 2 to 2½ feet tall. This helps develop finer pods.

Planting Guide in Brief

Recommended Varieties:

Early and Main Crops—Giant Windsor and Longpod Seville.
Mid-Season—Broad Windsor and Prolific Longpod.

How and When to Plant:

Plant seeds outdoors early in May; 4 to 6 inches deep; 6 to 8 inches apart; 2 to 2½ feet between rows. Thin when 6 inches high. Stake when 12 inches high. Pinch out growing tips when plants about 2 to 2½ feet high. Water at noon. Cultivate intensively.

Crops Available:

Early crop, in mid-July; mid-season, in August.

FRENCH BEANS

The French bean is a wax pod or butter bean. These half-hardy annuals are from South America, belonging to the pea family.

The French bean thrives best in a rich, light soil. The ground should be dug deeply and manured. A dressing of potash at the rate of two ounces to the square yard will prove beneficial.

These beans should be planted at a depth of 3 inches, 4 to 5 inches apart in rows, with 16 inches between rows.

Care should be taken to gather the pods while they are young and tender. Some persons leave the pods on the plants until seeds form, which is not good, because they become tough.

Don't plant French beans until the first week in June (even maybe June 10), because they are easily damaged by a light frost. Don't water French beans when the weather is cool, and especially not in the evenings. Watering in cool or cold weather will result in rust forming on the plants and may render them useless. French beans should be watered when it's hot, at noontime by irrigation for the best results.

Planting Guide in Brief

Recommended Varieties:
>Early—Canadian Wonder, Masterpiece, Cherokee Wax, Improved Golden.
>Mid-Season—Kinghorn Brittle Wax.
>Main Crop—Cherokee Wax.

How and When to Plant:
>Plant seeds outside between June 1 and 10; 3 inches deep; 4 to 5 inches apart; 16 inches between rows. Don't thin out. Water only around noontime when it's really hot.

Crops Available:
>Early crops starting about mid-July; mid-season, until about end of August; main crops, from late July until about end of August.

SCARLET RUNNERS

Scarlet runners are perhaps the choicest and most popular of the bean family. Being climbers, they should be trained on a wire fence or on stakes.

These beans should be planted 4 to 5 inches deep (4 if ground is heavy) and 9 to 10 inches apart, in rows 48 inches apart.

They should be planted in a rather protected part of the garden.

The scarlet flowers on the runner beans attract the elusive little humming birds, and I have known people grow scarlet runner beans especially for this attraction.

When the plants are about 9 to 10 inches high, place stakes behind each. The habit of the scarlet runner is to twine itself around the stake in the direction of the sun. It could be said they follow the sun.

When staking, start these beans in that direction, and the plants will continue in this manner until they reach the top of the stakes.

Planting Guide in Brief

Recommended Varieties:
>Early—Scarlet Runner, Kentucky Wonder Green, Early Blue Lake (for canning or freezing).
>Mid-Season—Scotia and Old Homestead.
>Main Crops—Kentucky Wonder or Old Homestead.

How and When to Plant:
>Plant seeds outside 4 to 5 inches deep in mid- or late May; 9 to 10 inches apart; 48 inches between rows. Stake when 9 inches high. Don't thin. Cultivate continually and water when hot, generally around noon.

Crops Available:
>Early crop, starting about late July; mid-season and main crops, generally during August.

DWARF BEANS

The tough green podded dwarf beans have flattish pods which become leathery when ripe. Edible green-podded or mange-tout beans never become stringy, even when ripe, and their pods are eaten whole when small.

The dwarf bean's botanical name is phaseolus vulgaris.

Planting Guide in Brief

Recommended Varieties:

Early—Contender and Tendergreen.
Mid-Season—Seminole and Tender Best.
Main Crop—Tender Best.

How and When to Plant:

Plant seeds outside between June 1 and 10; 4 to 5 inches deep; 6 inches apart; 15 inches between rows. Don't thin. Cultivate regularly and water around noon.

Crops Available:

Early crop, starting about end of July; mid-season, about mid-August; main crop, from about the end of July until toward end of August.

BEETS

Beetroot, another valuable root vegetable, is represented by numerous varieties. There are two principal types — the long beet, and the globe or round beet.

They may be sown outdoors after May 24, or earlier if the weather is fine and warm, in drills 2 inches deep; with 15 inches between rows. The seed should be scattered thinly along the rows, and covered.

When seedlings are 2 inches high, they should be thinned to 3 or even 6 inches apart. The thinning should be done gradually, the weakest plants being removed first. Many people like to cook the thinned-out young beets as a type of spinach.

As soon as the plants are above ground and can be seen easily, hoeing should be done frequently to keep down weeds and to encourage growth. Cultivation is of the utmost importance in the growing of all vegetables.

The long-rooted beets need deep, light, rich soil which should be free from lumps and free from fresh manure. If the ground has not been well-worked and if it remains lumpy, beets will be deformed, especially the long beets. It is a good idea to grow beets in a plot of ground that was deeply dug and manured the previous year.

When lifting beets in the fall, the top should be twisted off, not cut, or the beetroots will "bleed." Beets are easily stored in sand during the winter in a temperature of 35 degrees Fahrenheit.

Planting Guide in Brief

Recommended Varieties:

Early—Improved Dark Red, Red King, and Half Long Blood.
Mid-Season—Blood Red.
Late—Egyptian Turnip Rooted and Lutz Green Leaf.
Main Crop—Egyptian Turnip Rooted.

184

How and When to Plant:

Plant seeds outdoors about May 24; 2 inches deep; 16 inches apart; 15 inches between rows. Thin to 6 inches apart when seedlings 2 inches high. Cultivate frequently. Sprinkle lightly.

Crops Available:

Early crop, starting about July 10; mid-season, about Aug. 1; late, until about Sept. 1; main crop, from about Aug. 1 to Sept. 1.

CABBAGES

The cabbage, believe it or not, belongs to the wallflower family. It is often thought of as the commonest crop grown in the garden.

But because it is so easily grown, it is frequently cultivated in a haphazard fashion, and as a result often leaves only are produced and not firm heads.

The best way to raise cabbage here is to sow seeds indoors about the middle of April. They grow rapidly, in the greenhouse, and will be ready to plant outdoors by the middle of May provided the weather is favorable.

Early varieties of seed can be sown outdoors, but it's taking a big chance in this climate. If you insist, however, in seeding outside, then sow the seeds in the second week of May. But I would again warn you experience here generally has shown that it's wiser to seed indoors.

Cabbage seeds should be sown in a compost of two parts loam, one part peat moss, and one part sharp sand mixed well together. Sharp sand is coarse sand. Use flats about 2 inches deep for this purpose, and fill them with the compost, firming the soil and levelling it off with a piece of lath.

Sow the seeds and cover them in the usual manner with a mixture of soil and sand. Water with a fine spray and then cover the flats with paper, placing the flats in a warm, dark place until the seeds germinate.

They should then be brought gradually to the light, and later pricked off into larger flats when the third leaf appears. Cabbage plants, like most others, must be gradually hardened, especially if grown in the house or a greenhouse.

When they are about 3 inches, plant out of doors, 2 feet apart and 2 feet between rows.

Cabbage thrive outside best in a rich, fairly heavy soil, and require lots of water during the growing season.

Planting Guide in Brief

Recommended Varieties:

Early—Golden Acre, Golden Acre Elite, Canadian Acre, Copenhagen Market, Danish Ball Head, American Drumhead (savoy); Red Acre, and Mammoth Red Rock (red cabbage for pickling).

Mid-Season—Bonanza O-S Cross, Burpee's Allhead, Early Steins, and Flat Dutch.

Late—Penn State Ballhead, Perfection, Drumhead, Mammoth, and Red Rock.

Main Crop—Burpee's Allhead, or Early Steins, or Flat Dutch.

How and When to Plant:

Sow seeds indoors about middle of April; ½ inch deep. Plant seedlings outside about May 24 when they're 3 inches high; 3 inches deep; 2 feet apart and 2 feet between rows. Cultivate Continually. Water heavily.

Crops Available:

Early crops, starting about end of July; mid-season, from about mid-August; late, until Sept. 1; main crop, in August.

CAULIFLOWERS

This delicious vegetable of summer and fall closely resembles broccoli in appearance, though the edible heads are usually smaller and of finer flavor.

Cauliflowers thrive best in rich, loamy soil, but ordinary garden soil may be made suitable by deep digging and manuring. The ground should be dug in the fall, with manure added.

Seeds of cauliflower may be sown in April in a heated greenhouse or sun porch in a temperature of 60 degrees in a flat of sifted, sandy loam.

As soon as they are an inch high, the seedlings are pricked off, and put 2 inches apart in flats filled with equal parts of loam, peat moss and sand. They are then treated the same as cabbage plants.

When the plants are 3 to 4 inches tall they are set out in the garden about the end of May, but make sure they have been properly hardened. Plants are set out 20 inches apart, with 2 feet between rows.

Planting Guide in Brief

Recommended Varieties:

Early—Extra Early Snowball, Madsen's Super Snowball, and Snowball X.
Mid-Season—Improved Snowball and Walcheren.
Late—Conquest.
Main Crop—Improved Snowball.

How and When to Plant:

Sow seed in greenhouse about April 15. Prick off 1-inch seedlings into flats; harden off. Plant outdoors about May 24 when seedlings about 3 to 4 inches high; 20 inches apart; 2 feet between rows. Cultivate intensively. Water often.

Crops Available:

Early crops, starting about mid-July; mid-season, starting in August; late, until Sept. 15; main crop, during August.

CARROTS

One of the most popular and widely used vegetables is the carrot. The botanical name is daucus carota.

It has much-divided foliage and reddish-yellow roots which differ widely in size and shape.

Being a biennial, small whitish flowers don't appear until the year following that in which seeds are sown. But most people grow carrots only for the first-year root; the flowers are grown only if seeds are to be gathered from them. Here, because of our climate, they would have to be taken in for the winter and set out again the following spring so that they could produce flowers and seed.

Carrots, like other vegetable root crops, require a rich, sandy soil. It is usual to cultivate them on ground that was well-manured the previous year. The manure will be well decayed by spring, and the soil will be rich enough then for growing excellent carrots. If grown in lumpy soil, or that which contains fresh manure, the roots are likely to be misshapen.

Carrots may be grown, from seed outdoors, any time after May 24, or earlier if the weather is fine and warm. They are sown in small drills about 2 inches deep, with 15 inches between rows. The seeds must be sufficiently covered, and this is generally done by passing the back of a rake over the drill rows.

When the third, or permanent leaf appears, the seedlings should be thinned out to 2 inches apart and later to 3 inches apart. The seedlings pulled out at the second thinning will be large enough for cooking, and they are also deliciously sweet and tender eaten raw.

The best time to thin carrots, or any other vegetable that requires thinning, is when the soil is really moist after a heavy rain.

After the thinnings, the soil should be firmed along the rows. The soil between rows of carrots needs to be cultivated throughout the season; on an average of once a week should be sufficient. When cultivating between rows, it is a good idea to till the soil up toward the carrots to keep the roots covered. This will prevent the green shoulders so often seen on these vegetables.

Carrots are more easily stored throughout the winter than perhaps any other vegetable. They keep excellently in slightly damp sand and in a temperature of 35 degrees.

Planting Guide in Brief

Recommended Varieties:

Early—Early Short Horn, Early Nantes, Chantenay Half-Long, Nantes Improved, and Long Imperator.
Mid-Season—St. Valery and Intermediate Improved.
Late—Gold Pak.
Main Crop—Early Nantes.

How and When to Plant:

Plant seed outdoors after May 24 (or maybe earlier); 2 inches deep; scatter thinly; 15 inches between rows. Thin out when third leaf appears, to 2 inches apart, later to 3 inches. Cultivate continually. Water heavily.

Crops Available:

Early crops, starting about mid-July; mid-season, about mid-August; late, in September; main crop, during August.

CELERY

Another health-giving vegetable is celery, which for best results is grown in a prepared trench.

Seeds of celery first must be grown in the house or in a greenhouse, sown in early March at a temperature of 65 degrees in a flat filled with a sandy compost of loam, peat moss and sand.

The seeds are covered with the merest sprinkling of compost, and then treated the same way as other vegetable seeds.

187

When seedlings have formed two or three leaves, they are pricked off, at 3 or 4 inches apart, in flats filled 4 inches deep with a compost of equal parts of loam, peat moss and rotted manure, and placed near the glass in a temperature of 60 degrees.

They must be kept moist at the roots; if the soil is allowed to become dry, growth of the plants will be checked and that may prove disastrous.

The seedlings must be kept warm for a week or two, but as spring advances the greenhouse must be ventilated freely. About the first week of May the flats of celery are placed in a cold frame. There the plants will be hardened off, preparatory to being planted outside about the middle of May.

The usual method of cultivation is to set out the plants in trenches dug in deep, rich soil. The trenches should be a foot deep and a foot wide for a single row of celery. A good heavy layer of manure 4 to 5 inches deep is placed in the bottom of the trench and covered with 6 inches of soil.

Now the celery plants are set in, 10 inches apart, in the centre of the trench, and watered. If dry weather sets in, and it usually may in June and July in this part of the country, the celery must be watered periodically, for it is most necessary that the soil be kept moist to produce thick, succulent stalks.

When plants are well-established, occasional applications of liquid manure are beneficial.

No earthing up must be done until the plants are almost full grown, or their development will be retarded. Earthing up is the process of mounding up soil around the stems to blanch them and to render them fit for use.

Some people use cardboard collars around the celery stems to assist in blanching them, and this is to be recommended.

Planting Guide in Brief

Recommended Varieties:

Early—Golden Plume, Golden Self-Blanching (white), and Utah 15 (outstanding green).

Mid-Season—Burpee's Fordhook, Giant Red, and Gigantica Pink.

Late—Giant Pascal.

Main Crop—Giant Red or Gigantica Pink.

How and When to Plant:

Sow seed in greenhouse early in March; prick off when seedling have 2 or 3 leaves; plant in flat 3 to 4 inches apart; soil must always be moist; place flats in coldframe early in May; harden off. Plant seedlings outside about middle of May; plants 10 inches apart; soil always moist; apply liquid manure. Don't earth up until plants almost full grown.

Crops Available:

Early crop, about end of August; mid-season and late, from September until freeze-up.

CORN

There is difficulty in Calgary in ripening sweet corn because of our short growing season and early frosts. One way to try to overcome this difficulty is to start corn inside, planting the seed in individual 3-inch pots.

Seeds can be grown either in the greenhouse or home until they are a foot tall. Then harden them off, in a coldframe. After they're properly hardened, they may be planted outside about the first of June.

Corn loves a rich, light, sandy loam, and the sunniest, most sheltered location in the garden, protected from winds.

There should be 2 feet between plants and at least 3 feet between rows.

Try to buy the very best early variety of corn. Pull all suckers which grow from the base of the main stem, otherwise the main plant will fail to develop properly. Water during the heat of the day; watering during the cool of the evening is detrimental to growth and also may cause mildew.

Several excellent hybrid varieties of corn have been developed for this part of the country.

Planting Guide in Brief

Recommended Varieties:
> Early—Earliest Golden Sweet, Extra Early Golden Bantam, and Dorinny. Mid-Season and Main Crop—Golden Beauty.

How and When to Plant:
> Plant seed in pot in greenhouse about May 1; grow there until 12 inches high; harden in coldframe. Plant young plants outside about June 1; 3 to 4 inches deep; 2 feet between plants; 3 feet between rows. Only water during heat of day. Cultivate regularly.

Crops Available:
> Early crops, starting about Aug. 15; mid-season and main crop; from Aug. 31 until frost.

CUCUMBER

Cucumbers can be grown in a frame placed on a hotbed. The hotbed is made of fresh horse manure which has been turned several times. On the Prairies the stable manure is inclined to be on the dry side; therefore it must be wetted down with water from a hose.

The hotbed should be 12 inches longer and wider than the frame, and made firm by treading it down firmly.

A layer of soil 10 inches deep, consisting of fibrous loam mixed with one part of decayed manure, is spaded on top of the horse manure 10 days before cucumber planting time.

About the end of April or the beginning of May seed should be sown directly in the soil, or plants (from seed grown in the greenhouse a month previously) can be planted; two plants to each frame.

A glass sash must be put over them for a few days until they are properly rooted. They must be lightly shaded at first, using whitening, or lime and water mixed, to lightly coat the glass.

A temperature of 70 degrees Fahrenheit by day and 60 degrees by night is required. Soft water at the same temperature as the air in the frame must be used for watering, and the plants must be syringed twice daily with tepid water.

When the plants are 9 to 10 inches high, the tops are pinched off. When the shoots have four leaves, their points are pinched out to further ensure side growths.

No further pinching out is done until fruits are formed. Then the growing point of each fruiting shoot is nipped out at a point two leaves beyond the fruit.

Water in such a way that while there is an abundance of moisture at the roots, a saturated condition is avoided. Air must be admitted freely.

189

If the frame is heated by waterpipes, similar treatment should be followed. But a hotbed is not necessary.

Gherkins (which are only grown outdoors) and ridge cucumbers can both be grown outside in Calgary with care, and with some luck.

Cucumber plants are subject to several diseases, including leaf spot, leaf blot, mildew and cucumber wilt. But if careful attention is given to the plants, all these diseases may be avoided.

Planting Guide in Brief

Recommended Varieties:

Marketer, Mandarin, Palomar, Everbearing, Burpee's Hybrids, Sparta and Stockwood Ridge.

How and When to Plant:

Plant seed in a frame in a hotbed about end of April or early May. Shade with a glass sash; daytime temperature of 70 degrees F. and night-time temperature 60. Pinch off tops when plants 9 inches high. After fruits formed, pinch out shoot at a point two leaves above fruit. Water carefully.

Crops Available:

Starting about Aug. 31 and until frost.

HORSE-RADISH

Roast beef, in my opinion, is not complete without a touch of appetizing horse-radish.

A deep loam with good texture and moderately rich in humus, fairly open and sandy will produce horse-radish roots of the best quality and the largest size. Grown in dry soil the roots will be smaller, woody, and deficient in pungency, wet and strong tasting. But it will do fairly well in almost any type of soil with the exception of heavy clay.

Drainage is essential for the best results, Hard subsoil induces excessive shoots from the roots. Applications of nitrogenous manures should be given rather lightly. Commercial fertilizers, rich in potash, are recommended, using one large handful to the square yard.

Horse-radish should be kept well-cultivated after the roots are set out in the soil (maybe in April), but thorough preparation of the bed is essential before planting.

Since horse-radish rarely produces seeds, cuttings are made from the roots, not less than half an inch thick and about 4 inches long. To facilitate planting, the larger end should be up. This upper end is cut off square, and the lower end on a slope.

Shallow trenches are dug 4 inches deep and 2 feet between rows. The usual distance between the prepared root cuttings is 12 inches.

Cultivation is usually given a day or two after a good soaking of rain or of water from the hose. Horse-radish usually makes its best growth in the cooler August weather, and it steadily improves until the end of September.

Leave it in the ground as long as possible, but it may be damaged by 20 degrees of frost, so don't leave it undug too long.

Storage in a root cellar is best. Indoor storage causes horse-radish to lose much of its pungency.

In trimming for storage, the lateral roots are saved and buried in sand in boxes indoors for next year's planting. Exposure to air, sun and frost robs roots of their vitality.

The insect enemies of horse-radish are those that attack other members of the cabbage family — caterpillars and certain bugs. Only two diseases that I know of are troublesome to the plant, namely club root rot and dust.

Be careful to keep horse-radish within bounds; it spreads rapidly and will crowd out other nearby plants if given half a chance.

Horse-radish, or cochlearia armoracia, belongs to the wallflower family, the cruciferae.

Planting Guide in Brief

How and When to Plant:
Plant cuttings about 12 inches apart in spring in trench; rows about 24 inches apart; cover with about 4 inches of soil.

Crops Available:
Anytime.

KALE

There are many varieties of kale, a vitamin-rich green leafy vegetable which thrives in ordinary, well-cultivated garden soil, enriched with well-decayed manure. Treat like cabbage.

Kale requires a good deal of water.

Planting Guide in Brief

Recommended Varieties:
Early—Dwarf Green Scotch Curled, Middlestem Curled.
Mid-Season—Cottagers, Asparagus.
Late—Dwarf Siberian and Blue Curled Scotch.
Main Crop—Blue Curled Scotch.

How and When to Plant:
Sow seed in greenhouse early in April. Plant seedlings outdoors after May 24; 3 inches deep; 18 inches between plants; 24 inches between rows. Cultivate and water heavily.

Crops Available:
Early crop starting about end of June; mid-season, about mid-July; late, until freeze-up; main crop, from about mid-July until freeze-up.

KOHLRABI

Kohlrabi is a turnip-rooted cabbage with a very long botanical name, brassica oleracea canlo-rapa. Though a variety of cabbage, it is quite distinct in appearance, having a large rounded root with the leaves developing on its surface. The early varieties only are recommended for growing here.

Planting Guide in Brief

Recommended Varieties:
Early—Early Purple Vienna, White Vienna, and Earliest White.
Main Crop—Early Purple Vienna.

How and When to Plant:
Sow seed outdoors thinly in drills half an inch deep, about 16 inches between rows. When seedlings about 2 inches high, thin to 8 or 9 inches apart. Cultivate regularly and water heavily in noontime heat.

Crops Available:
Early crop, starting about Aug. 1; main crop, from Aug. 15 until frost.

LEEKS

The leek, which is not so commonly grown on the Prairies as many other vegetables, is, however, one of the most flavorful.

To grow leeks well, start them in the house or greenhouse, going through the usual greenhouse procedure of sowing seeds, pricking out the seedlings into larger flats when they are 2 inches high, hardening in a coldframe and then setting out.

The correct way to grow leeks in the garden is to plant the 4-inch seedlings in a trench, which should be from a foot to 18 inches deep and 18 inches in width for a single row of plants. Dig a heavy layer of manure into the bottom of the trench, and cover with approximately 9 inches of soil.

The leeks should be planted down the centre of the prepared trench at a distance of 9 inches apart. When they are a foot high, place cardboard collars around them, and pile the soil up around the collars as the leeks grow. This is to blanch the leeks and keep the stems clean.

This tasty vegetable lends an appetizing flavor to vegetable soups and may also be used as a whole vegetable. Any Welshman will sing the praises of the leek, which of course is Wales' national emblem.

Planting Guide in Brief

Recommended Varieties:
Early—Broad Flag, Musselboro, and Prize-Taker.
Late—Walton Mammoth and Large American Flag.
Main Crop—Large American Flag.

How and When to Plant:
Sow seed indoors about Feb. 1; prick out when seedlings 2 inches high; harden in coldframe. Plant seedlings outdoors about May 24 in a trench 12 to 18 inches deep; 9 inches apart; 18 inches between rows. Place cardboard collars around leeks when they're 12 inches high, and pile soil outside collars. Cultivate and water very heavily.

Crops Available:
Early crops, starting about July 31; late and main crop, about from Aug. 30 until freeze-up.

LETTUCE

Lettuce is a hardy annual invaluable for mixed salads at all times of the year, but especially during spring and summer.

The varieties are grouped into two main classes: cos and cabbage.

Cabbage lettuce has a round or flattened head. Cos lettuce usually is tall and elongated.

Sow lettuce seed outdoors after May 24 in ½-inch deep drills.

Planting Guide in Brief

Recommended Varieties:
Early—Tom Thumb, Grand Rapids, Bibb and Early Prizehead.
Mid-Season—Big Boston and Burpeeana.
Late—Great Lakes and Romaine.
Main Crop—Great Lakes

How and When to Plant:
Plant seed thinly after May 24 in the garden; in drills ½-inch deep; 12 inches between rows. When 2 inches high, thin to 2 or 3 inches apart, later

to 9 inches apart. The thinned-out lettuce may be either used as early salads, or transplanted. Cultivate well; water very heavily but in morning only.

Crops Available:
Early crop, starting about June 1; mid-season, about July; late, until Aug. 30; main crop, from July until late August.

ONIONS

More onions are more than likely grown in Calgary than any other vegetable. Even when the smallest space is set aside for a garden, invariably room is found for onions. The popularity of onions results, of course, from their potency in flavoring foods.

There are many types and varieties of onions, which may vary greatly in size, shape and color.

They are generally raised every year from seed, sown under glass or outdoors, but they can be grown earlier in the season from small bulbits called onion sets. These sets are merely ordinary onions which are arrested in their growth, and which, when planted, resume growing.

Onion sets are grown from seed which is sown very thickly on rather poor soil so that the young bulbs soon reach the limits of growth under such conditions. They mature when still small.

The small bulbs, or sets, are harvested, kept over winter, and used for planting next spring. They are usually purchased from stores. When re-planted, they grow rapidly, and early in the year you have onions for the kitchen.

Early February is the seeding time for those who plan to grow their large spring onions from seed. They should be grown indoors, of course, at a temperature of 60 degrees. As soon as the seedlings are an inch high the temperature should be reduced to 50 degrees. This should produce sturdy plants.

Some gardeners transplant young onion plants into 2-inch pots, but the usual practice is to prick them off into 3-inch-deep flats. Fill these flats with a mixture of two parts loam, one part peat moss and one part sharp sand, well mixed together. They are then set into the flats 2 inches apart each way, care being taken not to plant them too deeply in the soil — I recommend about 2 inches deep.

Now careful watering is necessary. The soil should be moistened only when it is fairly dry. When the onion plants are well rooted and established in the flats or pots, they should then be gradually hardened in a coldframe for a week or 10 days.

Plant out in the garden around May 24, if the weather is favorable. They should not be planted too deeply (again I suggested about 2 inches, or thick-necked onions which do not keep too well in storage will result. The plants should be set out in such a manner that the bulbs are practically sitting on top of the soil or only partly covered.

Hoeing too close to the plants during the summer in order to loosen the soil may result in roots being uncovered; so don't. The best growers know and stress that the soil must be kept firm along the sides of the bulbs. Hand-weeding between rows is preferable for onions.

To obtain fine, large onions in Alberta, with our short growing season, plants must be well-grown inside, and bedded out in the garden when all danger of frost has gone.

Onions are gross feeders, and should have regular applications of liquid or artificial manure, but not after Aug. 1. Through the summer the onions need little

193

attention other than to keep them fed and the weeds pulled, but remember, keep the soil firm around the bulbs at all times. They don't need much water; the soil should be on the dry side.

About the middle of August, when growth of bulbs is nearly complete, it is a good plan to draw the soil away from the base of the bulbs to expose them as much as possible to air and sunshine. This assists them to ripen. When tops begin to turn yellow, the stems should be twisted and bent down. This is best done by bruising the neck of the onions just above the bulbs, using the fore-finger and thumb.

As long as the weather remains fine, with no danger of frost, onions should be left in the ground to ripen as fully as time allows. With the first forecast of frost, onions should be lifted and set out each day in sunny, warm locations until they are thoroughly dry. This drying is most necessary if you have to take them up before they are fully ripened.

If it is wet, set them outside under cover. When completely dry, the tops will shrivel up.

The onions are then stored in a cool, frost-proof place for winter. There are many varieties of onions to pick from, and in this part of the country they are remarkably free from pests and diseases.

You can grow shallots for pickling from sets planted outside during the last two weeks of April. Just press the sets in the soil and they should root quickly. Harvest in July.

Planting Guide in Brief

Recommended Varieties:

Early—Early Globe, Large Red Wetherfield, Southport White Globe and Sweet Spanish; and Silver Skin and White Ebenezer (both excellent for pickling); and onion sets.

Mid-Season—Ailsa Craig Improved and Prize-Taker.

Main Crop—Ailsa Craig Improved.

How and When to Plant:

Plant seeds indoors about Feb. 28; prick 1-inch seedlings into flats; 2 inches apart each way; harden off in coldframes. Plant seedlings outside about May 24; 12 inches apart; 15 inches between rows; keep soil firm around onion bulb until mid-August, then draw away soil until bulbs practically sitting on top of ground. Feed heavily until Aug. 1. Keep soil on dry side. Onion sets may be pressed into outside garden toward end of April. If seeding outside, plant seeds thinly about May 24 in drills an inch or less deep.

Crops Available:

Early crop, starting about July 30; mid-season, about Aug. 15; main crop, from about August until freeze-up. Shallots may be harvested from sets in July.

PARSNIPS

The parsnip, a valuable and nourishing root vegetable, is one of the easiest to cultivate. It is hardy; so hardy, in fact, that it may be left in the garden all winter, and you can dig it up as you need throughout the winter and on into spring until growth starts again. But never pull to eat after growth has restarted— the root is bitter then.

Few vegetables give the gardener less trouble. But large, well-developed roots are obtained only by sowing seed on land which has been prepared by deep cultivation. In shallow, badly dug or stony ground, parsnips will be small and unshapely.

To grow parsnips for exhibition, one would need to trench the ground 2 feet deep. This, of course, applies to all deep-rooted vegetable plants such as carrots and long beets.

The amateur who wishes to have good-sized, well-shaped parsnips must have the ground dug the previous fall not less than two spits deep — about 20 inches. When digging, the ground should be well-broken to this depth, thus allowing roots to penetrate easily.

Fresh manure should not be used when preparing the ground, Well-decayed manure may be dug in again during the fall with advantage, but it should be mixed in with the lower layer of soil.

In spring, when forking over the garden you may apply bone meal flour, using one handful to the square yard of ground.

As parsnips need as long a growing season as possible, the seeds should be sown outdoors as soon as possible, that is, as soon as conditions of weather and soil allow, by the beginning of April if possible.

The seeds should be sprinkled thinly along the garden rows in a small trench about 2 inches deep, then covered. There should be 16 inches between rows. Use a line and draw-hoe to make the trench and to keep it straight.

When seedlings are about 3 inches high, they should be thinned to about 3 or 4 inches apart.

In fall, parsnips may be taken indoors and stored in sand, or left out in the ground all winter. But if they are left in the ground too long in spring they will produce flower heads, because they are biennials.

When they flower, they are no longer edible. I don't think they're poisonous, but they are certainly no longer fit for the table. Any vegetable which goes to flower and seed is rendered unfit for food.

Planting Guide in Brief

Recommended Varieties:
> Early—Hollow Crown, All America, and Short Thick.
> Mid-Season—Guernsey and Student.
> Late—Tender and True.
> Main Crop—Hollow Crown.

How and When to Plant:
> Plant seed outdoors as soon as frost is out of the ground, maybe in first week of April; sprinkle seed thinly along trench 2 inches deep; 16 inches between rows. Thin when seedlings 3 inches high, to 3 to 4 inches apart. Cultivate continually and water lightly.

Crops Available:
> Early crop, starting about Aug. 31; mid-season, about Sept. 30; late, until freeze-up; main crop, from about September until freeze-up.

PEAS

Garden peas, freshly picked, are delicious. The numerous varieties in cultivation have been improved over the years by crossbreeding.

Peas may be safely seeded outdoors in the Prairies after May 24, sometimes even earlier if the weather is settled and fine. Later sowings — ten days apart— may be made to provide a continuous supply of peas throughout the season.

Green peas can be grown well only in deep, fairly rich soil that is not allowed to dry out during the hot weather. They are not a success in poor or light soil.

The ideal way to prepare the ground is to dig a trench 2 feet deep in the fall. Add manure to the lower soil, because pea roots penetrate deeply. In early spring the soil will be friable and easily broken up with a garden fork.

Unless the soil already contains plenty of lime, a scattering of this should then be put on the surface, and lightly raked in.

As seeds of peas germinate quickly, it is wasteful to scatter them too thickly along the row. The best plan is to make a 6-inch-wide shallow trench seeding 3 inches deep on the prepared site. If the soil is heavier, and up to 6 inches deep if the soil is very light.

Then plant the seeds 2 or 3 inches apart and cover them with soil.

As soon as the seedlings show above ground they should be protected from birds, or considerable loss probably will occur. Sparrows are very fond of young peas. Black thread may be strung along the rows to scare off the birds. Wire netting may also be placed over the plans to try to stop birds.

It is important to support young pea vines when they are only 2 or 3 inches high with twiggy branches or netting wire supported by posts.

If this is neglected, pea vines will fall over for lack of support, and if that happens they never really do well afterwards.

Before staking, however, the soil should be drawn up with a draw-hoe around the bottom of the vines to a height of 2 or 3 inches to lend support to them while they begin to climb the stakes or wire.

Planting Guide in Brief

Recommended Varieties:
> Early—Little Marvel, Thomas Laxton, Hundredfold, Radio, and Alaska.
> Mid-Season—Stratagem, Early Abundance, Superb Laxton, Meteor, and Greater Progress.
> Late—Giant Stride.
> Main Crop—Greater Progress.

How and When to Plant:
> Plant seeds outside about May 24, sometimes earlier. Seed in trench 3 or 4 inches deep; 2 or 3 inches apart. Protect from birds as soon as seedlings appear; stake when 2 or 3 inches high; also drawing up soil then around vines almost to top of seedlings. Cultivate regularly; water heavily in mornings (not in evenings).

Crops Available:
> Early crop, starting about July 31; mid-season, starting about Aug. 1; late, until about Aug. 31; main crop, from about July 31 to Aug. 31.

POTATO

That ever popular and basic vegetable the potato is a tender (not hardy) perennial from South America, and is the principal vegetable crop in this and many other countries. Its botanical family name is solanum tuberosum.

Potatoes can be cultivated in all kinds of soil, but the finest crops are dug from well-drained, loamy earth that has been enriched with manure.

They may be planted in the same site year after year with good results, if the ground is maintained in a fertile condition by liming, manuring and keeping free from weeds.

In a moderate-sized garden, however, it is wise to include potatoes in any system of rotation of crops which may be practised, so that they have a change of soil periodically.

The best way to prepare soil for potato cultivation is to dig it in the fall, and turn it over in the form of ridging, leaving the soil in this state throughout winter. Towards the end of April or in May the soil will break down in small particles. In other words, it will be friable when forked over. Exposure to frost, snow and wind greatly benefits cultivation.

When choosing seed potatoes, purchase government-tested seed. Early varieties are best for this part of the country. Late kinds on no account should be chosen, because owing to our short growing season they will not ripen in time for storing.

If you select seed from your own crop of last season, pick medium-sized ones, healthy of course, and as shallow-eyed as possible. Deep-eyed potatoes are more wasteful, although there are some fine kinds which have rather deep eyes, such as Warba and the Irish Cobbler.

You can sprout your own seed potatoes earlier by placing them on trays in the greenhouse or anywhere indoors with the rose end up, and bringing them to the light. The rose end is that end containing most of the eyes. The opposite end — the root end — seldom if ever bears any eyes.

Large potatoes can be split for seed, making sure that there are at least two eyes on each split portion. Always cut the potato from the rose end down. From some large potatoes you may obtain as many as three and sometimes four splits, all of which must contain eyes.

Plant potatoes 8 inches deep, 18 inches between seeds and 2½ feet between rows.

When the potatoes break through the soil, it is most important they be cultivated, as this hastens growth. Earthing up the hill should be done by drawing soil on each side of the row, so that it supports the potato stems and leaves when they are about 8 inches high.

This also protects tubers from exposure to the sun. Hilling up should not be completed on one occasion but on several, as the crop grows.

When lifting and storing, potatoes must not be exposed to light for more than a few hours, but just give them time to dry out properly for storing. If left out too long they will turn greenish, rendering them bitter and unsuitable.

Potatoes are subject to many diseases, such as potato blight, blackleg, leaf roll, powdery scab, wart disease, and others. The potato beetle or Colorado beetle is troublesome in Prairie gardens, eating the foliage of the vines and depleting the crop.

It is imperative that the Colorado beetle be prevented from increasing on the Prairies. When infected, it is necessary to spray potato vines with arsenate of lead several times during the season.

Paris green is another effective method of clearing a garden of this pest. It is extremely important that any beetles resembling the Colorado be immediately dealt with by spraying vines with arsenate of lead or Paris green. The Colorado beetle is about a quarter of an inch long, bright yellow in color, and has 10 black stripes on the back. There are also black spots on the body and head.

Planting Guide in Brief

Recommended Varieties:
>Early—Early Ohio, Warba, Irish Cobbler, Green Mountain and Katahdin.
>Mid-Season—Kerr's Pink, Pontiac and Norland.
>Main Crop—Irish Cobbler, or Warba or Green Mountain.

How and When to Plant:
>Plant seed potatoes (or eyes) outdoors 8 inches deep about May 24; 18 inches between seeds; 30 inches between rows. Hill up earth when stems

about 8 inches high; keep on hilling as plant grows. Cultivate and water regularly.

Crops Available:
Early crop, starting about end of July; mid-season, about mid-August; main crop, from August until freeze-up.

PUMPKIN

Pumpkin is the common name given to cucurbita maxima, a half-hardy plant related to the vegetable marrow and the gourd.

Plants are raised from seed sown in warmth under glass in March. In our climate they can only be placed out of doors when they're in covered frames.

Planting Guide in Brief

Recommended Varieties:
Early—Small Sugar, Orange Winter, Jack O'Lantern.
Mid-Season—Golden Cushaw.
Main Crop—Small Sugar.

How and When to Plant:
Sow seed under glass in March. Continue to cultivate indoors or in covered frames outdoors.

Crops Available:
Early crop, starting about mid-June; mid-season, starting about July; main crop, during July and August.

RADISH

Radish, this familiar small red and white salad vegetable, whose botanical name is raphanus sativus, is a hardy annual found wild in parts of Europe.

The garden radish is easy to grow, and by making sowings at different times (several seedings at about ten-day intervals) it is possible to maintain a supply for a whole gardening season. With such continuous seeding, it isn't customary to specify radish as early or mid-season crops.

Sow in good, rich ground.

Planting Guide in Brief

Recommended Varieties:
French Breakfast, Comet, Early Scarlet Globe, and Icicle.
Main Crop—Early Scarlet Globe.

How and When to Plant:
Plant seed thinly outdoors about May 24; ½-inch deep in trench; 12 inches between rows. Thin out as required for salads. Cultivate and water heavily.

Crops Available:
Early crop, starting about June 24; then depending on interval of later seedings; main crop, from about July 1 until Aug. 31.

RHUBARB

Rhubarb, from which so many delicious preserves are made, is rather neglected in most gardens, although everybody seems to want rhubarb pie when spring comes.

Rhubarb delights in a very rich soil and a sunny location in the garden.

Large and brittle leaf stalks are obtained only from soil that is over-flowing with manure.

The rhubarb bed should be renewed every five years; if not the clump of roots become more numerous than desired. Take up the whole root and cut it into pieces, leaving only one or two strong eyes in each piece.

Plant the divisions in a newly-prepared bed, or even back in the old bed if it has been properly enriched and cultivated. This can be done better in the fall; but may be done in the spring.

Keep all flowering spikes cut down to ground level at all times. If this is not done the vitality of the plant is reduced.

Planting Guide in Brief

Recommended Varieties:
MacDonald's Red and Giant Victoria.

How and When to Plant:
To start a new bed, plant root cuttings containing at least one or two strong eyes outside in April. Divisions should be set 48 inches apart; crowns (or tops) just covered with soil. Top dress the soil with manure.

Crops Available:
Crops available from old beds all season starting in June. Only pull stems from second-year roots in moderation.

SPINACH

The common spinach (spinacia oleracea) is grown for its edible leaves. It is easily managed, providing suitable conditions are provided. It needs rich, moist soil, well fertilized with decayed manure.

Planting Guide in Brief

Recommended Varieties:
Early—American New, Viking, Long Stand.
Mid-Season—Nobel and Bloomsdale Long Standing.
Late—New Zealand and America.
Main Crop—America.

How and When to Plant
Plant seeds thinly outdoors after May 24; in drills ½ inch deep; 12 inches between rows. When seedlings about 2 inches high, thin to 4 inches apart. Cultivate regularly and water heavily.

Crops Available:
Early crop, starting in June; mid-season, in July; late, until August 31; main crop, from about mid-June until mid-August.

SQUASH

Squash cannot be grown here outdoors, only in greenhouses or in covered frames.

For best eating, summer squashes are taken up while very young and tender.

Planting Guide in Brief

Recommended Varieties:

    Early—Early White and Crystal Bell.

    Mid-Season—Butternut, Early Golden Summer, and Crookneck.

    Main Crops—Early Golden Summer or Crookneck.

How and When to Plant:

    Sow seed indoors about the end of April. When seedlings about 3 inches high, set them out in covered frames to ripen. Water and feed heavily.

Crops Available:

    Early crop, starting about Aug. 1; mid-season, about Aug. 30; main crop, from about Aug. 1 until Sept. 30.

TOMATO

The tomato, which is sometimes called a fruit, is a native of tropical America and is grown more extensively on the North American continent than elsewhere. And the varieties here have reached a higher perfection.

Seeds of tomatoes should be sown in a warm greenhouse during the latter part of April. As soon as the seedlings are large enough to handle they are transplanted into 3-inch pots. Later, and as soon as the roots gets around the pots, they should be moved into 5-inch pots. After this they are gradually hardened in a coldframe, providing the weather is not too cold, and providing frost cannot touch them.

You can grow tomato seedlings in the house in the same manner, taking care, however, to give them all the light and air possible.

If you buy tomato plants, look for healthy, short-jointed and stout-stemmed plants, if possible with the bottom truss of flowers showing.

Plants should be set outdoors the first week in June, 2 feet apart each way and should be supported by stakes, and tied right away. All side shoots should be removed as soon as they appear, and when plants reach a height of 3 feet the top ought to be nipped out. The reason for this, fruits seldom ripen on the upper trusses, and retard the ripening of the lower fruits.

During hot weather it is especially important plants don't suffer from lack of water.

A top-dressing of well-rotted manure spread over the surface roots will conserve valuable soil moisture and supply food to tomato plants, which need a lot of nourishment. They should be fed regularly with liquid or artificial manure, every 10 days or two weeks throughout the growing season.

To hasten growing and ripening of tomatoes, grow them close to a board fence where storm windows or sheets of glass can be slanted over them, forming a semi-greenhouse.

Last, a warning: tomatoes are subject to many diseases and insect pests, and must be tended with extreme care all through the growing season.

Planting Guide in Brief

Recommended Varieties:

    Early—Earliana Improved, Quebec 309, Cavalier Early Bounty, Bison, Bonny Best, Victor, and Beefsteak.

How and When to Plant:

    Plant seed indoors about April 15. Transplant seedlings from 3- to 5-inch pots; harden off in coldframe. Transplant outdoors these seedlings or purchased plants about June 1; plant 2 feet apart each way; stake. Prune off all side shoots; nip off top when plant is 3 feet high. Water well. Feed liquid manure every ten days.

Crops Available:

Early and main crops, starting about Sept. 1 until freeze-up.

TURNIPS

The garden turnip often is rather despised as a vegetable, possibly because it frequently is fed to cattle and sheep, though this should prove them high in nourishment.

The turnip, sometimes also called the golden or yellow turnip, belongs to the same family as cabbage.

Turnips should be raised in good soil enriched with manures before sowing time. The seed should be sown in drills an inch or so deep, and 2 feet between rows. If it's dry, the drills should be watered an hour or so before the seed is sown.

Seeds are dropped thinly along the rows and covered lightly with earth. A light scattering of sulphate of ammonia or nitrate of soda along the sides of the rows when the turnips are 6 inches high will greatly help turnips develop and make rapid growth.

Thin out when the plantlings are 2 inches high, leaving about 9 or 10 inches between roots.

Turnips here are not subject to many pests and diseases. Their chief needs are rich soil and lots of water.

Planting Guide in Brief

Recommended Varieties:

Early—Early Flat White Dutch, Yellow Aberdeen, Early Milan, Early Six Weeks, and Green Top Stone.
Mid-Season—Golden Ball.
Main Crop—Golden Ball.

How and When to Plant:

Sow seed thinly outdoors about May 24; in drills about 1 inch deep; 24 inches between rows. Thin when plants 2 inches high to 9 or 10 inches apart. Water heavily. Cultivate regularly.

Crops Available:

Early crop, starting about July 15; mid-season, about July 31; main crop; from July until about Aug. 15.

SWEDE TURNIPS

Similar gardening should apply to Swede turnips as to the golden garden ones. There are selected varieties of Swedes suitable for garden cultivation. The Swede roots are larger and of stronger flavor than garden turnips. Swedes are improved in flavor by a touch of about two or three degrees of frost before being harvested.

The swede turnip is very hardy, and is popular in the kitchen in winter because it is easily stored in sand in a root cellar, and keeps well at a temperature of 35 degrees.

It is not customary here, to plant Swedes by early or mid-season varieties.

Planting Guide in Brief

Recommended Varieties:

    Johnston's Purple Top, Early Purple Milan, Canadian Gem,
Jumbo Elephant and Laurentian Swede.

    Main Crop—Laurentian Swede.

How and When to Plant:

    Plant seeds thinly outdoors about May 24 in drills 1 inch deep; 24 inches between rows. Thin out when plants 2 inches high to 9 or 10 inches apart. Water and cultivate regularly.

Crops Available:

    Starting about Aug. 31 until freeze-up; main crop, same period.

VEGETABLE MARROW

The vegetable marrow gives little trouble to the gardener except sometimes it grows too luxuriantly — and then it doesn't bear fruit freely.

It is commonly planted on heaps of rotted manure and loam mixed well together. But it can also be grown on level ground, or even run up a fence. When the vines are entwined on a fence, the flowers are well exposed to sun and air, and are likely to produce more freely.

The risk in growing marrows on mounds of manure is that the growth is so vigorous that the flower are hidden (and lost) among the large, luxuriant leaves.

Gardeners often complain, especially during a damp, dull summer, that the crop is disappointing. The reasons may include: the soil is too rich, too much shade, failure to fertilize the blooms, and the flowers may be smothered by the leaves.

It is beneficial to thin out some of the shoots to expose the remainder to air and sunshine. Although fertilization by hand of flowers is not commonly practised, it is well to do this if there are prospects of a poor crop. Fertilize by transferring the pollen from the male (or staminate) bloom to the stigma of the female (or fruiting) bloom. The latter are distinguished from the male blooms by the swelling above the bloom — this is just a tiny marrow which requires fertilizing to make it grow.

As the marrow will not withstand frost, it is raised first in a greenhouse or in the home at a temperature of 60 degrees Fahrenheit. Late in April sow the seeds indoors singly in 3-inch pots filled with a compost of two-thirds loam and one-third peatmoss.

The pots are covered with glass, shaded, and the soil is kept moist.

When the seedlings are well rooted, transfer them to a coldframe as soon as the weather is mild enough. Plant them outdoors in June.

There are many varieties of marrow — some the trailing kind, some with large fruits, some with small fruits, and then the bush marrows. My favorites among the big marrows are Long Green and Long White. Excellent small varieties are Table Dainty and Rotherside Orange. The bush marrows, grown in the same way as the other two kinds, are excellent for pickling.

A delicious jam, something like marmalade, is made from the large marrows.

202

Planting Guide in Brief

Recommended Varieties:

Early—Long Green, Long White, Table Dainty and Rotherside Orange.
Mid-Season—Long Cream and Long Green Striped.
Main Crop—Long Green Striped.

How and When to Plant:

Plant seed indoors late in April in 3-inch pots. Transplant 3- to 6-inch seedlings in June. Leave in coldframe as long as possible, then remove frame. For outdoors planting, plant three seeds in each garden hill about June 1; hills 3 feet apart. Throw away the two weakest seedlings, keeping the strongest seedling only in each hill. Lots of sunshine and air needed. Thinning of foliage may be necessary if leaves too luxuriant. Cultivate, water and feed heavily.

Crops Available:

Early crop, starting mid-August; mid-season, at end of August; late, until danger of frost; main crop, from August until freeze-up.

GARDENING DEFINITIONS

Words sometimes mean different things to different people. Especially is this so about plants.

So to avoid more confusion, I'll briefly explain what I mean in this manual when I use a certain term, such as:

ALPINE—Plants from mountainous regions, usually of dwarf growth and generally for rock gardens.

ANNUAL—A plant which grows, flowers, sets and matures its seeds and dies within one year.

BIENNIAL—A plant which grows from seed one year, flowers the second year and then dies.

BULB—A plant in its resting stage, with a swollen stem enclosed within scales or plates.

COLDFRAME—An outdoors unheated boxed frame in which seedlings in flats may be gradually introduced to outside temperatures.

COMPOST—A compost heap is composed of manure, or decomposed or fermented garden refuse, or of soil and manure.

CORM—A bulb-like, scaleless underground stem; often called a bulb.

CUTTING—A severed part of a plant used to produce roots and new growth; in house plants often called a slip.

FLAT—A shallow box in which seeds may be sown indoors.

HARDENING OFF—"Toughening" young plants started indoors or under glass by exposing them gradually to outdoor conditions, generally by reducing the protection in coldframes.

HERBACEOUS BORDER—A floral border of perennials which die down each year.

HERB—Savory kitchen herbs such as mint and parsley; or also perennial herbs which are grown for the flowers, such as saxifrage and gentians.

HOTBED—A fermented bed of manure, 2 to 3 feet deep, on which, after reaching a temperature of 70 degrees Fahrenheit, soil is placed. An open-bottomed frame like a coldframe is then put over this bed. Plants in the soil are forced to earlier growth.

PERENNIAL—A plant which lives through more than two seasons of growth.

PRICKING OUT—Lifting small seedlings, and re-spacing them to promote sturdier growth.

SEEDLING—a young plant raised from seed.

SHRUB—A low, woody plant with several stems instead of one trunk. The latter is a tree.

VARIETY—A cultivated plant differing from others in its species in some minor permanent manner.

VINES

Vines if chosen wisley and planted carefully can add a great deal to a garden, especially a kind of background harmony. But you must pick the hardy ones which will grow here, and you should plant vines in the appropriate places —for instance, don't put a vine which may grow to a maximum height of 10 feet beside a 20-foot trellis you want covered.

Many vines are chosen for their foliage, others for their flowers, some for both.

They will grow in practically any good soil, but they all especially like lime, so be sure to feed this to vines.

They should never be planted on a north wall or trellis.

Vines by heights

Recommended hardy vines include the following:

Common Name	Botanical Name	Maximum Height (in feet)	Color of Flower (if any)
°American Bittersweet	Ceastrus Scandens	15	Orange berries
°Bower Actinidia	Actinidia Arguta	18	Yellow
°Canary Bird	Tropaeolum Peregrinum	20	Yellow, Red
°Donald Honeysuckle	Lonicera Glaucescens	10 to 12	Yellow berries
Golden (Chinese) Clematis	Clematis Tangutica	15	Gold
Hermitgold Clematis	Clematis Serratifolia	20	Gold
Jackman Clematis	Clematis Jackmanii	15	Blue
Oriental Bittersweet	Celastrus Articulatus	20	Orange berries
°Moon Flower	Calonyction Aculeatum	15	Blue
Perrenial Pea	Lathyrus Latifolius	6	Varied
°Purplebell Cobaea	Cobaea Scandens	10	Blue
Riverbank Grape	Vitis Riparia	2 to 3	—
Rock (or Purple) Clematis	Clematis Vertilaris	2 to 3	White, Blue
Virginia Creeper	Ampelopsis Aconitifolia (or)	24	—
	Partenocissus Quinquifolia	24	—
Western Virginsbower	Clematis Ligusticifolia	15	White

°Annuals. All others are perennials.

INDEX

INDEX — Continued

INDEX — Continued

INDEX — Continued

INDEX — Continued

This index did not appear in earlier editions. The book has been indexed to include all common and botanical names of plants as they appear in the text. However, no attempt has been made to match common with the botanical names. Rather, it is a simple index — compiled for the convenience of the layman gardener.